# A is *for* Almanac

**Complete Lessons
to Teach the Use of
Reference Sources
in Grades K–6**

*Susan L. Garvin* and *Annie Weissman*

# Neal-Schuman Publishers, Inc.
New York                     London

Published by Neal-Schuman Publishers, Inc.
100 William St., Suite 2004
New York, NY 10038

Printed and bound in the United States of America.

The paper used in this publication meets the minimum requirements of American National Standard for Information Sciences—Permanence of Paper for Printed Library Materials, ANSI Z39.48-1992.

**Library of Congress Cataloging-in-Publication Data**

Garvin, Susan L.
    A is for almanac: complete lessons to teach the use of reference sources in grades K–6 / Susan L. Garvin, Annie Weissman
        p. cm.
    Includes bibliographical references and index.
ISBN  978-1-55570-623-4 (alk. paper)
1. Library orientation for school children. 2. Reference sources—Study and teaching (Elementary)  I. Weissman, Annie, 1948– II. Title.

Z711.25.S36G37  2008
027.62'5—dc22

2007034861

Susan: to Lawanda McVey, who set me on the path of librarianship; to Annie Weissman, who guided me along the way; and to my family and friends, who have loved and encouraged me throughout my career.
Annie: to all the unique and spunky students who have taught me how to reach out, teach them, and get them the right books.

# Contents

## Part II: Curriculum Units Using Reference Sources

## Part III: Games and Contests

# CD-ROM Contents

### Games for Students to Practice Reference Skills

1. Monthly 10 Questions Reference Games
2. Monthly Matching Game
3. "Between the Pages" Weekly Game
4. "Use Your Brain" Weekly Game
5. The "Counting Corner" Estimation Jar Monthly Game

### Work Sheets, Internet Web Sites, and Letters to the Parents

1. Dictionary Lessons K–6
2. Thesaurus Lessons K–6
3. Encyclopedia Lessons K–6
4. Atlas Lessons K–6
5. Almanac Lessons K–6
6. Online Catalog Lessons K–6
7. Using the Internet Lessons K–6
8. Kindergarten Who Am I? Unit
9. First-Grade Animal Defenses Unit
10. Second-Grade Shelter Unit
11. Third-Grade Transportation Unit
12. Fourth-Grade Biomes Unit
13. Fifth-Grade Natural Weather Hazards Unit
14. Sixth-Grade War Unit

### Brochures

1. Dictionary
2. Thesaurus
3. Encyclopedia
4. Atlas
5. Almanac
6. Online Catalog
7. Internet

# Preface

An increasing emphasis on measurement and testing permeates today's schools. In this age of standards and assessments, librarians may worry that libraries will be left behind. In fact, information literacy instruction can have a measurable positive effect on student achievement. A study in Alaska demonstrated that the more often students received instruction on information skills from a library media specialist, the better their test scores (Lance, 2005). Another study showed that reading scores on the Colorado Student Assessment Program were 21 percent higher for students whose librarians and teachers collaborated the most than for students whose librarians and teachers collaborated the least (Lance, 2005).

*A is for Almanac: Complete Lessons to Teach the Use of Reference Sources in Grades K–6* contains over 200 lessons that collaborating librarians and teachers can use to teach information skills. Each one meets national standards in multiple areas, including information literacy, language arts, science, social studies, and technology. In the lessons in the first half of the book, students learn about the features of dictionaries, encyclopedias, thesauri, almanacs, atlases, online catalogs, and the Internet and how to use these reference sources. The science and social studies units in the second half of the book help students to apply and reinforce these skills.

One distinctive aspect of our approach is that we introduce reference sources in kindergarten and the primary grades. All too often students do not start learning research skills until third or fourth grade. Here, we encourage librarians and teachers to take reference books off the shelves, place them in the hands of students, and require them to think. The lessons target the higher cognitive levels of Bloom's taxonomy through active participation strategies, higher-level thinking, and having the students create their own reference materials.

We know that these approaches work because we have used them. We tested all of the lessons in *A is for Almanac* in real-life settings to ensure that they interested students and got them involved. One group of students attended an upper middle-class school in the suburbs of Phoenix. The other groups were in inner city schools with more than 90 percent of the students eligible for free and reduced lunch and with a large percentage of English language learners. Even though the populations varied greatly, the children in both environments enjoyed working with the reference materials, the subjects, and the products.

Librarians can use *A is for Almanac* as the basis of a curriculum in both fixed and flexible library schedules. Beginning librarians may wish to use the programs as is so that they can spend time focusing on learning their many other responsibilities, while experienced librarians may wish to do more modification and tailoring. Classroom teachers in schools without teaching librarians can also use the lessons in a stand-alone program. The plans explicitly state the objectives and standards, so they can be copied and handed in to the principal to meet lesson plan requirements.

Many activities can also carry over to the families at home. We encourage readers to reach out to families using the brochures and letters. For all lessons that use the Internet, we include letters inviting parents to peruse the sites with their children. We have gotten very positive feedback from parents about this component of the curriculum. One parent called the principal to let him know how much she appreciated knowing about the material and Web sites her kindergartener used.

## ORGANIZATION

*A is for Almanac: Complete Lessons to Teach the Use of Reference Sources in Grades K–6* explores the subject in two main parts. Part I, "Reference Resources Lessons," begins with an introduction discussing the theory behind the lessons and the strategies necessary for effective implementation.

Part I contains seven chapters, each dedicated to a specific tool. Each chapter includes lessons for every grade.

- Chapter 1, "The Dictionary"
- Chapter 2, "The Thesaurus"
- Chapter 3, "The Encyclopedia"
- Chapter 4, "The Atlas"
- Chapter 5, "The Almanac"
- Chapter 6, "The Online Catalog"
- Chapter 7, "The Internet"

Part II, "Curriculum Units Using Reference Sources," starts with an introduction to teaching strategies and unit design. The seven chapters each contain a unit of multiple lessons focusing on a particular topic for a particular grade.

- Chapter 8, "Kindergarten: Who Am I?"
- Chapter 9, "First Grade: Animal Defenses"
- Chapter 10, "Second Grade: Shelter"
- Chapter 11, "Third Grade: Transportation"
- Chapter 12, "Fourth Grade: Biomes"
- Chapter 13, "Fifth Grade: Natural Weather Hazards"
- Chapter 14, "Sixth Grade: War"

## THE CD-ROM

The accompanying CD includes work sheets, instructor support materials, brochures, games, and contests. The work sheets can be personalized for a specific setting and printed out. The instructor can use the brochures and letters to communicate with parents. The lessons on each reference source suggest a grade level in which to send home the brochure and letter for that source. Because of copyright limitations, the charts, brochures, and work sheets do not have graphics, but these can be easily added using clip art.

Students can practice their information literacy skills through the weekly and monthly contests and games. The CD provides enough challenges for three years' worth of contests. The CD also includes hot links to many Web sites, which instructors may wish to put on a launch page or bookmark on the computers being used. Launch pages are available at no cost through Google.

## REFERENCE

Lance, Keith Curry, and David V. Loertscher. 2005. *Powering Achievement: School Library Media Programs Make a Difference: The Evidence.* 3rd ed. Salt Lake City, Utah: Hi Willow Research and Publishing.

# Acknowledgments

Thanks to the learning communities of the Roosevelt, Alhambra, and Kyrene School Districts in Arizona. Thanks to Neal-Schuman Publishers for making this project a reality.

# PART I

# REFERENCE
# RESOURCES LESSONS

# Introduction

# Essential Background on Lessons, Teaching Strategies, and Format

Standards, accountability, and assessments are part of the environment in which school librarians exist. All of the lessons in this book contain all three of these elements.

## STANDARDS

The standards used in this book were from the national professional associations in that subject area. For language arts, the standards of The National Council of Teachers of English were used. The overview of these is available at www.ncte.org/about/over/standards/110846.htm. For information literacy, the American Association of School Librarians' *Standards for the 21st-Century Learner* (AASL, 2007) standards were used. They can be found on the Web at www.ala.org/ala/aasl/aaslproftools/learningstandards/standards.cfm. For science, the National Academy of Science Standards were used. An overview of these is available at http://books.nap.edu/readingroom/books/nses/html/overview.html. The National Council for the Social Studies has its curriculum standards available at www.socialstudies.org/standards/. For technology, the International Society for Technology in Education (ISTE) curriculum standards were used. They are available at http://cnets.iste.org/currstands/cstands-netss.html. These standards basically cover the questions asked about reference on most standardized tests, one of the measures of accountability used by administrators at building and district level. In addition to these standards, librarians and teachers may want to add district and state standards. All of the lessons were devised to require higher-level thinking skills.

If the school has not formally taught reference books and practicing information literacy skills, it may be very beneficial to disaggregate the data from last year's tests for all grade levels on questions that include reference books or skills. This is the baseline data. Teach the lessons and units in this book to one or more grade levels. At the end of the school year, disaggregate the data for that year's tests. It should show that there has been an increase in scores. This should be shared with the building and district administration. It can be used to justify library positions and materials budgets.

## FORMAT

The format for the lesson plans for this book are loosely based on Madeline Hunter's *Mastery Teaching* and Arizona State University's student teacher's lesson plan template found on page 95 in *Coaching the Student Teacher* by Enz, Hurwitz, and Carlile. The *standards* are listed first, then the specific *objective* for the lesson. The objective is written in behavioral terms: what the student will be able to do as a result of the lesson.

The *materials* are listed so that they can be gathered in advance. Many of the materials, including the work sheets and brochures, are available on the CD that accompanies this book. "Board-ready copy" means either a transparency for an overhead projector or the material made ready for an interactive white board, Proxima, or other means of projection so that the whole class can read the information at the same time. In the lessons on each reference source, a sign is indicated in the materials. Simply write the name of the reference source, such as "dictionary," in large letters and paste a picture of a dictionary on a piece of tag board or construction paper. Make two holes near the top, thread enough yarn or ribbon through them that you can wear the sign around your neck, and the sign is complete. Wear it during all lessons on that reference source. Visuals are included in many of the lessons to assist comprehension for English-language learners and visual learners. These visuals can be found easily on the Internet and printed out.

The *set* is the part of a lesson that introduces it. Its purpose is to engage the students and interest them in the topic of the lesson. In the *review*, the instructor reviews previously taught material in order to link it with the lesson of the day.

The *input* is the direct instruction from the instructor. In this section, the instructor introduces and models the skill or feature being taught. The *guided practice* is when the students practice the skill. Independent practice has not been included as a separate segment, because this is sometimes included in the guided practice, depending on how much assistance the instructor needs to provide.

The *assessment* is generally informal. The instructor circulates among the students and directly observes whether the students are able to complete the tasks or need reteaching. There are many work sheets that provide written evidence of understanding. These can be collected and assessed if a formal grade is necessary. The *closure* is a very important part of any lesson. It should include active participation on the part of the students. This summary of what has been learned allows students to chunk the new information into long-term memory.


## SOURCES

For this book, Wikipedia was used as a Web-based reference source. It has been validated recently in a special report by the journal *Nature*, dated December 15, 2005, with an update on March 28, 2006. The study reported on in *Nature*, conducted by Jim Giles, compared Wikipedia and *Encyclopaedia Britannica* on nature subjects and found four large errors in each encyclopedia and approximately the same number of smaller errors in each encyclopedia. Giles's study concluded that Wikipedia could be considered accurate enough to be worth using (Giles, 2005). Instructors may want to preface lessons that use Wikipedia as a source with the information that Wikipedia is an online free encyclopedia, founded in 2001, that allows anyone to contribute articles and add or correct information in articles over the Web. Wikipedia is used because its articles often appear within the first five hits on Google search results and can be read without a subscription. Google is the most common search engine used by elementary schools.

The index to the *World Book Encyclopedia* was not taught in the lessons in this book. There are several reasons. First, there is only one index for a set, so it cannot be used directly by students. All of the lessons in this book include hands-on activities. Second, the *World Book Encyclopedia* has mostly specific, not broad, articles, which makes the use of an index less necessary than when using an encyclopedia with only broad entries, such as *Encyclopedia Britannica*.

The Internet lessons were designed for limited searches, because most elementary schools have firewalls and other rules against free searching. The objectives for the Internet lessons were more concerned with familiarizing students with what is available, how to read for information, and how to evaluate the accuracy of Web sites.

The lessons in this book were created using specific reference books and sources. It is not necessary that you have these particular books and sources, but these are the ones that the lessons are keyed to.


### Dictionaries

K–1: *American Heritage Picture Dictionary*. 2007. Boston: Houghton Mifflin, 138 pp.
Grades 2–3: *Merriam-Webster's Elementary Dictionary*. 2005. Springfield, MA: Merriam-Webster, 595 pp.
Grades 4–6: *Merriam-Webster's Intermediate Dictionary*. 2004. Springfield, MA: Merriam-Webster, 1005 pp.

### Thesauri

K–2: Bollard, John K. 1998. *Scholastic Children's Thesaurus.* New York: Scholastic, 240 pp.
Grades 3–6: Hellweg, Paul, Joyce LeBaron, and Susannah LeBaron. 2007. *The American Heritage Student Thesaurus.* Boston: Houghton Mifflin, 378 pp.

### Almanacs

K–4: Kashman, Zoe, ed. 2006. *World Almanac for Kids 2007.* New York: World Almanac Books, 352 pp.
Grades 5–6: McGoveren, William A., ed. 2005. *The World Almanac and Book of Facts 2006.* New York: World Almanac Books, 1008 pp.

### Encyclopedias

*World Book Encyclopedia.* Chicago: World Book.

### Atlases

K–2: *National Geographic Beginner's World Atlas.* 2005. Washington, D.C.: National Geographic, 64 pp.
Grades 3–6: *National Geographic World Atlas for Young Explorers.* 2003. Washington, D.C.: National Geographic, 192 pp.

## TEACHING STRATEGIES

In order to implement the lessons in this book effectively, certain teaching strategies need to be employed. Most of them are directly related to active participation. As Fred Jones says in his book *Fred Jones Tools for Teaching*, research has found that teaching by telling is not effective. Modeling must be done, and students must have the opportunity to practice skills and use them in meaningful ways. Instructors should always model the skill that students are learning. That means going through the process with a specific example similar to the work they will be given. Most of the modeling is included in the "input" section of the lesson plan.

### Cooperative Learning: Small-Group Work

It would take many books to explain all the practices of cooperative learning. The following cooperative learning strategies are used in the lessons: small-group work, think-pair-share, jigsaw, and group composition.

Small-group work is when students are divided into groups of three to five each. Ideally, these groups should be heterogeneous. Each student in the group is given a number, and tasks are assigned. It is very helpful to have a chart with two columns: one for the number of the student and the other for the task assigned. The chart can be laminated so it can be used many times. Each student is made responsible for a specific part of the work. The groups work together on a product or process. It is necessary for the instructor to circulate constantly among the groups, assisting but also ensuring that the students remain on task. It's easiest to manage groups by making a folder for each, with the names of the members next to a number, and the group's assignment on the front. For instance, if four students are working on "airplanes," that word is printed on the front of their folder along with numbers one, two, three, and four. The students write their names next to the numbers. This allows the instructor to vary the tasks of each student, based on number. This strategy was used extensively for the units in this book.

## Jigsaw

The "jigsaw" strategy is used in several lessons. This involves students working in one group to become an "expert" on a part of the material. The students are then regrouped so that each new group has one "expert" for each part of the material. Students teach each other the material that they have learned. This allows students to become confident in knowing the material and then to understand it even better by teaching it to others.

## Think-Pair-Share

We began using this strategy more than 30 years ago when we were first conducting story times in the library. We were not happy with the quality of the discussion after a book was read. The same students participated every time, and the other students didn't have to think. Think-pair-share allows every student the opportunity and responsibility to answer a question. All too often, an instructor asks a question and one student responds. The instructor then assumes that everyone understands. To truly check for understanding, all students need to be held responsible for thinking of a response and verbalizing it. This is particularly true for English-language learners. Think-pair-share allows them to respond in a small and safe situation. It also allows students who do not understand to be taught by their partners. This cannot be used for all questions during a lesson, as it would bog down the pace. It should be used when asking questions for which there are divergent answers. If the answer is "yes" or "no," either choral response or hand signals (thumbs up and thumbs down at an appointed time) are better choices.

The lessons in this book alert the instructor when to use think-pair-share. The instructor asks the question, gives think time, and then has the partners share. The partners should be either students sitting next to each other (shoulder partners) or across from each other (eyeball partners). The pairs should be given a total of between one and three minutes of time to share for each question.

The instructor *must* circulate among the pairs, whether they are seated on the carpet or at tables and desks. If there is a pair that is not responding, go up to the pair and direct the question to one of the partners. When she or he begins to answer, says, "Tell your partner." Every once in while there is a student who does not like his or her partner and refuses to cooperate. A tactic to nip this in the bud is to explain that people do not choose their co-workers in the real world. Give the student the choice of cooperating or coming in during lunch to answer the questions with you. Halfway through the designated "pair" time, remind the students that it's the other student's turn to talk. After the pairs have discussed the questions, call the group together again and have some of the pairs share their answers. You should feel free to call on any student. If the student didn't understand before pair time, the other student should have explained the answer.

## ADDITIONAL ACTIVE PARTICIPATION STRATEGIES

Active participation strategies have been built into the lessons. For some lessons, students congregate at an area under a sign and discuss their research. In other lessons, students challenge each other on specific knowledge items.

## Working in Pairs

Many of the lessons call for students to work in pairs. This was done for two reasons. First, sometimes there are not sufficient reference sources (books or computers) or materials for each student. Another reason is to have students help each other with the assignment. These pairs can be random or purposely formed by the instructor so that nonreaders or English-language learners are paired with stronger students.

## Group Composition and Paraphrasing

The strategy for several of the lessons is group composition during the modeling phase of the lesson. This is accomplished by identifying the information that needs to be written and using think-pair-share to have students compose complete sentences. After listening to several suggestions, write one of them on the board. With kindergarten to second grade, you may choose to do some encoding aloud to model it for the students. For grades 3 through 6, the students should read along as you write the sentence. You and the students should always repeat the sentence that has been written. There are times when complete sentences are not appropriate, such as when notes are taken. Use think-pair-share for the students to come up with the information, which is then written in phrases on the board. After the activity is finished, read the sentences or notes aloud with the students, pointing out the ways in which the writing meets the criteria for the activity. This solidifies what the students are to do during guided practice.

## BLOOM'S TAXONOMY

The lessons in this book are aimed at the higher levels based on Benjamin Bloom's *Taxonomy of Educational Objectives*. A summary of these objectives are available on many Web sites and on pages 111–112 in Gronlund's *How to Write and Use Instructional Objectives*. The skills are hierarchical from understanding (remembering things learned) to comprehension (getting the meaning of what was learned) to analysis (breaking something down to smaller parts in order to understand its organization) to synthesis (putting together ideas in a new way) to evaluations (judging the value of something for a specific purpose).

An example of an understanding objective is that the student will recall that dictionaries are in alphabetical order. Students who demonstrate application should be able to find words in the dictionary using the alphabet. At the analysis level, the student should be able to use the dictionary to find spelling, part of speech, and meanings. At the synthesis level, students are able to make their own dictionaries using words that are important for a content area. At the evaluation level, the students assess their dictionaries, or commercial ones, to see whether they meet the criteria of a good dictionary.

## REFERENCES

American Association of School Librarians. 2007. *Standards for the 21st-Century Learner*. Chicago: American Library Association. Available: www.ala.org/ala/aasl/aaslproftools/learningstandards/standards.cfm

Bloom, Benjamin S. 1956. *Taxonomy of Educational Objectives: The Classification of Educational Goals*. New York: Susan Fauer Company.

Enz, Billie, Sally C. Hurwitz, and Barbie J. Carlile. 2007. *Coaching the Student Teacher*. Dubuque, IA: Kendall Hunt Publishing.

Giles, Jim. 2005. "Internet Encyclopedias Go Head to Head." *Nature* 438: 900-901.

Gronlund, Norman F. 2000. *How to Write and Use Instructional Objectives*. New York: Merrill.

Hunter, Madeline. 1982. *Mastery Teaching*. Thousand Oaks, CA: Corwin Press.

Jones, Fred. 2000. *Fred Jones Tools for Teaching*. Santa Cruz, CA: Fredric H. Jones and Associates.

# Chapter 1

# The Dictionary

## KINDERGARTEN DICTIONARY LESSON 1:  FUN WITH WORDS

**Standards:**

*AASL #1:*    Inquire, think critically, and gain knowledge. 1.1, Skills: 1.1.1, Follow an inquiry-based process in seeking knowledge in curricular subjects, and make the real-world connection for using this process in own life; 1.1.4, Find, evaluate, and select appropriate sources to answer questions.
*NCTE #8:*    Students use a variety of technological and information resources to gather and synthesize information and to create and communicate knowledge.
*Language Arts:*    Students recognize that print represents spoken language and conveys definition.

**Objective:**
Students are attentive while the instructor uses the dictionary to find the definition of a word.

**Materials:**

- one regular dictionary
- one picture dictionary
- picture book with a few words not known to most kindergarten students
- dictionary sign

**Set:** Read a short picture book with a few words not known to most kindergarten students, such as "ptarmigan," "ermine," "lemmings," and "mukluks" in *Mama, Do You Love Me?*

**Input:** Ask whether the students know a specific word from the book; allow some guesses using context or pictures. Look up the word in a regular dictionary, telling students each part of the process: letter in the alphabet, finding the word in the dictionary, reading the definition, and relating it to concepts they know. Compare the definition of the word with their guesses. Show the picture dictionary and its features, noting that the book is arranged alphabetically and gives a picture for the definition. Look up easily identifiable words the students know and guide them through the process: "bridge," "kindergarten," "rope," "strong," and "zipper." Reinforce the point that dictionaries are books people use to discover the definitions of words and are arranged in alphabetical order.

**Assessment:** Informally observe whether the students followed along as you modeled the procedure for finding words in the picture dictionary.

**Closure:** Using think-pair-share, ask the students, "What would you use a dictionary for?" (to look up words).

## KINDERGARTEN DICTIONARY LESSON 2: MAKING A PICTURE DICTIONARY

**Standards:**

*AASL #1:*    Inquire, think critically, and gain knowledge. 1.1, Skills: 1.1.1, Follow an inquiry-based process in seeking knowledge in curricular subjects, and make the real-world connection for using this process in own life; 1.1.4, Find, evaluate, and select appropriate sources to answer questions.
*NCTE #12:*    Students use spoken, written, and visual language to accomplish their own purposes.
*Language Arts:*    Students communicate by drawing, telling, or writing for a purpose.

**Objective:**

Students make a dictionary of their favorite words, using alphabetical order and picture dictionary skills. (The illustration matches the definition of the word.)

**Materials:**

- board and markers
- commercially prepared blank big book (available from www.barebooks.com/books.htm) or one made of 12″ × 18″ construction paper
- blank copy paper for students' illustrations
- crayons, two boxes per table
- a sample of a picture dictionary, either commercial or homemade
- dictionary sign

**Set:** Show the students a picture dictionary and look up a word in it. Note the word and the picture and ask, "Who thinks we can make our own picture dictionary?"

**Review:** Review with the students that dictionaries are books of words that contain the definition and the spelling of each word, and that they are arranged in alphabetical order.

**Input:** State two of your favorite words, ones that the students will recognize. Draw a picture to represent the words. Through think-pair-share, solicit the students' favorite words, recording them on the board and on blank pieces of paper at the same time. If there are duplicates, make sure there are enough words for each student to illustrate one.

**Guided practice:** Give each student a paper with a word on it and ask him or her to illustrate the word. Cut out the students' pictures so that mistakes can be corrected on the other side. Make sure that students put their names on the papers. Circulate to make sure students are drawing pictures that correctly illustrate the word. Reread the word to any student who forgets.

**Assessment:** Informally observe whether the students drew pictures appropriate for the words.

**Closure:** As the students line up to leave the library, call out and collect, in alphabetical order, the words they have illustrated, in order to ensure that they understand that dictionaries are arranged in alphabetical order.

**Instructor's homework:** Type the students' words, which should already be in alphabetical order, and put them in the big book that has been prepared. Cut out the students' illustrations and names, and affix them to the correct page. If more than one student illustrated a word, put all of the pictures on the same page. The students' dictionary can be shared by the class the next time they visit the library.

## FIRST-GRADE DICTIONARY LESSON 1: WORKING WITH WORDS

**Standards:**

*AASL #1:*  Inquire, think critically, and gain knowledge. 1.1, Skills: 1.1.1, Follow an inquiry-based process in seeking knowledge in curricular subjects, and make the real-world connection for using this process in own life; 1.1.4, Find, evaluate, and select appropriate sources to answer questions.
*NCTE #6:*  Students apply knowledge of language structure, language conventions, media techniques, figurative language, and genre to create, critique, and discuss print and non-print texts.
*Language Arts:*  Students communicate by drawing, telling, or writing for a purpose.

**Objectives:**

1.   Students illustrate a common definition for a word.
2.   Students give multiple definitions for common words.

**Materials:**

- 16 primary dictionaries
- 15 copies of the work sheet with words and page numbers (*Scholastic First Dictionary* was used for the work sheet from the CD)
- board-ready work sheet
- dictionary sign

**Set:** Say, "Please hand me the mouse." Use think-pair-share to elicit what the sentence means. Point out the different meanings of the sentence, based on two different definitions of mouse: "a small furry animal" or "a small hand-operated device used for computer input."

**Review:** Show the students a primary dictionary and ask through think-pair-share how the dictionary is organized.

**Input:** Display the words from the work sheet on the board. There are eight words, which have multiple definitions. The words and their page numbers in the dictionary are also provided on work sheets for the students, with plenty of space between the words so that the students can illustrate the definitions. Look up "along" in the primary dictionary, with pairs of students looking up the word in their own primary dictionaries.

Think aloud the steps to looking up the word: What is the first letter of the word, where is that letter in the alphabet, and how far into a dictionary would that letter be? Tell the students the page number for the word. Read the first definition of the word, the one the students know, emphasizing that the first definition is the most common. Draw a picture to illustrate the definition. Read another definition of the word and explain it. Illustrate that definition of the word.

**Guided practice:** Think aloud the steps for finding the next word. The students turn to that page of the dictionary. Read the common definition of the word, emphasizing that the first definition is the most common. Along with the students, draw an illustration for that word. Read a less common definition for the word and explain it. With the students, draw an illustration for that definition of the word. Repeat the procedure for the rest of the words.

**Assessment:** Collect the papers and assess whether the pictures reflect the different definitions of the words.

**Closure:** Students pretend they are words and line up in alphabetical order by their first names.

## FIRST-GRADE DICTIONARY LESSON 2:  DICTIONARY OF CONTENT WORDS, PART 1

**Standards:**

*AASL #1:*   Inquire, think critically, and gain knowledge. 1.1, Skills: 1.1.1, Follow an inquiry-based process in seeking knowledge in curricular subjects, and make the real-world connection for using this process in own life; 1.1.4, Find, evaluate, and select appropriate sources to answer questions.
*NCTE #6:*   Students apply knowledge of language structure, language conventions, media techniques, figurative language, and genre to create, critique, and discuss print and non-print texts.
*Language Arts:*   Students communicate by drawing, telling, or writing for a purpose.

**Objectives:**

1.   Students demonstrate an understanding that a dictionary is a reference source that gives the definitions of words and that it is arranged in alphabetical order.
2.   Students brainstorm the definitions of content words and create a content dictionary.

**Materials:**

- specialized dictionary, such as *A Visual Dictionary of Baseball* by James Buckley or *The New Illustrated Dinosaur Dictionary* by Helen Roney Sattler
- board and markers
- blank copy paper
- 10 to 15 content words from a targeted first-grade curriculum
- dictionary sign

**Set:** Show the students a specialized dictionary such as those noted above and look something up in it. Ask the students what they are studying in science, math, or social studies. (Before the lesson, confer with the classroom teacher and select the content area and words to be targeted.)

**Review:** Use think-pair-share to review that a dictionary is a book of words and their definitions and that it is in alphabetical order.

**Input:** Say a content word from the targeted curriculum. Write a definition of the word on the board and ask the students whether it is correct. Then ask the students for content words that are from the targeted area of the curriculum. Use the board to record the students' suggestions and also write them on blank copy paper. If the students can't think of enough content words, use the content words from the list provided by the classroom teacher. There should be 10 to 15 content words generated by your or the students' list.

**Guided practice:** Use think-pair-share to have students come up with a definition of another content word.

**Assessment:** Informally observe whether the students understand that giving a definition is not the same as using the word in a sentence.

**Closure:** Hand out the words, written on the copy paper. The students line up alphabetically according to the word each student holds. Collect the sheets as the students leave.

## FIRST-GRADE DICTIONARY LESSON 3: DICTIONARY OF CONTENT WORDS, PART 2

**Standards:**

*AASL #1:*   Inquire, think critically, and gain knowledge. 1.1, Skills: 1.1.1, Follow an inquiry-based process in seeking knowledge in curricular subjects, and make the real-world connection for using this process in own life; 1.1.4, Find, evaluate, and select appropriate sources to answer questions.
*NCTE #6:*   Students apply knowledge of language structure, language conventions, media techniques, figurative language, and genre to create, critique, and discuss print and non-print texts.
*Language Arts:*   Students communicate by drawing, telling, or writing for a purpose.

**Objectives:**

1.   Students demonstrate an understanding that a dictionary is a reference source that gives the definitions of words and that it is arranged in alphabetical order.
2.   Students brainstorm the definitions of content words and create a content dictionary.

**Materials:**

- board and markers
- commercially prepared blank book or one made of 12″ × 18″ construction paper
- lined paper for students' definitions with the content word already printed on each paper at the top
- crayons, two boxes per table
- a sample of a primary dictionary, either commercial or homemade
- dictionary sign

**Set:** Show a primary dictionary. State that the students have been studying [a particular content area]. "Today we are going to make a dictionary of words about [the content area]. You will be able to use the dictionary to write about [the content area]."

**Review:** State a word, and then read the most common definition of the word. Note that the definition does not contain the word itself.

**Input:** Teach the standards of a good definition (e.g., the definition makes the word understood by someone who doesn't know it, the definition doesn't use the word to define it). Model, using one of the content words, how to write a definition of the word. Say aloud the thinking process. What does the word mean? Give a non-example by using the word in a sentence, and explain that the definition cannot do that. Finish with a clear definition of the word. For example: "'Root' is the word I want to define. I can't say, 'A plant has roots,' because that's using it in a sentence, not defining it. You can't use the word to define it. How about, 'Root: The part of a plant that is usually underground. It gets food for the plant.'"

**Guided practice:** Students are paired. The pairs write definitions of the content words. (The modeled definition word can be given to students who struggle either academically or with English.) Circulate, and write down the students' ideas, if they cannot express themselves in writing. It may be very difficult for some students. You may have to supply these students with a simple definition.

**Assessment:** As you circulate, informally assess the students' skill in devising definitions.

**Closure:** Have some of the students share their definitions. Point out how these meet the criteria for a definition. Have the students line up alphabetically by the words they defined. As the students leave, collect their dictionary pages.

**Instructor's homework:** Type up the content "dictionary" and copy it for each student.

## FIRST-GRADE DICTIONARY LESSON 4: DICTIONARY OF CONTENT WORDS, PART 3

**Standards:**

*AASL #1:*    Inquire, think critically, and gain knowledge. 1.1, Skills: 1.1.1, Follow an inquiry-based process in seeking knowledge in curricular subjects, and make the real-world connection for using this process in own life; 1.1.4, Find, evaluate, and select appropriate sources to answer questions.
*NCTE #6:*    Students apply knowledge of language structure, language conventions, media techniques, figurative language, and genre to create, critique, and discuss print and non-print texts.
*Language Arts:*    Students communicate by drawing, telling, or writing for a purpose.

**Objective:**
Students illustrate the content dictionary to enhance the definitions.

**Materials:**

- board and markers
- crayons, two boxes per table
- a sample of a picture dictionary, either commercial or homemade
- dictionary sign

**Set:** Distribute the 10- to 15-page content dictionaries made from the students' work at the last lesson and have the students, together, read the dictionary out loud. If the students cannot independently read, do "echo reading": read a line and have the students repeat it.

**Review:** Use think-pair-share to review how a dictionary is organized and what makes a good definition.

**Input:** Use the board to illustrate a content word.

**Guided practice:** Tell the students to draw pictures of the definitions of the words in their copies of the class content dictionary. They can refer to their "dictionaries" for the definitions.

**Assessment:** Informally observe whether the students drew pictures that illustrated the definitions of the words.

**Closure:** Use think-pair-share and ask students to compare writing a definition and drawing an illustration for a word. Tell the students to take their content dictionary home and share it with their family.

## SECOND-GRADE DICTIONARY LESSON 1: INTRODUCTION TO GUIDE WORDS

**Standards:**

*AASL #1:* Inquire, think critically, and gain knowledge. 1.1, Skills: 1.1.1, Follow an inquiry-based process in seeking knowledge in curricular subjects, and make the real-world connection for using this process in own life; 1.1.4, Find, evaluate, and select appropriate sources to answer questions.
*NCTE #8:* Students use a variety of technological and information resources to gather and synthesize information and to create and communicate knowledge.
*Language Arts:* Students demonstrate understanding of print concept and alphabetize a series of words to the second letter.

**Objectives:**

1. Students use guide words to find the location of a word in a dictionary.
2. Students alphabetize to the first and second letter in order to find the location of a word in a dictionary.

**Materials:**

- sets of "pairs" of guide words and individual words printed on tag board by hand or printed from the CD
- the first sets of guide words and individual words should require the student to alphabetize to the first letter
- the second set of guide words and individual words should require the students to alphabetize to the second letter
- picture dictionary
- primary dictionary
- dictionary sign
- board

**Set:** Search for a word in the dictionary. Announce the word to the class, a word near the beginning of the alphabet, such as "cat." Search near the end of the dictionary, saying the words on the pages. Ask the students whether you're close. (They'll say, "NO!") Show the students the guide words and read them. Ask whether this is close to "c" for "cat." Then ask for suggestions. (Students will say different letter, farther forward.)

**Review:** Review that a dictionary is in alphabetical order and contains the definitions of words. Show a picture dictionary and a primary dictionary. Point out the guide words.

**Input:** Put two sets of guide words on the board. Explain that guide words tell whether a word falls between them or not on a page in a dictionary. Use non-examples as well: words that don't fall between either pair of guide words. This activity will *not* simulate an actual dictionary. This activity is to help students understand the concept of guide words and how to alphabetize between words. The guide words are "apple" and "farm" on the first set and "lamp" to "sack" on the second. The individual words are "bat," "cat," "egg," "dog," "money," "net," "pie," "run," "jump," and "work." These should *not* be presented in alphabetical order. Ask between which set of guide words each word belongs and places it in the correct position. If the word doesn't belong between either set of guide words, it is placed at the bottom of the board.

**Guided practice:** Select four students to be the "guide words," which are printed larger than the other words. The remaining students are each given a word and asked to stand "where they belong," between the correct guide words, four at a time. Once the students are standing between the correct guide words, have the students arrange themselves in alphabetical order. Repeat the input and the guided practice using the set of words and guide words that will require the students to alphabetize to the second letter.

**Assessment:** Informally assess by observing whether the students placed themselves between the correct guide words.

**Closure:** Use think-pair-share and ask, "How did you know where your word belonged?" Reinforce that they used the guide words.

## SECOND-GRADE DICTIONARY LESSON 2: CATEGORIES AND DICTIONARY PRACTICE

**Standards:**

*AASL #1:*   Inquire, think critically, and gain knowledge. 1.1, Skills: 1.1.1, Follow an inquiry-based process in seeking knowledge in curricular subjects, and make the real-world connection for using this process in own life; 1.1.4, Find, evaluate, and select appropriate sources to answer questions.
*NCTE #8:*   Students use a variety of technological and information resources to gather and synthesize information and to create and communicate knowledge.
*Language Arts:*   Students identify a variety of sources that may be used to answer specific questions and/or gather information.

**Objectives:**

1.   Students use guide words to find words in a dictionary.
2.   Students write the definition of words from a dictionary and put the words into categories.

**Materials:**

- 30 primary dictionaries
- one set of two category cards and four words for modeling
- five category cards on 11″ × 17″ paper
- 30 words (six words for each category) for guided practice from the CD
- 30 index cards
- dictionary sign

**Set:** Tell the class that you have a word that you are using in a letter to your mother, but you are not sure whether you are using the correct definition of the word. Ask the class, "How can I find the definition of the word?" Someone in the class will suggest using a dictionary. Model finding the word by using the guide words in the dictionary and reading the correct definition.

**Review:** Review that a dictionary is arranged in alphabetical order, and that it contains the definitions of words. Show a primary dictionary and point out the guide words.

**Input:** Place four words on the overhead or chart: "drill," "hammer," "salad," and "pizza." Assign four students to look up the words and have them write the *first* definition in the dictionary on an index card. Collect the cards and print the definition of each word on the board or affix them to a chart. Use think-pair-share and ask the questions, "Can these four words be placed into categories? If they can, how many categories, and what would the names of the categories be?" The students should give the categories of tools and food or something similar. Lead a discussion on how most words will have more than one definition, and how the first definition is the most commonly used definition.

**Guided practice:** Hand out one word on an index card per student. The students use their dictionaries to find the word and write the *first* definition. After all the students are done, tape five category cards around the room, and ask the students to stand by the category they think their word belongs under. After the students place themselves into the categories, tell each student in each category to say their word and definition. Then ask the rest of the class whether that word belongs in that category.

**Assessment:** Informally observe whether the students have written the first definition of the word and whether they have placed themselves in the correct category.

**Closure:** Use think-pair-share and ask, "How did using the guide words help you find your word in the dictionary?"

## SECOND-GRADE DICTIONARY LESSON 3: PARTS OF A MAIN ENTRY

**Standards:**

*AASL #1:* Inquire, think critically, and gain knowledge. 1.1, Skills: 1.1.1, Follow an inquiry-based process in seeking knowledge in curricular subjects, and make the real-world connection for using this process in own life; 1.1.4, Find, evaluate, and select appropriate sources to answer questions.

*NCTE #8:* Students use a variety of technological and information resources to gather and synthesize information and to create and communicate knowledge.

*Language Arts:*    Students identify a variety of sources that may be used to answer specific questions and/or gather information.

**Objective:**

Students identify the features (spelling, the word as main entry, pronunciation, definitions, part of speech, and guide words) of a dictionary.

**Materials:**

- board-ready pages from a primary dictionary
- brochure on the dictionary for students and parents from the CD
- 30 copies of a primary dictionary
- seven signs each of the parts of a main entry: word, spelling, pronunciation, definition, sample sentence, other definitions, and guide words from the CD
- dictionary sign

**Set:** Tell the class that people are tool makers. A tool is a very useful thing. A tool such as a hammer has several features: a handle and head, which has a face, eye, cheek, throat, crown, and a claw. A dictionary is a tool we use in the library and classroom, and it has its own special features.

**Review:** Review that a dictionary is arranged in alphabetical order and that it contains the definitions of words. Show a primary dictionary and point out the guide words.

**Input:** Display a board-ready page of a primary dictionary. Go over every feature of a main entry: guide words, word, spelling, pronunciation, definition, other definitions, and sample sentence.

**Guided practice:** Each student is given a card with the name of one of the features of a main entry on it. As you read a dictionary entry word, either from the board or the dictionary itself, the students stand up when they hear their part of the entry. For example, read the word "good" and the students with a "word" sign stand up. Then spell the word, and the students with the "spelling" signs stand up, and so on through all parts of a main entry. Do as many words as time allows.

**Assessment:** Informally observe whether the students stood up when their part of the main entry was read.

**Closure:** Use think-pair-share and ask, "How many features of a dictionary entry can you identify?"

## THIRD-GRADE DICTIONARY LESSON 1:  CREATING A MAIN ENTRY

**Standards:**

*AASL #1:*    Inquire, think critically, and gain knowledge. 1.1, Skills: 1.1.1, Follow an inquiry-based process in seeking knowledge in curricular subjects, and make the real-world connection for using this process in own life; 1.1.4, Find, evaluate, and select appropriate sources to answer questions.

*NCTE #8:*    Students use a variety of technological and information resources to gather and synthesize information and to create and communicate knowledge.

*Language Arts:* Students determine the definitions and other features of words (e.g., pronunciation, syllabication, synonyms, parts of speech) using the dictionary, thesaurus, and CD-ROM and Internet when available.

**Objectives:**

1. Students identify the parts of a dictionary main entry (word, parts of speech, and definition/s).
2. Students create a main entry for a given word.

**Materials:**

- 30 elementary dictionaries
- board-ready copy of the work sheet
- 30 paper strips with one word on each from the CD
- 30 copies of the work sheet from the CD
- dictionary sign
- 30 copies of the Dictionary brochure from the CD

**Set:** Show a pencil (or some other item in a library) and think aloud, "Are there any words that can describe and explain a pencil to someone who has never seen one?" The students give suggestions until an agreed upon definition is produced. Write the students' definition on the board. Look the word up in the dictionary and read the definition aloud. The class compares their definition with the dictionary definition.

**Review:** Review that a dictionary is arranged in alphabetical order and that it contains the definitions of words. Show an elementary dictionary and point out the guide words. Have two sets of guide words on the board. Leave spaces between each guide word set and give 10 students one word each. Ask them to put the words between the correct guide words.

**Input:** Put a word ("chair," "table," "paper," etc.) on the board and model making up a dictionary main entry: the word, the part of speech, and the definition/s. Write on the board the parts of a dictionary main entry: the word, the part of speech, and the definition/s, so that the students can use it to refer to during guided practice.

**Guided practice:** Distribute a paper strip and a work sheet to each student. Explain that the students are to make up a main entry for the word. After everyone at their table has finished, the students share the entries they created. Then explain that after the students have created their main entry, they are to look up their word in a dictionary and write the dictionary main entry on their work sheet. They are to compare and contrast it with the main entry they created.

**Assessment:** Ask some of the students to share their created entries and the dictionary entries with the class. Observe whether each student has included every part of a dictionary main entry, and how close to the common definition the students came.

**Closure:** Use think-pair-share and ask, "How many parts of a dictionary main entry can you identify?" Distribute the Dictionary brochure, go over it, and ask the students to share it with their families.

## THIRD-GRADE DICTIONARY LESSON 2:　WEATHER WORDS

**Standards:**

*AASL #1:*　Inquire, think critically, and gain knowledge. 1.1, Skills: 1.1.1, Follow an inquiry-based process in seeking knowledge in curricular subjects, and make the real-world connection for using this process in own life; 1.1.4, Find, evaluate, and select appropriate sources to answer questions.

*NCTE #8:*　Students use a variety of technological and information resources to gather and synthesize information and to create and communicate knowledge.

*Language Arts:*　Students determine the definitions and other features of words (e.g., pronunciation, syllabication, synonyms, parts of speech) using the dictionary, thesaurus, and CD-ROM and Internet when available.

**Objectives:**

1.　Students use a dictionary to find the definition of a specific "Weather Word."
2.　Students categorize the weather words into "Mild," "In-between," or "Severe."

**Materials:**

- 30 elementary dictionaries
- 30 paper strips with one weather word on each from the CD
- two weather words for modeling
- three chart papers titled "Mild," "In-between," and "Severe"
- dictionary sign
- board-ready copy of the paper strip

**Set:** Ask, "Does everyone remember Hurricane Katrina? What do you think caused more damage and loss of life: the hurricane or the flooding that came after the breaking of the levees?" Discuss the various answers and let the students know that if the levees hadn't broken, the hurricane damage wouldn't have been that bad.

**Review:** Review that a dictionary is arranged in alphabetical order, and that it contains the definitions of words. Show an elementary dictionary and point out the guide words.

**Input:** Explain that every field of study has its own bank of words. Weather is a field of study that has many interesting and unique words. Explain that each student will be given a "weather word" to look up in the dictionary. They are to write the definition of the word. If the word has multiple definitions, they are to use the one that deals with weather. Model the procedure with two weather words: "fog," a word with multiple definitions; and "drizzle," with only one definition.

**Guided practice:** Distribute the dictionaries and the paper strips with the weather words. As the students are working, hang three chart papers marked "Mild," "In-between," and "Severe," respectively. After the students have written their definitions from the dictionary, they share their words and definitions with the students at their table. As a group, the students decide in which category their words fall. Model a procedure, using the two weather words from the input. (Both "fog" and "drizzle" should be placed under "Mild.") Ask one table at a time to come up and place their words on the correct chart paper. They say their word and the definition as they place their word. Ask the class whether they agree with the placement. If time allows, lead a general discussion on which of the severe weather conditions the students think have caused the most damage and loss of life.

**Assessment:** Informally observe whether the students have found the correct definitions, and whether the words were placed in the correct categories.

**Closure:** Ask the students, "Where can we find the definitions of words?" The students answer chorally.

## THIRD-GRADE DICTIONARY LESSON 3:  USING INTERNET DICTIONARIES

**Standards:**

*AASL #1:*   Inquire, think critically, and gain knowledge. 1.1, Skills: 1.1.1, Follow an inquiry-based process in seeking knowledge in curricular subjects, and make the real-world connection for using this process in own life; 1.1.4, Find, evaluate, and select appropriate sources to answer questions.
*NCTE #8:*   Students use a variety of technological and information resources to gather and synthesize information and to create and communicate knowledge.
*Language Arts:*   Students determine the definitions and other features of words (e.g., pronunciation, syllabication, synonyms, parts of speech) using the dictionary, thesaurus, and CD-ROM and Internet when available.

**Objectives:**

1. Students demonstrate use of an Internet dictionary.
2. Students write definition of words from three different Internet dictionaries.

**Materials:**

- http://encarta.msn.com/encnet/features/dictionary/dictionaryhome.aspx
- www.wordcentral.com/
- www.m-w.com/
- projection of an Internet computer screen (must have access to computer, Internet, and means of projection)
- 15 computers with Internet access, or enough so that each pair can access the Internet dictionaries
- 15 paper strips with three words from the CD
- 15 copies of the work sheet from the CD
- board-ready copy of the work sheet
- dictionary sign

**Set:** Ask the students, "If you are at home and need to use a dictionary, but your dog ate it, is there another place where you could go to find the definition of a word?"

**Review:** Review the rules on using the Internet at school.

**Input:** Demonstrate how to access and use the three Internet dictionaries: Encarta, WordCentral.com, and Merriam-Webster Online. Point out the features of each Web site and compare and contrast them. Type in a different word in each of the Internet dictionaries.

**Guided practice:** Pair the students, give them a work sheet and a paper strip, and assign each pair a computer. Instruct the students to write the three words on the paper strip on the work sheet. They are then to look the words up using the appropriate Internet dictionary and write the definition on the work sheet.

**Assessment:** Informally assess whether the students were able to access and use the Internet dictionaries.

**Closure:** Ask the students, "Was it easier or harder to use the Internet dictionaries than a book dictionary? Why?"

## FOURTH-GRADE DICTIONARY LESSON I: MULTIPLE DEFINITIONS

**Standards:**

*AASL #1:*   Inquire, think critically, and gain knowledge. 1.1, Skills: 1.1.1, Follow an inquiry-based process in seeking knowledge in curricular subjects, and make the real-world connection for using this process in own life; 1.1.4, Find, evaluate, and select appropriate sources to answer questions.
*NCTE #8:*   Students use a variety of technological and information resources to gather and synthesize information and to create and communicate knowledge.
*Language Arts:*   Students determine the definitions and parts of speech of words by using a variety of reference aids.

**Objectives:**

1.   Students demonstrate an understanding that many words have multiple definitions.
2.   Students guess the multiple definitions of a word and then use a dictionary to find all the multiple definitions.

**Materials:**

- board-ready copy of the work sheet from the CD
- 15 intermediate dictionaries
- visual of a person running, a baseball diamond, and a clock
- word list from the CD
- 15 copies of the work sheets from the CD
- dictionary sign

**Set:** Ask, "How many definitions do you think there are for the word 'run'?" Show the visual of a person running and ask the students to explain this definition of the word "run" (to go fast). Show the visual of the baseball diamond and ask the students for another definition for the word "run" (to go around all four bases). Finally, show the visual of a clock and ask the students whether they can think of two other definitions of the word "run" (the clock is running, meaning that the clock works or that time is passing). Write down their suggestions on the board.

**Review:** Review that a dictionary is arranged in alphabetical order and that it contains the definitions of words. Show an intermediate dictionary and point out the guide words.

**Input:** Look up "run" in the dictionary and write the numerous definitions on the board. The class compares them with their previous scripted definitions.

**Guided practice:** Pair the students and distribute an intermediate dictionary to each pair. Give each pair a work sheet with a word from the word list on it. The assignment is for the pairs to think of as many definitions of the word as they can and then look up the word in the dictionary and write down all the definitions. After the pair is finished at the table, they can challenge the other pair at their table to think of all the definitions of their word.

**Assessment:** Circulate and observe the guided practice to assess whether students understand all the definitions of their words.

**Closure:** Ask who found a word with three definitions. (Students name the word.) With four? With five? and so on. "Is there any trend in the words?" (Usually the simplest words have the most definitions.)

## FOURTH-GRADE DICTIONARY LESSON 2: STUMP YOUR INSTRUCTOR OR FRIEND DICTIONARY GAME

**Standards:**

*AASL #1:*    Inquire, think critically, and gain knowledge. 1.1, Skills: 1.1.1, Follow an inquiry-based process in seeking knowledge in curricular subjects, and make the real-world connection for using this process in own life; 1.1.4, Find, evaluate, and select appropriate sources to answer questions.
*NCTE #8:*    Students use a variety of technological and information resources to gather and synthesize information and to create and communicate knowledge.
*Language Arts:*    Students determine the definitions and parts of speech of words by using a variety of reference aids.

**Objectives:**

1.    Students use the dictionary to find words unknown to them.
2.    Students use the new word in a sentence that has context clues.

**Materials:**

- 15 intermediate dictionaries
- 60 copies of the "Stump Your Friend . . ." work sheet from the CD
- dictionary sign

**Set:** Ask students whether they know the definition of the word "gratified." Write on the board the students' answers. Then quote the sentence from the book *Sylvester and the Magic Pebble,* "In all his young life Sylvester had never had a wish gratified so quickly." Ask the students whether they have more ideas of what the word means now that they have heard it used in a sentence. Look the word up in an intermediate dictionary, read the definition, and discuss how close the students' guesses were to the dictionary definition.

**Review:** Review that a dictionary is arranged in alphabetical order and that it contains the definitions of words. Show an intermediate dictionary and point out the guide words.

**Input:** Pair the students and distribute an intermediate dictionary to each pair. Ask one student to look in the dictionary and find a word for which they think you may not know the definition. Ask the student to try and "stump" you with the word. Try to guess the definition. Then ask the student to use the word in a sentence to help you guess the definition. Try again to define the word. The student reads the definition. If you did not provide a correct definition, the student has stumped you.

**Guided practice:** Hand out four "Stump Your Friend . . ." work sheets to each pair. Go over the work sheet and make sure every student understands how to fill it out. Have each pair use the dictionary to look up a word they can use to stump the other pair at their table. They must write the most common definition and use it in a sentence, which may be the one in the dictionary. Have the pairs challenge each other as to the definition of the word, first by asking the word alone, and then by giving the word in a sentence with context clues. After they try to stump each other, each pair looks up another two words and writes a sentence for each. One word is to stump you and one is to stump their parents. Students each need a paper to take home to stump their parents. Pairs that stump earn a bookmark.

**Assessment:** Informally observe whether the students were able to find words unknown to them and write sentences with context clues.

**Closure:** Have some of the pairs report which words were known and which words stumped the other pair. Use think-pair-share to ask, "How did hearing the word in a sentence help in guessing the definition of the word?"

## FOURTH-GRADE DICTIONARY LESSON 3: USING AN INTERNET DICTIONARY

**Standards:**

*AASL #1:*  Inquire, think critically, and gain knowledge. 1.1, Skills: 1.1.1, Follow an inquiry-based process in seeking knowledge in curricular subjects, and make the real-world connection for using this process in own life; 1.1.4, Find, evaluate, and select appropriate sources to answer questions.
*NCTE #7:*  Students gather, evaluate, and synthesize data from a variety of sources to communicate their discoveries in ways that suit their purpose and audience.
*NETS Technology #3: Research and Information Fluency:*  Students apply digital tools to gather, evaluate, and use information.
*Language Arts:*  Students interpret details from functional text for a specific purpose.

**Objectives:**

1.  Students become familiar with a new content area by looking up key words using an Internet dictionary.
2.  Students create flashcards for the key words they look up.

**Materials:**

- projection of an Internet computer screen (must have access to computer, Internet, and means of projection)
- 15 computers with Internet access, or enough so that each pair can access the Internet dictionaries
- paper strips with geography context words from the CD
- http://encarta.msn.com/encnet/features/dictionary/dictionaryhome.aspx
- 30 index cards
- dictionary sign

**Set:** Say the word "meridian" and ask the students to guess, using think-pair-share, what the word might mean.

**Review:** Review the rules on using the Internet at school.

**Input:** Access the Internet and demonstrate how to look up the word "meridian" on the bookmarked Internet dictionary. Write the word in large letters on one side of an index card, write the definition on the other side, and explain that the students are going to make flashcards to learn the definitions of words used in the study of geography. Remind the students that the geographical definition may not be the first definition of the word.

**Guided practice:** The students are paired and assigned a computer per pair. Distribute a paper strip with two geography words and two index cards to each pair. The pairs look up the two words using the bookmarked Internet dictionary, making two flashcards; one member of the pair writes the flashcard while the other looks up the word, and then they switch tasks for the second word. Pairs try the flashcards out on other pairs.

**Assessment:** Informally observe whether the students are able to use the Internet dictionary and to write definitions that are understandable to the other students.

**Closure:** Ask several pairs to share the flashcards they have created.

## FIFTH-GRADE DICTIONARY LESSON 1: REVIEWING THE DICTIONARY

**Standards:**

*AASL #1:* Inquire, think critically, and gain knowledge. 1.1, Skills: 1.1.1, Follow an inquiry-based process in seeking knowledge in curricular subjects, and make the real-world connection for using this process in own life; 1.1.4, Find, evaluate, and select appropriate sources to answer questions.
*NCTE #8:* Students use a variety of technological and information resources to gather and synthesize information and to create and communicate knowledge.
*Language Arts:* Students determine the definitions of words by using a variety of reference sources.

**Objectives:**

1. Students use guide words to locate a specific word in an intermediate dictionary.
2. Students use an intermediate dictionary to find the definitions of words.

**Materials:**

- 15 intermediate dictionaries
- paper strips of the word list, from the CD or from the content the students are studying
- 30 index cards
- dictionary sign

**Set:** Say, "I recently told a student I was glad I was an avid reader. The student didn't know whether that was good or bad. How could the student find out?" (Students will say, "Look in the dictionary.")

**Review:** Review that a dictionary is arranged in alphabetical order and that it contains the definitions of words. Show an intermediate dictionary and show the guide words.

**Input:** Pair students and distribute an intermediate dictionary to each pair. Ask each pair to look up the word "avid," read the definition, and decide whether it is a compliment or an insult. Have the students identify the parts of the entry for "avid": spelling, pronunciation, part of speech, and definitions. Have them identify the guide words.

**Guided practice:** Hand the paper strips with two words from the word list and two index cards to each pair. Model the game procedure by using the set sentence. Put "avid" on one side of the card and "enthusiastic" on the other side of the index card.

Explain the game rules to the students:

- The pairs look up each word. They write a word on one side of an index card and the definition of the word on the other side of the index card.
- The pairs challenge the pair at their table, with one saying the word and the other pair trying to provide the definition. If time allows, the pairs can challenge pairs at other tables.

**Assessment:** Informally assess by observing the students' facility in using the dictionary to complete the task.

**Closure:** Use think-pair-share and ask students to name as many parts of the dictionary entry as possible.

## FIFTH-GRADE DICTIONARY LESSON 2: CONTENT WORDS

**Standards:**

*AASL #1:*   Inquire, think critically, and gain knowledge. 1.1, Skills: 1.1.1, Follow an inquiry-based process in seeking knowledge in curricular subjects, and make the real-world connection for using this process in own life; 1.1.4, Find, evaluate, and select appropriate sources to answer questions.
*NCTE #8:*   Students use a variety of technological and information resources to gather and synthesize information and to create and communicate knowledge.
*Language Arts:*   Students determine the definitions of words by using a variety of reference sources.

**Objective:**
Students use guide words to locate the definitions of specific content words.

**Materials:**

- 15 intermediate dictionaries
- 30 index cards
- paper strips with words from the CD or from the content the students are studying
- dictionary sign

**Set:** Say, "I had a snickerdoodle last night. Can anyone tell me what it is?" If no one can, give hints about it: cinnamon, crunchy, round, snack. Show the students a snickerdoodle cookie and explain that it is from the colonial era. Some words from history are still in common use while others have become less used.

**Review:** Review that a dictionary is arranged in alphabetical order and that it contains the definitions of words. Show an intermediate dictionary and point out the guide words.

**Input:** Pair students and distribute a student dictionary to each pair. Explain that the class is going to see which words are still in use from the American Colonial period. Look up "quarter" with the students and have them search for the definition that would relate to the colonial period (lodging for soldiers). Write the word on one side of an index card, and the definition on the other side.

**Guided practice:** Hand a paper strip with two words from the American Colonial period and two index cards to each pair. The pairs look up the words and see whether their words have a definition that is not used today. They write their index cards with the word on one side and the definition on the other side. They challenge the pair at their table to guess the definition of the words. If time allows, the pairs can challenge pairs at other tables.

**Assessment:** Informally assess by observing the students' facility in using the dictionary to complete the task.

**Closure:** Ask, "Which words are still commonly used? Which ones are less common or obsolete now?"

## FIFTH-GRADE DICTIONARY LESSON 3: ETYMOLOGY OF WORDS

**Standards:**

*AASL #1:*  Inquire, think critically, and gain knowledge. 1.1, Skills: 1.1.1, Follow an inquiry-based process in seeking knowledge in curricular subjects, and make the real-world connection for using this process in own life; 1.1.4, Find, evaluate, and select appropriate sources to answer questions.
*NCTE #8:*  Students use a variety of technological and information resources to gather and synthesize information and to create and communicate knowledge.
*Language Arts:*  Students determine the definitions of words by using a variety of reference sources.

**Objectives:**

1.  Students demonstrate knowledge of the word "etymology."
2.  Students use the dictionary to find the etymology of specific words.

**Materials:**

- 15 intermediate dictionaries
- board-ready copy of a dictionary page with the word "psychology"

- paper strips with two words from the CD
- 15 copies of the work sheet from the CD
- board-ready copy of the work sheet
- four paper banners, with the words "Greek," "Latin," "French," and "Middle English"
- dictionary sign

**Set:** Use think-pair-share to elicit answers to the following question: "Who came up with the word 'cyber-space' and what does it mean?" After their suggestions, tell them the story about who coined the word "cyber-space." (It was coined by William Gibson in his 1984 novel *Neuromancer.* In this book, "cyberspace" is a futuristic computer network that people use by plugging their minds into it. The term now refers to the Internet or to the online or digital world in general.)

**Review:** Review that a dictionary is arranged in alphabetical order and that it contains the definitions of words. Show a student dictionary and point out the guide words.

**Input:** Put the word "etymology" on the board. Put "etymon" and "logia" next to it. Explain that most English words came from other languages, particularly Greek and Latin. "Etymology" comes from "etymon," a Greek word that means "the true definition of a word." "Logia" is a Greek word that means "study." Put these together and you have the definition of the word "etymology," the study of a word by looking at its history. Tell about the *Oxford English Dictionary*, which was many years in the making and contains the etymology of many English words.

Pair the students and give each pair an intermediate dictionary. Have each pair look up the word "psychology." Project the board-ready work sheet. Have them note that the etymology is often at the end of the entry, and that not all of the entries in dictionaries have a word's etymology. Each pair traces the etymology of the word. (Greek "psyche" means "mind or soul," and "logia" means "study or science," but the dictionary also mentions Latin as a source of the word.) Sometimes more than one language is in the chain of the development of the word. Project the board-ready work sheet and model how to fill it out.

**Guided practice:** Give each pair a paper strip with two words and a student work sheet and ask the students to trace the etymology of the two words. Explain that the students must note from what language the words came. After they have researched the words, ask the students, by table, to stand under a banner of the language from which the word *first* originated. Have the students under each banner read their words.

**Assessment:** Informally assess by observing the students' facility in using the dictionary to complete the task.

**Closure:** Use think-pair-share and ask, "From what language did most of the English words we looked up today originate?"

## SIXTH-GRADE DICTIONARY LESSON 1: REVIEWING THE DICTIONARY

**Standards:**

*AASL #1:*   Inquire, think critically, and gain knowledge. 1.1, Skills: 1.1.1, Follow an inquiry-based process in seeking knowledge in curricular subjects, and make the real-world connection for using this process in own life; 1.1.4, Find, evaluate, and select appropriate sources to answer questions.

*NCTE #8:* Students use a variety of technological and information resources to gather and synthesize information and to create and communicate knowledge.
*Language Arts:* Students determine the definitions of words by using a variety of reference sources.

**Objective:**
Students use guide words and identify the parts of a dictionary entry, including multiple definitions.

**Materials:**

- 15 intermediate dictionaries
- poster board or paper for each group of four students
- dictionary sign
- markers at each table

**Set:** Ask, "How many of you think you know how to use the dictionary?"

**Review:** None, as this will be done by the groups.

**Input:** Say, "Since most of you are sure you understand using the dictionary, each group of four students is going to be assigned a concept to review for the rest of the class. Please number yourselves from one to four. All of the people in the group will think of the ideas on what to present to the rest of the class. Student one will get the materials and keep the group on task. Student two will write the ideas on the poster paper with markers. Student three will draw figures or pictures to help put the ideas across, and student four will present the poster and ideas. Each group's presentation will be less than three minutes." Give each group a concept: arrangement of the dictionary, guide words, spelling, pronunciation, part of speech, most common and multiple definitions, and etymology.

**Guided practice:** Circulate among the groups to ensure that they are reviewing the concepts correctly. After each table is finished designing their presentation, call the groups one at a time to present to the rest of the class.

**Assessment:** Informally assess by observing whether the students' understanding of the concepts was complete enough to prepare a review for the group.

**Closure:** Use think-pair-share and ask, "What was the difference in being in the teaching and the learning positions?"

## SIXTH-GRADE DICTIONARY LESSON 2: SCIENTIFIC TERMS

**Standards:**

*AASL #1:* Inquire, think critically, and gain knowledge. 1.1, Skills: 1.1.1, Follow an inquiry-based process in seeking knowledge in curricular subjects, and make the real-world connection for using this process in own life; 1.1.4, Find, evaluate, and select appropriate sources to answer questions.
*NCTE #8:* Students use a variety of technological and information resources to gather and synthesize information and to create and communicate knowledge.

*Science:*    Apply the following scientific processes to other problem solving or decision making situations: observing, questioning, communicating, comparing, measuring, classifying, predicting, organizing, inferring, generating, variables.

**Objectives:**

1.    Students efficiently use the dictionary to look up the definitions of words.
2.    Students apply the definitions to everyday problems.

**Materials:**

- 15 intermediate dictionaries
- 11 paper strips with one word written on each. The words are "observing," "questioning," "communicating," "comparing," "measuring," "classifying," "predicting," "organizing," "inferring," "generating," "variables"
- dictionary sign

**Set:** Ask, "You want to buy some new jeans. How can you figure out the best place and price?"

**Review:** Review that a dictionary is arranged in alphabetical order and that it contains the definitions of words. Show an intermediate dictionary and show the guide words.

**Input:** Say, "I have a problem. I want to buy the best jeans for the least money. We're going to look up words that will assist us in solving problems, whether personal or scientific. I'll do the first one, 'measuring.' I'm going to the middle of the dictionary because it starts with 'm.' looking at the guide words; I see it's on page XXX." (Read the appropriate definition.) "How would this apply to my problem? I need to take careful measurements of my waist and the inseam to make sure that I try on the right size of jeans."

**Guided practice:** Each pair looks up a word and writes several ideas on how it relates to the solving of the problem of finding the best jeans for the least amount of money. Each pair reports out the definition of the word and how they related it to the problem.

**Assessment:** Informally assess through observation whether the students could easily look up the words and whether they understood the words well enough to use them in problem solving.

**Closure:** Using think-pair-share, ask, **"**How do these words and process differ from how you usually would solve the problem of finding new jeans?"

## SIXTH-GRADE DICTIONARY LESSON 3: STUMP YOUR INSTRUCTOR OR FRIEND DICTIONARY GAME

**Standards:**

*AASL #1:*    Inquire, think critically, and gain knowledge. 1.1, Skills: 1.1.1, Follow an inquiry-based process in seeking knowledge in curricular subjects, and make the real-world connection for using this process in own life; 1.1.4, Find, evaluate, and select appropriate sources to answer questions.

*NCTE #8:* Students use a variety of technological and information resources to gather and synthesize information and to create and communicate knowledge.

*Language Arts:* Students determine the definitions and parts of speech of words by using a variety of reference aids.

**Objectives:**

1. Students use an intermediate dictionary to find words unknown to them.
2. Students use the new word in a sentence that has context clues.

**Materials:**

- 15 intermediate dictionaries
- 30 copies of the work sheet from the CD
- 60 copies of the "Stump Your Friend . . ." work sheet from the CD
- dictionary sign

**Set:** Ask students whether they know the word "naphtha." Script on the board the students' guesses. Then use the word in a sentence: "The naphtha used to dissolve the substance was stored away from paper products and heat." Ask the students whether they have more ideas of what the word means, now that they have heard it used in a sentence. Look the word up in an intermediate dictionary, Read the definition and discuss how close the student guesses were to the definition in the dictionary.

**Review:** Review that a dictionary is arranged in alphabetical order and that it contains the definitions of words. Show an intermediate dictionary and point out the guide words.

**Input:** Pair the students and distribute a student dictionary to each pair. Ask a student to look in the dictionary and find a word for which the student thinks that you may not know the definition. Ask the student to try and "stump" you with the word. Try to guess the definition. Then ask the student to use the word in a sentence to help you guess the definition. Again, try to define the word. Have the student read the definition. If you did not provide a correct definition, the student has stumped you.

**Guided practice:** Hand out four "Stump Your Friend, Instructor, and Parent" work sheets to each pair. Go over the work sheet and make sure every student understands how to fill it out. Have each pair use the dictionary to look up a word they can use to stump the other pair at their table. They must write the most common definition and use it in a sentence, which may be the one in the dictionary. Have the pairs challenge each other as to the definition of the word, first by asking the word alone, and then by giving the word in a sentence with context clues. After they try to stump each other, each pair looks up another two words, and writes a sentence for each. One word is to stump you and one is to stump their parents. Students each need a paper to take home to stump their parents. Pairs that stump earn a bookmark.

**Assessment:** Informally observe whether the students were able to find words unknown to them and write effective sentences with context clues.

**Closure:** Have some of the pairs report out which words were known and which words stumped the other pair. Use think-pair-share to ask, "How did hearing the word in a sentence help in guessing the definition of the word?"

# Chapter 2

# The Thesaurus

## KINDERGARTEN THESAURUS LESSON 1: CLASSROOM THESAURUS

**Standards:**

*AASL #1:*   Inquire, think critically, and gain knowledge. 1.1, Skills: 1.1.1, Follow an inquiry-based process in seeking knowledge in curricular subjects, and make the real-world connection for using this process in own life; 1.1.4, Find, evaluate, and select appropriate sources to answer questions.
*NCTE #6:*   Students apply knowledge of language structure, language conventions, media techniques, figurative language, and genre to create, critique, and discuss print and non-print texts.
*Language Arts:*   Students acquire and use new vocabulary in relevant contexts.

**Objective:**
Students will provide synonyms for words in order to create a classroom thesaurus.

**Materials:**

- student-made or trade picture dictionary
- a primary thesaurus
- 10–15 blank pieces of copy paper and a thick-point marker
- A cover of 9″ × 12″ construction paper. The front has "Our Thesaurus by _____'s Kindergarten Class." The back cover is blank.
- thesaurus sign

**Set:** Read the picture dictionary made during the kindergarten lesson on the dictionary from this book. If this is a stand-alone lesson, read a few pages of a picture dictionary.

**Review:** Point out to the students that the dictionary is arranged in alphabetical order, and the pictures show the meaning of the words.

**Input:** Show the students a thesaurus and state that these are special dictionaries that give words of similar meanings, synonyms. Students repeat the word "synonym" several times. Tell the students that every time you say the word "synonym" they are to stand up. Choose one of the words from the student-made or trade dictionary that is in the primary thesaurus. Explain how to look up the synonyms, using the word "synonym" often, so students have a chance to recognize it and stand up. For example, "I'm choosing the word 'cold' to find a *synonym*. I'm looking the word up in a thesaurus, a book of *synonyms*. I look it up under the first letter, 'c.' I've found it in the thesaurus, a book of *synonyms*. The following words are *synonyms* for cold: cool, chilly, frosty, icy, freezing, and frigid." Pick a few words from the student-made or trade dictionary, write them each on a separate piece of paper, and look them up in the thesaurus. (This will require checking for the words in the primary thesaurus ahead of time.) Write the synonyms found.

**Guided practice:** Pick 10 to 15 more words for which the students will know the synonyms. Write each word on a piece of paper and use think-pair-share to ask the students for a synonym. Record the correct ones on the papers. If the students cannot come up with a synonym, look up the word in the thesaurus. Repeat the procedure until there are 10 to 15 pages for a classroom thesaurus.

**Assessment:** Informally observe whether students are supplying words that are synonyms.

**Closure:** Have the students put the new "thesaurus" in alphabetical order. Staple the pages together with the cover and give it to the classroom teacher, along with the student-made dictionary.

## FIRST-GRADE THESAURUS LESSON 1: WHAT ARE SYNONYMS?

**Standards:**

*AASL #1:*   Inquire, think critically, and gain knowledge. 1.1, Skills: 1.1.1, Follow an inquiry-based process in seeking knowledge in curricular subjects, and make the real-world connection for using this process in own life; 1.1.4, Find, evaluate, and select appropriate sources to answer questions.
*NCTE #4:*   Students adjust their use of spoken, written, and visual language to communicate effectively with a variety of audiences for different purposes.
*Language Arts:*   Students acquire and use new vocabulary in relevant contexts.

**Objective:**
Students provide synonyms for common words such as "cold, "street," and "cheerful."

**Materials:**

- the students' dictionary of content words or a trade dictionary
- a primary thesaurus
- 15 primary thesauri (optional)
- work sheet from the CD
- board-ready copy of the work sheet (optional)
- thesaurus sign

**Set:** Start the lesson with a sentence using the same word many times, such as, "I'm going to start, begin, get going, and open the lesson today with this sentence." Ask what is unusual about the sentence and repeat it. Use think-pair-share to elicit answers.

**Review:** Review that a thesaurus is a book that provide the synonyms of words and is arranged in alphabetical order.

**Input:** Explain that synonyms are words that are similar in meaning, but not exactly alike. Model thinking of a synonym from the students' content dictionary or a trade dictionary. Model again using a common word, such as "quiet." Think aloud while coming up with "silent," "still," and "noiseless." Explain how the words are synonyms.

**Guided practice:** Pair students. Each pair is given a common word, such as "cold," "street," "coat," "cheerful," "clean," "car," "bump," "scare," "look," "pebble," "catch," "money," "shop," "pitch," "vanish," "crash," "yell." The assignment is to think of a synonym for that word.

An optional activity is to distribute primary thesauri and Work Sheet 2 from the CD. The page number in the *Scholastic Children's Thesaurus* is given for each word. The students look up the words and find at least one synonym for each word.

**Assessment:** Informally assess by circulating as the pairs work on the synonyms and observe whether they understand that synonyms are words that are similar in meaning.

**Closure:** Each pair presents, one student saying the given word, the other student saying the synonym.

## SECOND-GRADE THESAURUS LESSON I: ANNOYING ADJECTIVES

**Standards:**

*AASL #1:*   Inquire, think critically, and gain knowledge. 1.1, Skills: 1.1.1, Follow an inquiry-based process in seeking knowledge in curricular subjects, and make the real-world connection for using this process in own life; 1.1.4, Find, evaluate, and select appropriate sources to answer questions.
*NCTE #4:*   Students adjust their use of spoken, written, and visual language to communicate effectively with a variety of audiences and for different purposes.
*Language Arts:*   Students select words that convey the intended meaning and create a picture in the reader's mind.

**Objectives:**

1.   Students understand the features of a thesaurus (alphabetical order, words with similar meaning, entries that give parts of speech and definitions of the word, sample sentences, and words with opposite meanings).
2.   Students use a thesaurus to determine better word choices for adjectives in a writing selection.

**Materials:**

- board-ready page from a primary-grade thesaurus
- board-ready input sentence from the CD
- work sheet Guided practice sentence lists, with sentences with a redundant adjective, from the CD (*Note:* The sentences need to be copied enough times that all pairs receive two sentences; the sentences are differentiated to support student achievement levels)
- 15 primary thesauri
- thesaurus sign

**Set:** Ask the students to listen to two sentences and by a show of hands indicate which sentence they like better. "The students in this class are smart. The students in this class are brilliant."

**Review:** Show a primary thesaurus and discuss its alphabetical arrangement and its use as a reference source to find synonyms: words that have similar meanings. Also review that an adjective is a word that describes a noun.

**Input:** Pair students and distribute a primary thesaurus to each pair. Point out that the entries in a thesaurus include the word, the part of speech, the definition, a sample sentence, and synonyms. Project the board-ready sentence "The <u>dirty</u> dog had <u>dirty</u> paws." The pairs use their thesaurus to find the word "dirty" and see how many synonyms the thesaurus gives. Together the class crosses out the word "dirty" and writes above it a synonym that you and the students decide fits the meaning best. The new sentence is read, and think-pair-share is used to compare it to the original.

**Guided practice:** Give each pair two sentences with an overused adjective. The pairs use their thesaurus to look up the adjective and replace it with an appropriate synonym. Students share their original and reworded sentences. If there is additional time, you can hand out more sentences to the pairs.

**Assessment:** Informally assess by observing whether the students locate the underlined adjective, and whether they are able to use the thesaurus to find synonyms.

**Closure:** Use think-pair-share to discuss how a piece of writing changes when synonyms for overused adjectives are used.

## SECOND-GRADE THESAURUS LESSON 2:  VITAL VERBS

**Standards:**

*AASL #1:*    Inquire, think critically, and gain knowledge. 1.1, Skills: 1.1.1, Follow an inquiry-based process in seeking knowledge in curricular subjects, and make the real-world connection for using this process in own life; 1.1.4, Find, evaluate, and select appropriate sources to answer questions.
*NCTE #4:*    Students adjust their use of spoken, written, and visual language to communicate effectively with a variety of audiences and for different purposes.
*Language Arts:*    Students select words that convey the intended meaning and create a picture in the reader's mind.

**Objectives:**

1.    Students understand the features of a thesaurus (alphabetical order, words with similar meaning, entries that give parts of speech, definition of the word, sample sentence, and words with opposite meanings).
2.    Students use a thesaurus to determine better word choices for verbs in a writing selection.

**Materials:**

• board-ready page from a primary thesaurus (optional)
• board-ready copy of input paragraph from the CD

- guided practice paragraph list, containing work sheet paragraphs with a redundant verb, from the CD (*Note:* The lists need to be copied enough times so all pairs receive two paragraphs; the paragraphs are differentiated to support student achievement levels)
- 15 student primary thesauri
- thesaurus sign

**Set:** Say, "Which sentence gives you a better picture? Maria walked to the school, walked to her class, and walked to her desk. Maria hiked to her school, marched to her class, and staggered to her desk."

**Review:** Show a primary thesaurus and discuss its use as a reference source to find words that have similar meanings. Explain that it is in alphabetical order and will give the part of speech, the definition of the word, a sample sentence, and synonyms.

**Input:** Pair students and distribute a primary thesaurus to each pair. Project the board-ready paragraph that has the redundant verb "run." The pairs use their thesaurus to find the word "run" and see how many synonyms it gives. Cross out "run." The students decide where the synonyms fit in the best. They chorally read the amended paragraph.

**Guided practice:** Give each pair two paragraphs with a redundant verb. The students use their thesauri to look up the redundant verb, cross out the overused verb, and write a new verb above it.

**Assessment:** Select pairs to read their paragraph with the new verbs.

**Closure:** Use think-pair-share and ask "How was the paragraph different with the new verbs?"

---

## THIRD-GRADE THESAURUS LESSON 1: FROM THE COMMON TO THE UNUSUAL

**Standards:**

*AASL #1:* Inquire, think critically, and gain knowledge. 1.1, Skills: 1.1.1, Follow an inquiry-based process in seeking knowledge in curricular subjects, and make the real-world connection for using this process in own life; 1.1.4, Find, evaluate, and select appropriate sources to answer questions.
*NCTE #8:* Students use a variety of technological and information resources to gather and synthesize information and to create and communicate knowledge.
*Language Arts:* Students determine the meanings and other features of words (e.g., pronunciation, syllabication, synonyms, parts of speech) using the dictionary, thesaurus, and CD-ROM and Internet when available.

**Objectives:**

1. Students use the thesaurus to encode sentences from everyday language to less common words.
2. Students use guide words to locate synonyms in the thesaurus.

**Materials:**

- 15 student thesauri
- copies of the guided practice sentence list work sheet, enough for each pair to have two sentences to encode, from the CD

- board-ready copy of input sentence from the CD
- thesaurus sign
- 30 copies of the Thesaurus brochure from the CD

**Set:** Read from the board the following sentence: "The giant *shows greed* when he *steals* the town's *treasure*." Ask, "How could you make this sentence less understandable to your friends?"

**Review:** Review that the thesaurus is a book of synonyms that is arranged alphabetically and has guide words on each page.

**Input:** Pair students and distribute a thesaurus to each pair. Read from the board the set sentence, "The giant shows greed when he steals the town's treasure." Underline the words "giant," "show," "greed," "steal," and "treasure." Have every pair look up "giant." Have the students suggest more difficult synonyms. Each table is assigned an underlined word to look up in their thesaurus. Remind the students to use the guide words. Students find and choose a synonym to substitute for the more common word. The students say the words they want to substitute. Rewrite the sentence using their suggestions such as, "The titan displays avarice when he pilfers the town's hoard." Ask the students which sentence is more understandable.

**Guided practice:** Distribute a paper strip with two sentences to each pair. Ask the pairs to use their thesaurus to replace the common underlined words with a more unusual synonym. (Before the lesson, you must check that the students' thesauri have the underlined words. Note that the sentences will have between two and four words underlined. The sentences can be distributed to the students according to their achievement levels.) The students use their thesauri to locate more unusual synonyms and rewrite the sentences. Each pair reads the rewritten sentence to the other pair at their table, who try to guess what the sentence means. If they can't guess, they are told. If there is additional time, you can hand out more sentences to the pairs.

**Assessment:** Observe whether the students use the guide words in the thesaurus, and whether they make the sentences difficult enough to stump their friends.

**Closure:** Ask which pairs were able to stump the other pair at the table. They read the more unusual sentence and have the class guess at its meaning. Distribute the Thesaurus brochure, go over it, and ask the students to share it with their families.

## THIRD-GRADE THESAURUS LESSON 2: ANTONYMS: OPPOSITES ATTRACT

**Standards:**

*AASL #1:*   Inquire, think critically, and gain knowledge. 1.1, Skills: 1.1.1, Follow an inquiry-based process in seeking knowledge in curricular subjects, and make the real-world connection for using this process in own life; 1.1.4, Find, evaluate, and select appropriate sources to answer questions.
*NCTE #8:*   Students use a variety of technological and information resources to gather and synthesize information and to create and communicate knowledge.
*Language Arts:*   Students determine the meanings and other features of words (e.g., pronunciation, syllabication, synonyms, parts of speech) using the dictionary, thesaurus, and CD-ROM and Internet when available.

**Objectives:**

1. Students identify where antonyms are located in a thesaurus entry.
2. Students play with language and write a sentence opposite to the original meaning.

**Materials:**

- 15 student thesauri
- 15 paper strips, each with two sentences (see Guided practice)
- thesaurus sign
- board-ready copy of the input sentence

**Set:** Present the following sentence by either saying it or having it on a board: "The old man was proud of his wealth."

**Review:** Review that the thesaurus is a book of synonyms that is arranged alphabetically and has guide words on each page.

**Input:** Pair students and distribute a student thesaurus to each pair. Direct the students to use the guide words to find the pages in the thesaurus that contain the words "old," "proud," and "wealth." Point out that the antonyms are at the end of the entry, and note that not all entries contain antonyms.

The students find the antonyms that change the meaning of the sentence. Rewrite the new sentence, "The young man was ashamed of his poverty" on the board.

**Guided practice:** Give each pair a paper strip with two sentences on it. The assignment is for the students to look up the underlined words in the two sentences and find an antonym for each. They then rewrite the sentences so that the sentence has an opposite meaning. You can use the sentences from the guided practice sentences list on the CD or take sentences from one of the third-grade textbooks.

**Assessment:** Informally observe whether the students can locate the antonyms and use them appropriately. A formal assessment can be done to determine whether the new sentences are the opposite of the originals.

**Closure:** Several pairs read the opposite sentences. The students chorally response to the question, "Where do you find antonyms in a thesaurus entry?"

## FOURTH-GRADE THESAURUS LESSON 1: ELIMINATING OVERUSED ADJECTIVES

**Standards:**

*AASL #1:* Inquire, think critically, and gain knowledge. 1.1, Skills: 1.1.1, Follow an inquiry-based process in seeking knowledge in curricular subjects, and make the real-world connection for using this process in own life; 1.1.4, Find, evaluate, and select appropriate sources to answer questions.
*NCTE #4:* Students adjust their use of spoken, written, and visual language to communicate effectively with a variety of audiences and for different purposes.
*Language Arts:* Students use descriptive words and phrases that energize the writing.

**Objectives:**

1. Students identify the features of a thesaurus (alphabetical order, words with similar meaning, entries that give parts of speech, definition of the word, sample sentences, and words with opposite meanings).
2. Students use a thesaurus to determine better word choices for adjectives in a writing selection.

**Materials:**

- board-ready page from a student thesaurus (optional)
- board-ready copy of input sentences available from the CD
- 15 student work sheets with three paragraphs with redundant adjectives from the CD
- 15 student thesauri
- thesaurus sign

**Set:** Say, "I saw a cute boy holding a very cute puppy." Then discuss the problem of overused adjectives.

**Review:** Review the basic features of a thesaurus: alphabetical order, a book of synonyms, parts of speech, guide words, and sample sentences.

**Input:** Pair students and distribute a thesaurus to each pair. Write a sentence with boring words on the board. Examples: The *old* man walked home. The *small* boy started to run when he saw the *mean* dog. Underline the boring adjectives and model how to look them up in the thesaurus, giving the students the page numbers if they have problems locating the word. Ask for suggestions of different words to energize the sentence. Rewrite the sentence with the new words.

**Guided practice:** Distribute the work sheets with three paragraphs and instruct the students to look up the overused words. The pairs use the thesauri to find synonyms for better word choices for adjectives. The pairs fill in the blanks in the paragraph using the new words.

**Assessment:** Observe whether students can substitute synonyms for the overused words.

**Closure:** Several pairs read the old and new paragraphs. Use think-pair-share to compare the paragraphs.

## FOURTH-GRADE THESAURUS LESSON 2: ANTONYMS: CHANGING MEANING

**Standards:**

*AASL #1:*   Inquire, think critically, and gain knowledge. 1.1, Skills: 1.1.1, Follow an inquiry-based process in seeking knowledge in curricular subjects, and make the real-world connection for using this process in own life; 1.1.4, Find, evaluate, and select appropriate sources to answer questions.
*NCTE #8:*   Students use a variety of technological and information resources to gather and synthesize information and to create and communicate knowledge.
*Language Arts:*   Students determine the meanings and other features of words (e.g., pronunciation, syllabication, synonyms, parts of speech) using the dictionary, thesaurus, and CD-ROM and Internet when available.

**Objectives:**

1.   Students identify where the antonyms are located in a thesaurus entry.
2.   Students play with language and write a sentence opposite to the original meaning.

**Materials:**

- 15 student thesauri
- 15 paper strips with two sentences each (see Guided practice)
- board-ready copy of the input sentences from the CD
- thesaurus sign

**Set:** Present the following sentence by either saying it or having it on a board: "The helpful hero was hesitant to give his sword to the youthful person."

**Review:** Review that the thesaurus is a book of synonyms and antonyms, is arranged alphabetically, and has guide words on each page.

**Input:** Pair students and distribute a student thesaurus to each pair. Direct the students to use the guide words to find the pages in the thesaurus that contain the words "helpful," "hesitant," and "youthful." Point out that the antonyms are at the end of the entry, and note that not all entries contain antonyms. The students find the antonyms that change the meaning of the sentence. Rewrite the new sentence, for instance, "The useless hero was confident to give his sword to the elderly person" on the board.

**Guided practice:** Give each pair a paper strip with two sentences on it. The assignment is for the students to look up the underlined words in the two sentences and find an antonym for each. They then rewrite the sentences so that the sentence has an opposite meaning. You can use the sentences from the guided practice sentences list on the CD or take sentences from one of the fourth-grade textbooks.

**Assessment:** Informally observe whether the students can locate antonyms and use them appropriately. A formal assessment can be done to determine whether the new sentences are the opposite of the originals.

**Closure:** Several pairs read their opposite sentences. The students chorally respond to the question, "Where do you find antonyms in a thesaurus entry?"

## FIFTH-GRADE THESAURUS LESSON 1:  SYNONYMS AND WORD MAPS

**Standards:**

*AASL #1:*   Inquire, think critically, and gain knowledge. 1.1, Skills: 1.1.1, Follow an inquiry-based process in seeking knowledge in curricular subjects, and make the real-world connection for using this process in own life; 1.1.4, Find, evaluate, and select appropriate sources to answer questions.
*NCTE #8:*   Students use a variety of technological and information resources to gather and synthesize information and to create and communicate knowledge.
*Language Arts:*   Students determine the meanings of words by using a variety of reference sources.

**Objective:**
Students demonstrate how to use a thesaurus to find synonyms of words with multiple meanings.

**Materials:**

- 15 student dictionaries and thesauri
- board and markers
- word map example from the CD
- thesaurus sign

**Set:** Ask the students whether they have ever mapped a word or its synonyms.

**Review:** Review that dictionaries give the meanings (definitions) of words. Most words have several meanings. Thesauri give synonyms and antonyms. Remind students to use the guide words.

**Input:** Pair students. The students are to look up the word "plot" in the dictionary. Write the word "plot" in a circle in the middle of the board. The students chorally read the first, most common, meaning of the word as a noun. Write "1" and have a student write the first meaning of the word. Put a circle around it. The students are directed to look up the word "plot" in the thesaurus. Ask them whether the first meaning matches the one on the board. If so, have a student write each of the words near the meaning. Draw circles around them and connect them to the circle with the meaning. This continues with all the meanings of the word as a noun. A separate map is made for the meanings as a verb. (*Webster's Intermediate Dictionary* and the *American Heritage Student Thesaurus* match perfectly for this entry.)

**Assessment:** Informally observe whether the students can make suggestions for the map.

**Closure:** Students use think-pair-share to draw conclusions based on the map. (Some examples are: words have different meanings as different parts of speech, synonyms are not exactly the same as the word, synonyms come in clusters of the meanings of the word.)

## FIFTH-GRADE THESAURUS LESSON 2:  ANTONYMS:  FLASHCARDS

**Standards:**

*AASL #1:*   Inquire, think critically, and gain knowledge. 1.1, Skills: 1.1.1, Follow an inquiry-based process in seeking knowledge in curricular subjects, and make the real-world connection for using this process in own life; 1.1.4, Find, evaluate, and select appropriate sources to answer questions.
*NCTE #8:*   Students use a variety of technological and information resources to gather and synthesize information and to create and communicate knowledge.
*Language Arts:*   Students determine the meanings of words by using a variety of reference sources.

**Objectives:**

1.   Students identify where the antonyms are located in a thesaurus entry.
2.   Students make flashcards for words and their antonyms.
3.   Students use the flashcards to practice antonyms.

**Materials:**

- 15 student thesauri
- paper strips with four words each from the CD
- index cards
- thesaurus sign

**Set:** Ask the students whether they know the antonym of "disparate." (Most probably won't know it.)

**Review:** Review that a thesaurus contains synonyms and antonyms. The latter are at the end of the entry and mean the opposite of the entry word. Remind students to use guide words.

**Input:** Pair students and distribute a thesaurus to each pair. Each pair is directed to use the thesaurus to look up the word "disparate." Guide the students to the antonym and ask them to read it chorally. Write "disparate" on one side of an index card, and "similar" on the other.

Explain that the pairs are going to create four flashcards by using their thesaurus to find words and their antonyms. They will write the word on one side of the card and the antonym on the other side of the card.

**Guided practice:** Each pair is given a paper strip with four words and four index cards. The students take turns being the scribe. The pairs look in the thesaurus and find the words and their antonyms. After the pairs at each table have created their flashcards, they can challenge each other to come up with the correct antonyms.

**Assessment:** Informally observe whether the students are able to find the words and their antonyms, and whether they used the guide words.

**Closure:** A few pairs challenge the whole class to guess the antonym. The class chorally responds to the question, "What is an antonym?"

## SIXTH-GRADE THESAURUS LESSON 1: ENERGIZING VERBS

**Standards:**

*AASL #1:* Inquire, think critically, and gain knowledge. 1.1, Skills: 1.1.1, Follow an inquiry-based process in seeking knowledge in curricular subjects, and make the real-world connection for using this process in own life; 1.1.4, Find, evaluate, and select appropriate sources to answer questions.
*NCTE #4:* Students adjust their use of spoken, written, and visual language to communicate effectively with a variety of audiences and for different purposes.
*Language Arts:* Students use descriptive words and phrases that energize the writing.

**Objectives:**

1. Students identify the features of a thesaurus (alphabetical order, synonyms, part of speech, definition of words, sample sentences, and antonyms).
2. Students use a thesaurus to determine better word choice for verbs in a writing selection.

**Materials:**

- board-ready copy of a page from a student thesaurus (optional)
- board-ready copy of the input paragraph from the CD
- 15 copies of the student work sheets with guided practice paragraphs (containing a redundant verb) from the CD
- 15 student thesauri
- thesaurus sign

**Set:** Project and read the board-ready copy of the input paragraph with the redundant verbs, stressing the word "follow." Ask the students why they're laughing.

**Review:** Review the basic features of a thesaurus: alphabetical order, a book of synonyms, antonyms, parts of speech, guide words, and sample sentence. Also review that a verb either is an action word or indicates a state of being.

**Input:** Pair students and distribute a thesaurus to each pair. Read a sentence from the input paragraph. Ask, "Which verb has been overused in this paragraph?" Underline the words the students suggest. Model how to look the verb up in the thesaurus, having the students follow along. Ask for suggestions of different words to energize the paragraph. Students chorally read the new paragraph and compare it to the original.

**Guided practice:** Distribute the work sheets with the guided practice paragraphs. Instruct the students to look up the overused verb. They work with a partner to look up the verbs and figure out better word choices. The students rewrite the paragraph using the new words.

**Assessment:** Informally assess whether the pairs can locate the words in the thesaurus and replace them with appropriate synonyms.

**Closure:** Several pairs read the old and new paragraphs and compare them.

## SIXTH-GRADE THESAURUS LESSON 2: ADJUSTING ADVERBS

**Standards:**

*AASL #1:*   Inquire, think critically, and gain knowledge. 1.1, Skills: 1.1.1, Follow an inquiry-based process in seeking knowledge in curricular subjects, and make the real-world connection for using this process in own life; 1.1.4, Find, evaluate, and select appropriate sources to answer questions.
*NCTE #4:*   Students adjust their use of spoken, written, and visual language to communicate effectively with a variety of audiences and for different purposes.
*Language Arts:*   Use descriptive words and phrases that energize the writing.

**Objectives:**

1.   Students identify the features of thesaurus (alphabetical order, synonyms, parts of speech, definition of words, sample sentences, and antonyms).
2.   Students use a thesaurus to determine better word choice for adverbs in a writing selection.

**Materials:**

- board-ready copy of a page from a student thesaurus (optional)
- board-ready copy of the input paragraph from the CD
- 15 copies of the student work sheet containing sentences with a redundant adverb from the CD
- 15 student thesauri
- thesaurus sign

**Set:** Project and read the input paragraph with the redundant adverb, stressing the word "very." Ask the students why they're laughing.

**Review:** Review the basic features of a thesaurus: alphabetical order, a book of synonyms, antonyms, parts of speech, guide words, and sample sentences. Also review that an adverb is a word that modifies (describes) a verb, an adjective, or another adverb.

**Input:** Pair students and distribute a thesaurus to each pair. Read a sentence from the input paragraph. Ask "Which adverb has been overused in this paragraph?" and underline the word the students suggest. Model how to look it up in the thesaurus, having them follow along. Ask for suggestions of different adverbs to energize the paragraph. Students chorally read the new paragraph and compare it to the original.

**Guided practice:** Distribute the work sheets with the guided practice sentences. Instruct the students to look up the overused adverb. They work with a partner to look up the adverbs and figure out better word choices. The students rewrite the sentences using the new words.

**Assessment:** Informally assess whether the pairs can locate the words in the thesaurus and replace them with appropriate synonyms.

**Closure:** Several pairs read the old and new paragraphs and compare them.

# Chapter 3

# The Encyclopedia

## KINDERGARTEN ENCYCLOPEDIA LESSON 1: *WORLD BOOK* WONDERS

**Standards:**

*AASL #1:*   Inquire, think critically, and gain knowledge. 1.1, Skills: 1.1.1, Follow an inquiry-based process in seeking knowledge in curricular subjects, and make the real-world connection for using this process in own life; 1.1.4, Find, evaluate, and select appropriate sources to answer questions.
*NCTE #7:*   Students conduct research on issues and interests by generating ideas and questions, and by posing problems. They gather, evaluate, and synthesize data from a variety of sources to communicate their discoveries in ways that suit their purpose and audience.
*Language Arts:*   Students use alphabetical order.

**Objectives:**

1.   Students examine the content of encyclopedias by perusing them.
2.   Students understand that encyclopedias are arranged in alphabetical order by replacing volumes on the shelves or cart in the correct order.

**Materials:**

- set of the *World Book Encyclopedia*
- encyclopedia sign

**Set:** Lead the class in singing the alphabet song. (That's the review, too.)

**Input:** Show the shelves or cart of encyclopedias and point out how they are arranged, with the letter on the spine. Open a volume and explain that encyclopedias contain information on people, places, and things. Some articles have many pages and some articles are part of a page. Model how to look through the volume, noting favorite pictures.

**Guided practice:** Pass out an encyclopedia volume to each student and give them seven minutes to look at the volume. The assignment is to remember a picture they saw in the volume. Students use think-pair-share to tell their partners something they saw in the encyclopedia. A few students share with the whole group. Students replace the volumes on the shelf or cart as you call each letter.

**Assessment:** Informally observe whether students notice what's in an encyclopedia and whether they replace the volumes on the shelf or cart with minimal help.

**Closure:** Say, "Encyclopedias have information about people, places, and things, and are in alphabetical order."

## KINDERGARTEN ENCYCLOPEDIA LESSON 2: WHAT'S THE BIGGEST DINOSAUR?

**Standards:**

*AASL #1:* Inquire, think critically, and gain knowledge. 1.1, Skills: 1.1.1, Follow an inquiry-based process in seeking knowledge in curricular subjects, and make the real-world connection for using this process in own life; 1.1.4, Find, evaluate, and select appropriate sources to answer questions.

*NCTE #7:* Students conduct research on issues and interests by generating ideas and questions, and by posing problems. They gather, evaluate, and synthesize data from a variety of sources to communicate their discoveries in ways that suit their purpose and audience.

*Language Arts:* Students respond appropriately to questions based on facts after listening to expository text.

**Objectives:**

1. Students understand that the encyclopedia contains factual information.
2. Students restate the lengths of dinosaurs after being read to from the encyclopedia.
3. Students discover which is the biggest dinosaur based on the information gleaned from the encyclopedia.

**Materials:**

- set of the *World Book Encyclopedia*
- board with a chart that has columns for the name of the dinosaur and its length
- colored tape (*Note:* Mark the length of 90 feet in the hallway, on the sidewalk, or on the playground before teaching this lesson.)
- visual of a dinosaur
- encyclopedia sign

**Set:** Say, "Who knows which is the biggest dinosaur?"

**Review:** Encyclopedias are in alphabetical order and contain information about people, places, and things.

**Input:** After repeating the set question, write down at least four of the students' suggestions. Think aloud about what volume to look in, select the "D" volume, find the article on "dinosaurs," and then read from the picture chart the pertinent information on the dinosaurs the students suggested. Students restate the length of the dinosaur as you record it on a chart. Repeat the process for each dinosaur. After the research, the students use think-pair-share to decide which is the longest dinosaur. (The answer is *Diplodocus* at 90 feet long.)

**Assessment:** Informally observe whether students restate the information when it's read to them.

**Closure:** With the students, go out to the hallway, playground, or sidewalk and stand between the lines that show the length of the biggest dinosaur.

## FIRST-GRADE ENCYCLOPEDIA LESSON 1: ENCYCLOPEDIA A TO Z

**Standards:**

*AASL #1:*   Inquire, think critically, and gain knowledge. 1.1, Skills: 1.1.1, Follow an inquiry-based process in seeking knowledge in curricular subjects, and make the real-world connection for using this process in own life; 1.1.4, Find, evaluate, and select appropriate sources to answer questions.

*NCTE #7:*   Students conduct research on issues and interests by generating ideas and questions, and by posing problems. They gather, evaluate, and synthesize data from a variety of sources to communicate their discoveries in ways that suit their purpose and audience.

*Language Arts:*   Students alphabetize to the first letter.

**Objectives:**

1.   Students examine the content of encyclopedias by perusing them.
2.   Students select the correct volume of an encyclopedia when given a word on a paper strip.

**Materials:**

- two sets of the *World Book Encyclopedia*
- paper strip words that have the first letter underlined from the CD
- encyclopedia sign
- windows of words that pinpoint the information needed. The "window of words" is accomplished by cutting out a small space in a sticky note that shows the word that is on the index card. (Optional.)

**Set:** Lead the class in singing the alphabet song. (That's the review, too.)

**Input:** Show the shelves or carts of encyclopedias and point out how they are arranged, and also point out the letter on the spine of each volume. Show and read a paper strip that says "dinosaur." Ask the students the beginning letter of "dinosaur." Go over to the encyclopedia shelves and talk aloud as you find the correct volume. Find the page, which is bookmarked, and the "window" and compare it to the word on the card. Reshelve the encyclopedia volume in the correct place.

**Guided practice:** Pass out to each student a card with a paper strip on it and tell him or her to look at the underlined letter to determine which volume to get. Call the students, by table, to find the correct encyclopedia volume. Students look for the bookmarked "windowed" word and compare it to the word on the paper strip. After the students complete the task and are waiting for others to finish, they are to look through the volume they have, remembering to keep the bookmark in the right place. The students replace the volumes on the shelves or carts as you call each letter. Each student is given another paper strip and the exercise is repeated.

**Assessment:** Informally observe whether students pick the correct volume, find the article, and replace the encyclopedia volume on the library shelf or cart with minimal help.

**Closure:** Ask the students to respond chorally to the question, "How are encyclopedia volumes arranged?"

## FIRST-GRADE ENCYCLOPEDIA LESSON 2:  LIFE CYCLE OF A FLY

**Standards:**

*AASL #1:*   Inquire, think critically, and gain knowledge. 1.1, Skills: 1.1.1, Follow an inquiry-based process in seeking knowledge in curricular subjects, and make the real-world connection for using this process in own life; 1.1.4, Find, evaluate, and select appropriate sources to answer questions.
*NCTE #7:*   Students conduct research on issues and interests by generating ideas and questions, and by posing problems. They gather, evaluate, and synthesize data from a variety of sources to communicate their discoveries in ways that suit their purpose and audience.
*Content (National Science Standard):*   The life cycles of organisms (reproduction).
*Language Arts:*   Students respond appropriately to questions based on facts after listening to expository text.

**Objectives:**

1.   Students understand that encyclopedias contain factual information.
2.   Students restate important information from the encyclopedia text.
3.   Students categorize information about the life cycle of the fly under "egg," "larva," "pupa," and "adult."

**Materials:**

- "F" volume of the *World Book Encyclopedia*
- sentence strips with the important information about each stage of a fly's life cycle from the CD
- chart paper or a board on which to affix the strips
- visual of a fly
- *Old Black Fly* by Jim Aylesworth
- encyclopedia sign

*Note: You must read ahead to decide which sentences are pertinent to read to the students for the life cycle of a fly and to write the sentence strips. A sample is given on the CD.*

**Set:** Read *Old Black Fly* by Jim Aylesworth and sing the words using the tune of "Joshua fought the Battle of Jericho." After the book is read, state, "Today we will learn about the life cycle of a fly."

**Review:** Multivolume encyclopedias are arranged in alphabetical order with some volumes having several letters of the alphabet. Encyclopedias contain information about people, places, and things.

**Input:** Model how to locate an article on the "fly" (thinking of the first letter of the word, selecting the correct volume, and using guide words). Look for the section on the life of the fly and point out, by walking around the room or projecting the pages on a board, the four stages that are in bold print. Show the students the chart or board that has already been labeled "egg," "larva," "pupa," and "adult." Read some sentences from the "egg" section of the article and think aloud about what's important. Read the sentence strip of the information.

**Guided practice:** Continue to read sentences under each section and use think-pair-share to elicit important information. After all the information on the sentence strips has been shared, randomly pick one and read it. Using think-pair-share, have the students identify the category in which the information belongs. This continues until all the sentence strips are placed.

**Assessment:** Informally observe whether students restate the important information and identify under which category it should be placed.

**Closure:** The students read the chart the class has made.

## FIRST-GRADE ENCYCLOPEDIA LESSON 3: HOW MANY YOUNG?

**Standards:**

*AASL #1:* Inquire, think critically, and gain knowledge. 1.1, Skills: 1.1.1, Follow an inquiry-based process in seeking knowledge in curricular subjects, and make the real-world connection for using this process in own life; 1.1.4, Find, evaluate, and select appropriate sources to answer questions.
*NCTE #7:* Students conduct research on issues and interests by generating ideas and questions, and by posing problems. They gather, evaluate, and synthesize data from a variety of sources to communicate their discoveries in ways that suit their purpose and audience.
*Content (National Science Standard):* The life cycles of organisms (reproduction).
*Language Arts:* Students identify facts in nonfiction.

**Objectives:**

1. Students find specific information in articles in the encyclopedia when provided with the name of an animal.
2. Students create a chart comparing the number of young of different animals.

**Materials:**

- set of the *World Book Encyclopedia* with bookmarks in each volume to assist students in locating the article
- encyclopedia sign
- paper strips with the names of animals from the CD
- butcher paper for a chart or board-ready copy of the chart from the CD, with two columns drawn and labeled "animal" and "number of young"

- "windows of words" placed to show the maximum number of young for each of the animals listed on the paper strips (to make a window of words, cut out a small rectangular hole in a sticky note and place the note on the encyclopedia page so that the numbers that answer the question show through the window) (Optional.)
- visual of a wolf

**Set:** Start the lesson with a short comparison of the number of siblings in the students' families by asking for a show of hands: "How many of you have no brothers or sisters? Only one brother or sister?" and so forth. Voice the conclusion that the data says that, in this class, families of humans have between one and six children. "Today we're going to find out how many babies many different animals have."

**Review:** Multivolume encyclopedias are arranged in alphabetical order with some volumes having several letters of the alphabet. Encyclopedias contain information about people, places, and things.

**Input:** Model the assignment by showing the visual of the wolf and the paper strip with "wolf." Notice aloud the beginning letter, reinforcing that you are selecting the encyclopedia volume that has that letter on its spine. Demonstrate opening the encyclopedia to the page that is marked with a bookmark. Show the students the window of words to find out the most young that the wolf has and write that number on the paper strip.

**Guided practice:** Pair students and give each pair a paper strip with the name of an animal. The pairs, called by table, select the correct volume, take it to their seats, and look for the animal using the bookmark. After finding the window of words and the answer, students write on the paper strip the most young that the animal has. The pairs place their paper strips on the chart under the corresponding maximum number of young.

**Assessment:** Informally observe whether students select the correct volume of the encyclopedia and locate the required information.

**Closure:** Students use think-pair-share to ask and answer questions that require them to think about ideas brought up by the data: "Why do flies have more young than elephants?" "Does the size of the animal have an influence on how many babies?"

## SECOND-GRADE ENCYCLOPEDIA LESSON 1: INTRODUCING GUIDE WORDS

**Standards:**

*AASL #1:* Inquire, think critically, and gain knowledge. 1.1, Skills: 1.1.1, Follow an inquiry-based process in seeking knowledge in curricular subjects, and make the real-world connection for using this process in own life; 1.1.4, Find, evaluate, and select appropriate sources to answer questions.
*Language Arts:* Students alphabetize to the second and third letter.

**Objective:**
Students alphabetize to the second letter and third letter to find the correct placement of a word between two guide words.

**Materials:**

- sets of "pairs" of guide words and individual words printed on tag board by hand or copied from the CD; the first set of guide words and individual words should require the student to alphabetize to the second letter; the second set of guide words and individual words should require the students to alphabetize to the third letter
- visual of a cat
- encyclopedia sign

**Set:** Show the visual of a cat and then search for an article on "cats" in the encyclopedia as you announce the word to the class. Search near the end of the volume, saying the words. Ask the students whether you're close. (They'll say, "NO!") Show the students the guide words and read them. Ask whether this is close to "ca" for "cat." Then ask for suggestions. (Students will say "different letter," "further forward.")

**Review:** Encyclopedias are in alphabetical order, and they have information about people, places, and things.

**Input:** Put two sets of guide words on the board. Explain that guide words tell whether an encyclopedia article falls between them or not. Use non-examples as well—words that don't fall between either pair of guide words. This will not simulate an actual encyclopedia. This is to help students understand the concept of guide words and how to alphabetize between words. In the CD, the guide words are "bat" and "bird" for the input and the individual words are: "bed," "bee," "beetle," "blood," "boxing," and "brain." These should *not* be presented in alphabetical order. Ask between which set of guide words each word belongs and place it in the correct position. If the word doesn't belong between either set of guide words, it is placed at the bottom of the chart.

**Guided practice:** Four students are selected to be the guide words "dinosaur," "duck," "map," and "money," which are printed larger than the other words. The remaining students are each given a word and asked to stand where they belong between the correct guide words, four at a time. Words that do not belong on the page are placed on a table. Once the students are standing between the correct guide words, have them arrange themselves in alphabetical order. Repeat the guided practice using the set of words and guide words that will require the students to alphabetize to the third letter.

**Assessment:** Informally observe whether the students can alphabetize to the second and third letter of a word.

**Closure:** Students use think-pair-share to answer the question, "How did you know where your word belonged?" This reinforces that they used the guide words.

*Note: This lesson, with different words, can be used as an introduction for third, fourth, fifth, and sixth grades.*

## SECOND-GRADE ENCYCLOPEDIA LESSON 2: WHO'S WHO?

**Standards:**

*AASL #1:* Inquire, think critically, and gain knowledge. 1.1, Skills: 1.1.1, Follow an inquiry-based process in seeking knowledge in curricular subjects, and make the real-world connection for using this process in own life; 1.1.4, Find, evaluate, and select appropriate sources to answer questions.
*Language Arts:* Students put words in alphabetical order.

**Objectives:**

1. Students select the correct volumes of the encyclopedia and find people by their last names.
2. Students find the beginning of the article and locate the birth and death dates of the person.

**Materials:**

- two sets of *The World Book Encyclopedia*
- 30 paper strips from the CD
- board-ready copy of the input paper strip and first page of the article on Walt Disney
- visual of Walt Disney
- encyclopedia sign

**Set:** State, "When you're young, people call you by your first name or nickname. As you become an adult, people will call you by your last name. For instance, when I was growing up, everyone called me ____. Now that I'm an educator and an adult, I am called Ms. or Mr. _____."

**Review:** Encyclopedias are multivolume, arranged in alphabetical order, and contain information about people, places, and things. The articles are sometimes short, sometimes very long.

**Input:** Show the visual of Walt Disney and a paper strip with "Walt Disney" and read it aloud. Think aloud about identifying the last name and then the first letter of the last name. Go to the shelf and select the correct volume and find the article using the guide words. Project the board-ready copy of the article and show where the article begins. Explain birth and death dates, or the lack thereof, and that question marks indicate an estimated birth or death date.

**Guided practice:** Pass out a paper strip to each student. The students identify the last name and which volume of the encyclopedia is needed. Call the students, by table, to find the correct volume. The students locate the name using the guide words and compare it to the name on the paper strip. Students write down the birth and death dates of the person. If students finish early, they are to look through the article noting charts, photos, pictures, and facts in brief, and see whether they can find an interesting fact to share. After the research phase is completed, students at each table share the information they found. The students replace the books as you call for each letter. Repeat the exercise if time allows.

**Assessment:** Informally observe whether students identify the last name of the person, select the correct volume, find the article, write the requested information, and replace the volumes on the library shelf or cart with minimal help.

**Closure:** Ask, "How many of you found a person who is still alive? How did you know?"

## SECOND-GRADE ENCYCLOPEDIA LESSON 3: MATCHING THE ATHLETE WITH THE SPORT

**Standards:**

*AASL #1:* Inquire, think critically, and gain knowledge. 1.1, Skills: 1.1.1, Follow an inquiry-based process in seeking knowledge in curricular subjects, and make the real-world connection for using this process in own life; 1.1.4, Find, evaluate, and select appropriate sources to answer questions.

*NCTE #7:* Students conduct research on issues and interests by generating ideas and questions, and by posing problems. They gather, evaluate, and synthesize data from a variety of sources to communicate their discoveries in ways that suit their purpose and audience.

*Language Arts:* Students locate specific information from an article in an encyclopedia.

**Objectives:**

1.  Using guide words, students select the correct encyclopedia volume and locate an article on an athlete by his or her last name.
2.  Students find the beginning of the article, write the birth and death dates, and the sport in which their person excelled.
3.  Students categorize the athletes under their sports.

**Materials:**

*   two sets of *The World Book Encyclopedia*
*   30 paper strips and work sheets from the CD
*   board-ready copy of the work sheet
*   signs of six sports categories, from the CD, posted around the room
*   display of biographies about athletes
*   visual of Mickey Mantle
*   encyclopedia sign

**Set:** Do a one-minute book talk on one of the biographies.

**Review:** Encyclopedias are multivolume, in alphabetical order, and contain information about people, places, and things. Articles on people are located under the person's last name. The articles are sometimes short, sometimes very long. Review how to use guide words and where to find the birth and death dates. Remind students that living people will not have a death date; the space will be blank.

**Input:** Show the visual of "Mickey Mantle" and project the board-ready copy of the work sheet. Select "Mickey Mantle" to look up in the encyclopedia. Think aloud and demonstrate how to identify the last name and then the first letter of the last name. Using the guide words, select the correct volume to find the article on the athlete. Demonstrate how to find the beginning of the article and the location of the person's birth and death dates. Read the first sentence of the article to identify the sport in which this person excelled.

**Guided practice:** Each student is given a paper strip and work sheet. Students identify the last name, the first letter of the last name, and select the correct volume of the encyclopedia. Students use guide words to find the article and where it begins. They write down the birth and death dates of the person. They read the first sentence to find the sport in which the athlete excelled and write the information on the work sheet. If they are early finishers, students can peruse the article for interesting facts and add these to the work sheet. When the research is completed, point out the six sport category signs posted around the room. Students gather under the name of the sport in which their person excelled. The students share the birth dates and death dates of the individuals and interesting facts with the other students in their category.

**Assessment:** Informally observe whether students identify the last name of the person, locate the article using the guide words, and find the sport and birth and death dates of the person.

**Closure:** Ask the students to say the name of their person, emphasizing the last name.

## THIRD-GRADE ENCYCLOPEDIA LESSON 1: INVENTION TIMELINE

**Standards:**

*AASL #1:* Inquire, think critically, and gain knowledge. 1.1, Skills: 1.1.1, Follow an inquiry-based process in seeking knowledge in curricular subjects, and make the real-world connection for using this process in own life; 1.1.4, Find, evaluate, and select appropriate sources to answer questions.

*NCTE #7:* Students conduct research on issues and interests by generating ideas and questions, and by posing problems. They gather, evaluate, and synthesize data from a variety of sources to communicate their discoveries in ways that suit their purpose and audience.

*NETS II:* Time, continuity, and change.

*Language Arts:* Students extract pertinent information from a reference source.

**Objectives:**

1.  Students use guide words to locate specific information on inventors.
2.  Students create a timeline of the inventions.

**Materials:**

- set of *The World Book Encyclopedia*
- 15 paper strip work sheets from the CD
- board-ready copy of an encyclopedia article on Johannes Gutenberg
- board-ready copy of the paper strip work sheet
- timeline on a chart or board that covers the eras of the inventions
- visual of Johannes Gutenberg
- encyclopedia sign
- 30 copies of the Encyclopedia brochure from the CD

**Set:** Ask how long ago microwave ovens were invented. Say the answer (invented in 1950s, sold en masse in 1970s) after the students guess. Using think-pair-share, students think about how long ago that was in comparison to the ages of their parents and grandparents.

**Review:** Encyclopedias are multivolume, in alphabetical order, and contain information about people, places, and things. The articles are sometimes short, sometimes very long. People are looked up under their last names. Guide words on each page help locate articles.

**Input:** Introduce Johannes Gutenberg by showing a visual. Think aloud about how to identify the last name and then the first letter of the last name. Go to the shelf, pick out the correct volume, and find the article using guide words. Project the board-ready copy of the article on Johannes Gutenberg. Explain the question mark by the birth and death dates. Read aloud the parts of the article that explain how the invention of movable type made printing practical. Project the board-ready copy of the paper strip work sheet and write the invention and the date. Explain that all books were hand copied when Gutenberg was born. Ask the students how long ago the mid-1400s were. Say, "His invention was not patented because there was no such process in the 1400s. Now, when a new product or process is created, the United States allows the inventor to apply for a patent. The patent gives them the sole right to make and sell the invention. Most of the inventors you will research have patent dates for their inventions."

**Guided practice:** Pair students and distribute a paper strip work sheet to each pair. Students identify the last name and which volume of the encyclopedia is needed. Call the students, by table, to find the correct volume. The pairs look for their inventor and write down the invention and the approximate date of the invention on the work sheet. After they finish the assignment, the pairs are to look through the article, noting charts, photos, pictures, facts in brief, and interesting facts to share. When called by table, the pairs post their inventions work sheet on the time line in chronological order. Using think-pair-share, read the timeline and discuss it.

**Assessment:** Informally observe whether students locate the last name of the person, select the correct volume, find the article, write the requested information, and replace the volumes on the library shelf or cart with minimal help.

**Closure:** Using think-pair-share, the students discuss how they found the information. Distribute the Encyclopedia brochure, go over it, and ask the students to share it with their families.

## THIRD-GRADE ENCYCLOPEDIA LESSON 2: IMPORTANT INVENTIONS

**Standards:**

*AASL #1:*  Inquire, think critically, and gain knowledge. 1.1, Skills: 1.1.1, Follow an inquiry-based process in seeking knowledge in curricular subjects, and make the real-world connection for using this process in own life; 1.1.4, Find, evaluate, and select appropriate sources to answer questions.
*NCTE #7:*  Students conduct research on issues and interests by generating ideas and questions, and by posing problems. They gather, evaluate, and synthesize data from a variety of sources to communicate their discoveries in ways that suit their purpose and audience.
*NETS VIII:*  Science, technology and society.
*Language Arts:*  Students extract information from a variety of reference sources.

**Objectives:**

1.  Students extract information from an encyclopedia article.
2.  Students hypothesize how an invention changed ordinary people's lives.

**Materials:**

- two sets of *The World Book Encyclopedia*
- 15 work sheets from the CD
- board-ready copy of the work sheet
- encyclopedia sign
- visual of a printing press
- timeline from last lesson

**Set:** Say, "Today we are going to hypothesize how inventions changed the everyday lives of people." Using think-pair-share, the students ponder how the microwave oven changed our daily lives.

**Review:** Say, "Last time we researched inventors, their inventions, and the dates of the inventions." Show the timeline. Review that encyclopedias are multivolume, in alphabetical order, and contain information about people, places, and things. The articles are sometimes short, sometimes very long. Guide words on each page help locate articles. Topics and subtopics are in bold face. Pictures, charts, tables, and "facts in brief" should be perused before reading the information in the article.

**Input:** Show a visual of the printing press and model finding the article on printing in the "P" encyclopedia volume. Look for the subheading of "invention of movable type" and read several paragraphs about it. Fill in the work sheet with the appropriate information. Explain how movable type made a difference, since books had to be copied by hand before the invention of the printing press. Think aloud how the printing press changed the lives of ordinary people. (Examples are that books were available to a larger part of the population, and it was much cheaper and faster to make copies of a book.) The most famous book printed by Gutenberg was the Bible.

**Guided practice:** Pair students and give each pair a work sheet with the name of an invention. Students locate the article on the invention in the encyclopedia. Students fill out the work sheet with information about the invention and analyze its impact. Each pair reports their information orally.

**Assessment:** Informally observe whether students locate the articles and find and record the information required. Also "eavesdrop" on the students' discussions about how the invention affected people.

**Closure:** Using think-pair-share, the students discuss which invention changed people's lives the most.

## THIRD-GRADE ENCYCLOPEDIA LESSON 3: NOTE TAKING AND SUMMARIES

**Standards:**

*AASL #1:* Inquire, think critically, and gain knowledge. 1.1, Skills: 1.1.1, Follow an inquiry-based process in seeking knowledge in curricular subjects, and make the real-world connection for using this process in own life; 1.3, Responsibilities: 1.3.3, Follow ethical and legal guidelines in gathering and using information.
*NCTE #7:* Students conduct research on issues and interests by generating ideas and questions, and by posing problems. They gather, evaluate, and synthesize data from a variety of sources to communicate their discoveries in ways that suit their purpose and audience.
*Language Arts:* Students write summaries from expository text.

**Objectives:**

1. As a whole class, students analyze a paragraph to extract important words.
2. As a whole class, students use these words and their own to create a summary of the paragraph.

**Materials:**

- 30 copies of an information-packed paragraph from an encyclopedia article on a topic the class is studying
- pencils and lined paper

- board-ready copy of the paragraph
- markers for the board
- *Once Upon a Time, The End* by Geoffrey Kloske and Barry Blitt
- encyclopedia sign

**Set:** Read one of the stories from *Once Upon a Time, The End* by Geoffrey Kloske and Barry Blitt. Point out how the story is a summary of a longer folktale.

**Review:** Encyclopedias are multivolume, in alphabetical order, and contain information about people, places, and things. The articles are sometimes short, sometimes very long. Guide words on each page help locate articles. Topics and subtopics are in bold face. Pictures, charts, tables, and "facts in brief" should be perused before reading the information in the article.

**Input:** Explain that when anyone does research, it is important to get the main ideas from the reference source, such as an encyclopedia, but it must be rewritten in the students' own words. Explain that students need to decide which are the important ideas and words. Distribute a copy of the encyclopedia paragraph to each student and project a board-ready copy. Read it aloud. The second time, the students chorally read the paragraph. Go back to the first sentence and use think-pair-share to decide on the important words. After the discussion, the students write the words deemed important on the lined paper. You should also write the words on the board. This is repeated for the balance of the paragraph. The students hand in the paper with the encyclopedia paragraph, leaving them only their notes. Use think-pair-share to elicit the topic sentence. Write the sentence on the board as the students write it on their lined paper. This continues until the summary is complete.

**Assessment:** Observe whether students locate the important words, take notes, and contribute to the writing of the summary.

**Closure:** Read aloud the encyclopedia paragraph and the students chorally read their summary of the paragraph and compare the two.

*Note: This lesson can be also be taught for fourth, fifth, and sixth grades and repeated for third grade.*

## FOURTH-GRADE ENCYCLOPEDIA LESSON 1: WOMEN WHO WIN

**Standards:**

*AASL #1:* Inquire, think critically, and gain knowledge. 1.1, Skills: 1.1.1, Follow an inquiry-based process in seeking knowledge in curricular subjects, and make the real-world connection for using this process in own life; 1.1.4, Find, evaluate, and select appropriate sources to answer questions.
*NCTE #7:* Students conduct research on issues and interests by generating ideas and questions, and by posing problems. They gather, evaluate, and synthesize data from a variety of sources to communicate their discoveries in ways that suit their purpose and audience.
*Language Arts:* Students extract information from a variety of reference sources.

**Objectives:**

1. Students use an encyclopedia to research and record the contributions of specific women.
2. Students compare the accomplishments of the two women they researched.

**Materials:**

- two sets of *The World Book Encyclopedia*
- 15 work sheets from the CD
- board-ready work sheet
- encyclopedia sign
- visuals of Amelia Earhart and Sally Ride

**Set:** Tell students that throughout history women have made great contributions. Some were rulers, like Cleopatra; some were scientists, like Marie Curie; and some were athletes, like Diana Turasi, the professional basketball player.

**Review:** Encyclopedias are multivolume, in alphabetical order, and contain information about people, places, and things. The articles are sometimes short, sometimes very long. Guide words are used to locate articles. People are found under their last names. Topics and subtopics are in bold face. Pictures, charts, tables, and "facts in brief" should be perused before reading the information in the article.

**Input:** Show the visuals of Amelia Earhart and Sally Ride. Think aloud about how to identify the last name and then the first letter of the last name. Go to the shelf and select the two correct volumes and find the articles using the guide words. In the article on Amelia Earhart, read the first three sentences and ask students what her achievements were. Project the board-ready work sheet and fill in the information on Amelia Earhart. This is repeated for Sally Ride. Using think-pair-share, ask, "What do the two women have in common?" Fill in that section of the work sheet.

**Guided practice:** Pair students and distribute a work sheet with the names of two women already written on the work sheet. Students identify the last names and which two volumes of the encyclopedia are needed. Call the students, by table, to find the correct volumes. Students look for each woman and write down her achievement and then figure out what the two women have in common. The pair shares their information with the other pair at their table.

**Assessment:** Informally observe whether students identify the last name of the person, select the correct volume, find the article, write the requested information, and replace the volumes on the library shelf or cart with minimal help.

**Closure:** Using think-pair-share, the students discuss reasons why there has never been a woman president of the United States and whether there will be one in the future.

## FOURTH-GRADE ENCYCLOPEDIA LESSON 2: NATIVE AMERICAN TRIBES TODAY

**Standards:**

*AASL #1:*  Inquire, think critically, and gain knowledge. 1.1, Skills: 1.1.1, Follow an inquiry-based process in seeking knowledge in curricular subjects, and make the real-world connection for using this process in own life; 1.1.4, Find, evaluate, and select appropriate sources to answer questions.

*NCTE #7:*  Students conduct research on issues and interests by generating ideas and questions, and by posing problems. They gather, evaluate, and synthesize data from a variety of sources to communicate their discoveries in ways that suit their purpose and audience.

*Language Arts:*  Students take notes on pertinent information in a reference source.

**Objectives:**

1. Students extract information from the encyclopedia and restate it in their own words.
2. Students create a chart on the populations of some Native American tribes.

**Materials:**

- two sets of *The World Book Encyclopedia*
- 15 paper strips from the CD
- chart from the CD
- visual of an Inuit
- encyclopedia sign

**Set:** Say, "There are more than 562 tribes of Native Americans in the United States. Today we're going to look up information about where some of them live and how many people belong to the different tribes."

**Review:** Encyclopedias are multivolume, in alphabetical order, and contain information about people, places, and things. The articles are sometimes short, sometimes very long. Guide words are used to locate articles. Topics and subtopics are in bold face. Pictures, charts, tables, and "facts in brief" should be perused before the information in the article is read.

**Input:** Show the visual of the Inuit and look up "Inuit" in the encyclopedia by using the guide words. Before reading the article, review the information that is needed: population and geographic location. Model reading the article and finding the population and geographical location information. Project the board-ready copy of the paper strip and model recording the information.

**Guided practice:** Pair students and give each pair a paper strip. Students identify which volume of the encyclopedia is needed. Call the students, by table, to locate the correct volumes. Students look for the Native American tribe and write down the required information on the paper strip. After the research has been completed, ask the pairs to state the population of their assigned tribe. With the students, arrange the paper strips on a chart in order from the smallest to the largest.

**Assessment:** Informally observe whether students locate the article, use the guide words, and find and record the information required.

**Closure:** Using think-pair-share, the students discuss why some tribes were so small and some were so large.

## FOURTH-GRADE ENCYCLOPEDIA LESSON 3: PREDATOR AND PREY

*Note: If enough computers are available, try this lesson with the online encyclopedias such as* World Book *or* Encarta.

**Standards:**

*AASL #1:* Inquire, think critically, and gain knowledge. 1.1, Skills: 1.1.1, Follow an inquiry-based process in seeking knowledge in curricular subjects, and make the real-world connection for using this process in own life; 1.1.4, Find, evaluate, and select appropriate sources to answer questions.

*NCTE #7:*   Students conduct research on issues and interests by generating ideas and questions, and by posing problems. They gather, evaluate, and synthesize data from a variety of sources to communicate their discoveries in ways that suit their purpose and audience.

*Content (National Science Standard):*   The life cycles of organisms (reproduction).

*Language Arts:*   Students take notes on pertinent information in a reference source.

**Objectives:**

1.   Students locate specific information from an encyclopedia and decide what is important.
2.   Students use this information to categorize the eating habits of animals.

**Materials:**

- two sets of *The World Book Encyclopedia*
- 30 copies of the work sheet from the CD
- signs that say "herbivore," "carnivore," and omnivore," to place on three tables
- three copies of the chart for the animals' weights and food, from the CD
- visual of a bear
- encyclopedia sign

**Set:** Say, "I went to the zoo last week and saw a bear. I couldn't remember if a bear was a carnivore, an herbivore, or an omnivore." The students guess and you record the guesses. "How much do you think a bear weighs?" The students guess and you record the guesses.

**Review:** Encyclopedias are multivolume, in alphabetical order, and contain information about people, places, and things. The articles are sometimes short, sometimes very long. Guide words are used to locate articles. Topics and subtopics are in bold face. Pictures, charts, tables, and "facts in brief" should be perused before the information in the article is read.

**Input:** Show the visual of a bear. Project a board-ready work sheet, and model how to look up "bear" in the encyclopedia. Check whether there is a "facts in brief" about bears and report what they eat and how much they weigh. Then circle whether the bear is a carnivore, herbivore, or omnivore. Students find out whether they were right about their guesses.

**Guided practice:** Each student is given a work sheet with an animal's name on it. They are instructed to look up the animal, what they eat, and how much they weigh. Students are to fill out the work sheet and circle what type of eater the animal is. After the research is complete, the students go to the table with the word that represents what their animal eats: herbivore, carnivore, and omnivore. In each group, the students discuss the weights of the animals and decide which is the lightest and which is the heaviest. One student records the data on the chart. Ask the three tables to report on the information on their charts.

**Assessment:** Informally observe whether students locate the information and correctly fill out the charts.

**Closure:** Using think-pair-share, the students discuss whether there is any correlation between the weight of animals and what they eat.

## FIFTH-GRADE ENCYCLOPEDIA LESSON 1:  WHERE IS THAT IN OUR BODIES?

**Standards:**

*AASL #1:*    Inquire, think critically, and gain knowledge. 1.1, Skills: 1.1.1, Follow an inquiry-based process in seeking knowledge in curricular subjects, and make the real-world connection for using this process in own life; 1.3, Responsibilities: 1.3.3, Follow ethical and legal guidelines in gathering and using information.
*NCTE #7:*    Students conduct research on issues and interests by generating ideas and questions, and by posing problems. They gather, evaluate, and synthesize data from a variety of sources to communicate their discoveries in ways that suit their purpose and audience.
*NSES Standard 6.9:*    Structure and function in living organisms.
*Language Arts:*    Students extract pertinent information from a reference source.

**Objectives:**

1.   Students research a human body part and write two sentences, from notes, about it. One sentence is about its function, one about its location.
2.   Students locate the body part on a large chart of the human body.
3.   Students write a bibliographic entry for the encyclopedia article they used.

**Materials:**

- two sets of *The World Book Encyclopedia*
- work sheets from the CD, with body parts written in
- board-ready work sheet
- sticky notes on the tables
- visual of an esophagus
- large outline of the top part of the human body
- encyclopedia sign

**Set:** Say, "I had some burning in my esophagus last night. Should I be concerned?"

**Review:** Encyclopedias are multivolume, in alphabetical order, and contain information about people, places, and things. The articles are sometimes short, sometimes very long. Guide words are used to locate articles. Take notes by writing down only important words.

**Input:** Show the visual of an esophagus and model looking up "esophagus" in the encyclopedia. Think aloud about how to identify which volume to use and select the correct volume. Using the guide words, find the article. Read the pertinent section about the function of the esophagus. Decide on the important information and take notes. Project the board-ready work sheet and model how to write a sentence in your own words and record it on the appropriate section of the work sheet. The same is done for the location of the esophagus. Write "esophagus" on a sticky note and attach it to its correct location on the chart of the human body. Model what information to record on the bibliographic information on the work sheet: title of encyclopedia, date of edition, volume, article title, author, and the page numbers. Point out the format of a bibliographic entry on the work sheet.

**Guided practice:** Pair students and distribute a work sheet to each pair with the name of the body part already filled in. Students identify which volume of the encyclopedia is needed. Call students, by table, to find the correct volumes. Students locate the article and write the notes and sentences required on the work sheet. They write the name of the body part on a sticky note. Students attach the sticky notes in the correct place on the chart of the body. Students complete the bibliographic entry for the article they used.

**Assessment:** Informally observe whether students find the correct volume and the article, and write the requested information in sentences using their own words. Observe whether the students correctly place the body part on the chart. The work sheets can be collected for a formal evaluation, so you can determine whether the sentences were well written and whether the bibliographic entries were correct.

**Closure:** Students compare the chart they made with a blowup of a medical chart of the body, available from an online visual dictionary.

## FIFTH-GRADE ENCYCLOPEDIA LESSON 2:  DEADLY DISEASES

**Standards:**

*AASL #1:*    Inquire, think critically, and gain knowledge. 1.1, Skills: 1.1.1, Follow an inquiry-based process in seeking knowledge in curricular subjects, and make the real-world connection for using this process in own life; 1.3, Responsibilities: 1.3.3, Follow ethical and legal guidelines in gathering and using information.

*NCTE #7:*    Students conduct research on issues and interests by generating ideas and questions, and by posing problems. They gather, evaluate, and synthesize data from a variety of sources to communicate their discoveries in ways that suit their purpose and audience.

*NSES Standard 6.9:*    Structure and function in living organisms.

*Language Arts:*    Students take notes on pertinent information in a reference source.

**Objectives:**

1.    Students extract information from the encyclopedia and restate it using their own words.
2.    Students write a bibliographic entry for the encyclopedia article they used.

**Materials:**

- two sets of *The World Book Encyclopedia*
- class chart from the CD
- 15 work sheet charts from the CD
- board-ready copy of the work sheet chart
- visual of the bubonic plague
- encyclopedia sign
- scissors and glue sticks on the tables

**Set:** Sing the song "Ring around the rosie, pocket full of posies, ashes, ashes, all fall down." Explain that there is a legend that the rhyme is about a disease common in the Middle Ages. According to Wikipedia, an interpretation of the rhyme is that the roses represent the look of the splotches that appear when son has bubonic plague. "Today we're going to be looking up information about human diseases."

**Review:** Encyclopedias are multivolume, in alphabetical order, and contain information about people, and things. The articles are sometimes short, sometimes very long. Guide words are used to locate a Topics and subtopics are in bold face. Pictures, charts, tables, and "facts in brief" should be perused reading the information in the article. Review also the information needed for a bibliographic entry.

**Input:** Show a visual of the bubonic plague and look up "bubonic plague" under "plague" in the encyclopedia using the guide words. Before reading the article, review the information that is needed: cause, symptoms, contagion, and cure. Point out that these are the categories on the chart. Model using headings and subheadings to find the information. The headings and subheadings may not be in every article on a disease. Project the board-ready work sheet chart and model reading the article and taking notes on the required information. State that complete sentences are not always required on a chart. Model what information to record for the bibliographic information on the work sheet: title of encyclopedia, date of edition, volume, article title, author, and the page numbers. Point out the format of a bibliographic entry on the work sheet. Cut the sections of the work sheet chart apart, place them on the class chart, and explain the rest of the rhyme: "The 'pocket full of posies' refers to the disease victims' clothes pockets, which were filled with flowers to mask the smell of the sores. The 'ashes' refer to the fact that they burned the bodies, bedding, and clothes. 'All fall down,' comes from the number of people who were killed by the bubonic plague."

**Guided practice:** Pair students and give each pair a work sheet chart with the name of a disease on it. Students identify which volume of the encyclopedia is needed. Call the students, by table, to find the correct volume. Students locate the article on their disease and write down the required information on the work sheet chart. Students cut the sections of the work sheet chart apart and place the information on the class chart and share it with the class.

**Assessment:** Informally observe whether students locate the article using the guide words, and find and record the information required.

**Closure:** Use think-pair-share to make observations and conclusions, such as which diseases are currently threats to people, what percentage of the diseases have vaccinations against them, and which are the deadliest.

## FIFTH-GRADE ENCYCLOPEDIA LESSON 3: MEDICAL MARVELS

*Note: If enough computers are available, try this lesson with online encyclopedias such as* World Book *or* Encarta.

**Standards:**

*AASL #1:* Inquire, think critically, and gain knowledge. 1.1, Skills: 1.1.1, Follow an inquiry-based process in seeking knowledge in curricular subjects, and make the real-world connection for using this process in own life; 1.1.4, Find, evaluate, and select appropriate sources to answer questions.

*NCTE #7:* Students conduct research on issues and interests by generating ideas and questions, and by posing problems. They gather, evaluate, and synthesize data from a variety of sources to communicate their discoveries in ways that suit their purpose and audience.

*NSES 6.3:*    Structure and function in living systems.

*Language Arts:*    Students write summaries from expository text.

**Objectives:**

1. Students analyze an encyclopedia article to extract important information.
2. Students use these notes to write complete sentences, in their own words, about the research.

**Materials:**

- two sets of *The World Book Encyclopedia*
- 15 work sheets from the CD
- board-ready work sheet
- visual of Sir Frederick Grant Banting
- encyclopedia sign

**Set:** Say, "With type 1 diabetes, the body stops making insulin, which is necessary for nutrition to get to the cells of the body. Before 1922, anyone who had type 1 diabetes died within a few years of diagnosis because there was no treatment."

**Review:** Encyclopedias contain information about people, places, and things. The articles are sometimes short, sometimes very long. Use guide words to locate articles. People are located by their last names. Topics and subtopics are in bold face. Pictures, charts, tables, and "facts in brief" should be perused before reading the information in the article. Take notes by writing down only important words. Remind students of the information necessary to write a bibliographic entry from an encyclopedia article.

**Input:** Project the board-ready copy of the work sheet and explain what information must be researched. Show the visual of Sir Frederick Grant Banting and model how to look him up in the encyclopedia. Read the pertinent information and decide on the important words to answer each question. (Answers: b. 1891, d. 1941; Canada; discovered insulin, the hormone that can control diabetes, worked with Rickard McLeod, Charles Best, and James Collip.) Model how to write a paragraph from the notes and go over the bibliographic entry example.

**Paragraph for work sheet:** Sir Frederick Grant Banting was born in 1891 in Ontario, Canada. He did his research in Canada with three other men. They discovered insulin, a hormone that could control diabetes. After this, many people were able to live with diabetes instead of it being a death sentence.

**Guided practice:** Pair students and give each pair a work sheet with the name of a person who made a medical discovery. The pairs select the correct volume, locate the article, and read for information. The students take notes and write a paragraph that contains the answers to the questions. The pairs write a bibliographic entry for the information. The pairs read out their paragraphs.

**Assessment:** Informally observe whether students locate the article using the guide words, find and record the information required, and write a paragraph using their own words. A formal assessment can be done if the work sheets are collected.

**Closure:** Use think-pair-share to have the students evaluate which were the two most important medical discoveries.

## SIXTH-GRADE ENCYCLOPEDIA LESSON 1:  FAMOUS FOR WHAT?

**Standards:**

*AASL #1:*    Inquire, think critically, and gain knowledge. 1.1, Skills: 1.1.1, Follow an inquiry-based process in seeking knowledge in curricular subjects, and make the real-world connection for using this process in own life; 1.3, Responsibilities: 1.3.3, Follow ethical and legal guidelines in gathering and using information.

*NCTE #7:*    Students conduct research on issues and interests by generating ideas and questions, and by posing problems. They gather, evaluate, and synthesize data from a variety of sources to communicate their discoveries in ways that suit their purpose and audience.

*Language Arts:*    Students take notes on pertinent information in a reference source.

**Objectives:**

1.    Using guide words, students select the correct volume and locate the article on the person in the encyclopedia by his or her last name.
2.    Students take notes while reading the article.
3.    Using their own words, students write a summary about a person's major achievement.

**Materials:**

- two sets of *The World Book Encyclopedia*
- 30 paper strips and work sheets from the CD
- board-ready copy of the work sheet
- six fields of achievement signs posted around the room, from the CD
- display of biographies about some of the people
- visual of Martin Luther King, Jr.
- encyclopedia sign

**Set:** Do a one-minute book talk on one of the biographies.

**Review:** Encyclopedias contain information about people, places, and things. The articles are sometimes short, sometimes very long. Use guide words to locate articles. People are located by their last names. Topics and subtopics are in bold face. Look over the pictures, charts, tables, and "facts in brief" before reading the information in the article. Take notes by writing down only important words. Remind students of the information necessary to write a bibliographic entry from an encyclopedia article.

**Input:** Show the visual of Martin Luther King, Jr., and look him up in the encyclopedia. Thinking aloud, demonstrate how to identify the last name. Select the correct volume to find the article, using the guide words. Demonstrate how to locate the beginning of the article and the location of the birth and death dates.

Model how to skim the article, looking for the person's major achievement and identifying the field. Using the board-ready work sheet, model taking notes and writing a one-paragraph summary about the person's achievement, including the field.

**Sample paragraph:**

Martin Luther King, Jr., was born in 1929 in Atlanta, Georgia. He was a civil rights leader who helped the United States break down racial barriers. He supported a boycott of Montgomery, Alabama's segregated bus system. He wanted to achieve racial equality peacefully so that all people could share in the American Dream. The 1964 Civil Rights Act was one of the important laws that his movement brought about. He continued to work for all races and the poor until he was shot and killed in 1968.

Remind students of the information necessary for a bibliographic entry from an encyclopedia and go over the example on the work sheet. Post the six fields of achievement signs around the library.

**Guided practice:** Each student receives a paper strip with the name of a famous person and a work sheet. Students find the correct volume, locate the article, skim the article, take notes of the important information, and write a paragraph on the person in their own words. After all the paragraphs are completed, students stand under the correct field of achievement and read their paragraphs to the other students in the same field.

**Assessment:** Informally observe whether students locate the article, use the guide words, find and record the information required, write the paragraphs using their own words, and write a bibliographic entry for the article used. A formal assessment can be done if the work sheets are collected.

**Closure:** The students in each group choose the top two achievers and share these with the whole group.

## SIXTH-GRADE ENCYCLOPEDIA LESSON 2: FAMOUS STRUCTURES

**Standards:**

*AASL #1:*   Inquire, think critically, and gain knowledge. 1.1, Skills: 1.1.1, Follow an inquiry-based process in seeking knowledge in curricular subjects, and make the real-world connection for using this process in own life; 1.3, Responsibilities: 1.3.3, Follow ethical and legal guidelines in gathering and using information.
*NCTE #7:*   Students conduct research on issues and interests by generating ideas and questions, and by posing problems. They gather, evaluate, and synthesize data from a variety of sources to communicate their discoveries in ways that suit their purpose and audience.
*NETS I:   Culture: c.* Explain and give examples of how . . . architecture . . . contributes to the development and transmission of culture.
*Language Arts:*   Students take notes on pertinent information using a reference source.

**Objectives:**

1.   Students extract information from the encyclopedia and restate it in their own words.
2.   Students write a bibliographic entry for the encyclopedia article they used.

**Materials:**

- two sets of *The World Book Encyclopedia*
- 15 work sheets from the CD
- board-ready copy of the work sheet
- map of the world
- sticky notes on the table
- encyclopedia sign
- visual of the Notre Dame Cathedral

**Set:** Show a picture of the Notre Dame Cathedral. Ask whether the students recognize it, and give hints such as "bell tower," "church," and "hunchback."

**Review:** Encyclopedias are multivolume, in alphabetical order, and contain information about people, places, and things. The articles are sometimes short, sometimes very long. Guide words are used to locate articles. Topics and subtopics are in bold face. Pictures, charts, tables, and "facts in brief" should be perused before reading the information in the article. Review also the information needed for a bibliographic entry.

**Input:** Look up "Notre Dame Cathedral" in the encyclopedia by using the guide words. Before reading the article, project the board-ready work sheet and review the information that is needed: name of building, location, when built, the purpose for the building, and whether it is still in use. Model how to find the required information and write a summary paragraph.

**Sample paragraph:**

The Cathedral of Notre Dame is in Paris, France. It was built between 1163 and 1250. Notre Dame was one of the first buildings to have flying buttresses, which are wall supports that are arched. The buttresses allow the cathedral to have huge stained glass windows. It was built as a Catholic church and is still in use today.

Write the name of the structure and its location on a sticky note and place it on the world map. Model how to gather the information for a bibliographic entry and its format and go over the sample bibliographic entry on the work sheet.

**Guided practice:** Pair students and give each pair the work sheet with the name of the structure already filled in. Students identify which volume of the encyclopedia is needed. Call students, by table, to find the correct volume. Students locate the article about the structure and write down the required information on the work sheet and on a sticky note. Students write a paragraph from their notes about the structure as well as a bibliographic entry. Students place the sticky notes with the name of the structure and its location on the world map. The pairs share their paragraph with the whole group.

**Assessment:** Informally observe whether students locate the article using the guide words, find and record the information required, write the paragraphs using their own words, and correctly format the bibliographic entry. A formal assessment can be done by collecting the work sheet.

**Closure:** Each pair points out the location of their assigned building on the world map.

## SIXTH-GRADE ENCYCLOPEDIA LESSON 3: FACTS IN BRIEF OF TWO COUNTRIES

**Standards:**

*AASL #1:* Inquire, think critically, and gain knowledge. 1.1, Skills: 1.1.1, Follow an inquiry-based process in seeking knowledge in curricular subjects, and make the real-world connection for using this process in own life; 1.3, Responsibilities: 1.3.3, Follow ethical and legal guidelines in gathering and using information.

*NCTE #7:* Students conduct research on issues and interests by generating ideas and questions, and by posing problems. They gather, evaluate, and synthesize data from a variety of sources to communicate their discoveries in ways that suit their purpose and audience.

*NETS IX:* *Global Connections: d.* Economic development.

*Language Arts:* Students write summaries from expository text.

**Objectives:**

1. Students locate an article on a country in the correct volume of the encyclopedia.
2. Students use the "facts in brief" to find specific information.
3. Students make a chart comparing the economies of two countries.
4. Students make inferences from the chart.

**Materials:**

- set of *The World Book Encyclopedia*
- 15 work sheets from the CD
- board-ready copy of the work sheet
- board-ready copy of the "facts in brief" of Uganda and the United States from the encyclopedia
- visuals of Uganda and the United States
- encyclopedia sign

**Set:** Say, "How many different crops are grown worldwide? Can you name some?"

**Review:** Review the parts of an economy: agriculture, mining, manufacturing, and fishing. Encyclopedias contain information about people, places, and things. The articles are sometimes short, sometimes very long. Use guide words to locate articles. Topics and subtopics are in bold face. Pictures, charts, tables, and "facts in brief" should be perused before reading the information in the article. Take notes by writing down only important information. Remind students of the information necessary to write a bibliographic entry from an encyclopedia article and how to format the entry.

**Input:** Show visuals of Uganda and the United States and project a board-ready copies of the "facts in brief" of Uganda and the United States from the encyclopedia and go over the information. Project a board-ready copy of the work sheet and model how to record the information required for the chart: agriculture, mining, manufacturing, and fishing.

|  | **Uganda** | **United States** |
|---|---|---|
| Agriculture | Bananas, cassava, coffee | Beef cattle, milk, chicken, corn |
| Mining | Copper | Petroleum, natural gas, coal |
| Manufacturing | — | Transportation equipment, metal products, processed foods |
| Fishing | — | Salmon, shrimp, crabs |

Use think-pair-share to elicit conclusions comparing the economies of Uganda and the United States, and write a two-sentence conclusion about the economies.

**Sample conclusion:**

Both the United States and Uganda grow crops, but crops are the most important part of the economy in Uganda. The United States produces beef cattle, milk, chickens, and corn, while Uganda grows bananas, cassava, and coffee. Uganda does not manufacture products, while this is a major part of the United States' economy. The main manufacturing products are transportation equipment, metal products, and processed food.

Model how to write the bibliographic entries to include the information for both countries. Sample:

Davidson, Roger H. "United States." *World Book Encyclopedia 2006.* Vol. 20, p. 100.
Rowe, John A. "Uganda." *World Book Encyclopedia 2006.* Vol. 20, p. 3.

**Guided practice:** Pair students and give each pair a work sheet with two countries filled in. The students identify the correct volume, locate the article, and read the "facts in brief" for information. They fill in the chart with the required information. They review the chart and write two sentences comparing the economies of the two countries.

**Assessment:** Informally observe whether students locate the article using the guide words, find and record the information required, and write the conclusion using their own words. A formal assessment can be done if the work sheets are collected.

**Closure:** Students share their conclusions with the other pair at their table. A few share with the whole group while you point out in what ways the students successfully completed the assignment.

# Chapter 4

# The Atlas

---

## KINDERGARTEN ATLAS LESSON 1: WHERE DO I LIVE?

---

**Standards:**

*AASL #1:* Inquire, think critically, and gain knowledge. 1.1, Skills: 1.1.1, Follow an inquiry-based process in seeking knowledge in curricular subjects, and make the real-world connection for using this process in own life; 1.1.4, Find, evaluate, and select appropriate sources to answer questions.

*NCTE #7:* Students conduct research on issues and interests by generating ideas and questions, and by posing problems. They gather, evaluate, and synthesize data from a variety of sources to communicate their discoveries in ways that suit their purpose and audience.

*NETS #3a:* The learner can construct and use mental maps of locales, regions, and the world that demonstrate understanding of relative location, direction, size, and shape.

**Objectives:**

1. Students recite in order: home, street, city, state, country, continent, Earth, solar system, and galaxy.
2. Students apply objective #1 to their own situation, stating their homes, streets, city, states, country, continent, Earth, solar system, and galaxy.
3. Students understand that atlases are books of maps.

**Materials:**

- *Where in the World Is Henry?* by Lorna and Lecia Balian or *Where Do I Live?* by Neil Chesanow
- atlas sign
- globe, wall map, and primary atlas (the atlas used for the lesson was the *National Geographic Beginner's World Atlas*)

**Set:** Ask, "Where do we live?" and record the answers.

**Input:** Read either *Where in the World Is Henry?* by Lorna and Lecia Balian or *Where Do I Live?* by Neil Chesanow. Go back through the books, reiterating the pattern of home, street, city (or town), state, country, Earth, solar system, and galaxy. Putting these to a tune or chant is recommended. For example, for "Row, Row, Row Your Boat" it would be:

Home, home, home and street,
City or town and state,
Country, continent, Earth, solar system
Tell us where we are.


The students repeat the pattern. With the students, compare the list of where they live from the input, labeling as many as possible from the pattern. Redo the pattern to fit the geographical situation of the class. For example:


Home, home, home, and Broadway,
Phoenix, Arizona,
USA, North America, Earth, solar system
Tell us where we are.


Show the students a primary atlas and point out the map of the United States and where they are on the map. Also show their location on a globe and wall map. Browse through the atlas so students can understand that an atlas is a book of maps.

**Assessment:** Informally observe whether students can follow the generic pattern as well as understand that an atlas is a book of maps.

**Closure:** With the students, sing or chant the generic pattern and the one that reflects their specific place in the world.


## KINDERGARTEN ATLAS LESSON 2:  MAKING A KEY TO A SCHOOL MAP

**Standards:**

*AASL #1:*   Inquire, think critically, and gain knowledge. 1.1, Skills: 1.1.1, Follow an inquiry-based process in seeking knowledge in curricular subjects, and make the real-world connection for using this process in own life; 1.1.4, Find, evaluate, and select appropriate sources to answer questions.
*NCTE #7:*   Students conduct research on issues and interests by generating ideas and questions and by posing problems. They gather, evaluate, and synthesize data from a variety of sources to communicate their discoveries in ways that suit their purpose and audience.
*NETS #3a:*   The learner can construct and use mental maps of locales, regions, and the world that demonstrate understanding of relative location, direction, size, and shape.


**Objectives:**

1.   Students recognize a map of their environment.
2.   Students create a key for the map to show different classrooms, the office, the health office, the library, the cafeteria, and so on.
3.   Students label their copies of the school map to reflect the key.

**Materials:**

- 30 copies of a map of the school
- atlas sign
- board-ready copy of the map of the school
- *Me on the Map* by Joan Sweeney or *As the Crow Flies* by Gail Hartman
- crayons and pencils
- primary atlas (the atlas used for the lesson was the *National Geographic Beginner's World Atlas*)

**Set:** Read either the book *Me on the Map* by Joan Sweeney or *As the Crow Flies* by Gail Hartman, pointing out the maps of local places.

**Review:** Review that an atlas is a reference book with maps, showing the primary atlas. Also review the generic pattern from the first lesson.

**Input:** Show the board-ready copy of the school map. Point out the library or classroom where the lesson is being taught. Use think-pair-share to name other places of interest at the school, and record their ideas, such as cafeteria, health office, and so on. Explain that a "key" for a map is where the author of the key tells the readers of the map how to find special places or things. Model making the first item in the school map: a spoon to indicate the cafeteria. At this point, distribute school maps to all students. The students draw the spoon on the room that is the cafeteria. Use think-pair-share to elicit ideas on how to indicate the places previously brainstormed. Write the keys, and model the drawing of the identifying marks. Students draw the identifying marks where they are indicated.

**Assessment:** Informally observe whether students label their individual maps according to the key the class constructs.

**Closure:** "Read" your map, saying and showing the labeled rooms and areas. Students "read" their maps to partners, explaining the labels as you circulate.

## FIRST-GRADE ATLAS LESSON 1: WHERE DO I LIVE?

**Standards:**

*AASL #1:*  Inquire, think critically, and gain knowledge. 1.1, Skills: 1.1.1, Follow an inquiry-based process in seeking knowledge in curricular subjects, and make the real-world connection for using this process in own life; 1.1.4, Find, evaluate, and select appropriate sources to answer questions.
*NCTE #7:*  Students conduct research on issues and interests by generating ideas and questions, and by posing problems. They gather, evaluate, and synthesize data from a variety of sources to communicate their discoveries in ways that suit their purpose and audience.
*NETS #3a:*  The learner can construct and use mental maps of locales, regions, and the world that demonstrate understanding of relative location, direction, size, and shape.

**Objectives:**

1. Students locate their town and state on an outline map of the United States.
2. Students describe locations using directionality (north, south, east, west).
3. Students understand that atlases are books of maps.

**Materials:**

- atlas sign
- primary atlas (the atlas used for the lesson was the *National Geographic Beginner's World Atlas*)
- 30 copies of an outline map of the United States, available from www.infoplease.com/statemaps.html (under U.S. regions)
- board-ready copy of the outline map
- colored pencils
- road map of the state where the lesson is being taught

**Set:** Ask, "Where do we live?" and record the answers.

**Review:** Review that an atlas is a book of maps. Also review the directions of north, south, east, and west.

**Input:** Open the primary atlas and point to the political map of the United States. Then point to your state and ask the students where the state is with respect to the rest of the country (north, south, east, or west). Emphasize the shape of the state. Show the board-ready outline map and distribute the same map to the students. Using think-pair-share, ask the students to locate their state on the outline map by pointing at it with a finger. Check the students for accuracy before outlining the state with a colored pen. Students outline their state in colored pencil on their individual maps. Show a road map of the state and locate your town or city by using the alphabetical list of cities and towns, noting the coordinates. Locate the town or city on the board-ready outline map. Students point to the same place on their maps. Circulate as students label their town or city after being checked. Using think-pair-share, ask, "Where is our city or town with respect to our state (north, south, east, or west)?"

**Assessment:** Informally observe whether students label their maps with their town or city and state as well as understand that an atlas is a book of maps.

**Closure:** Show your map and say, "I live in _____, _____," while pointing to the town or city and state. The students do the same with their partners.

## FIRST-GRADE ATLAS LESSON 2:  NEIGHBORS AND BORDERS

**Standards:**

*AASL #1:*   Inquire, think critically, and gain knowledge. 1.1, Skills: 1.1.1, Follow an inquiry-based process in seeking knowledge in curricular subjects, and make the real-world connection for using this process in own life; 1.1.4, Find, evaluate, and select appropriate sources to answer questions.
*NCTE #7:*   Students conduct research on issues and interests by generating ideas and questions, and by posing problems. They gather, evaluate, and synthesize data from a variety of sources to communicate their discoveries in ways that suit their purpose and audience.
*NETS #3a:*   The learner can construct and use mental maps of locales, regions, and the world that demonstrate understanding of relative location, direction, size, and shape.

**Objectives:**

1.   Students locate Canada, Mexico, and the Atlantic and Pacific Oceans on an outline map of the United States.

2.  Students describe locations using directionality (north, south, east, west).
3.  Students understand that atlases are books of maps.

**Materials:**

*   atlas sign
*   15 primary atlases (the atlas used for the lesson was the *National Geographic Beginner's World Atlas*)
*   30 copies of an outline map of North America, available from www.infoplease.com/statemaps.html (under continents)
*   board-ready copy of the outline map
*   crayons and pencils

**Set:** Using think-pair-share, ask, "Who is your neighbor at school?" and "Who is your neighbor at home?"

**Review:** Review that an atlas is a book of maps. Also review the directions of north, south, east, and west.

**Input:** Show the students a political map of North America in the primary atlas. (If there are 15 atlases, pair the students and give each pair an atlas. Give the page numbers as the class explores the different maps.) Ask, "Where on the map is the United States?" then ask what country is north of the United States. Point to the border and identify it, saying that Canada is our neighbor to the north. This is repeated for Mexico. Point to the Atlantic Ocean and using think-pair-share, ask whether it is north, south, east or west of the United States. This is repeated for the Pacific Ocean.

**Guided practice:** Show the board-ready outline map and distribute the same map to the students. Using think-pair-share, ask the students to locate the United States on the outline map with their fingers. Check the students for accuracy before printing "United States" in the correct location. The students label their individual maps. This is repeated for Canada, Mexico, and the Atlantic and Pacific Oceans. Giving think time and using choral response, ask directionality questions such as "What country is north of the United States?"

**Assessment:** Informally observe whether students label their maps and answer the directionality questions as well as understand that an atlas is a book of maps.

**Closure:** Show the map and say, "Canada is our neighbor to the north. Mexico is our neighbor to the south. The Atlantic Ocean is east of the United States, and the Pacific Ocean is west of the United States," pointing to each location as you say it. The students do the same with their partners.

## SECOND-GRADE ATLAS LESSON 1: USING THE INDEX IN A PRIMARY ATLAS

**Standards:**

*AASL #1:*   Inquire, think critically, and gain knowledge. 1.1, Skills: 1.1.1, Follow an inquiry-based process in seeking knowledge in curricular subjects, and make the real-world connection for using this process in own life; 1.1.4, Find, evaluate, and select appropriate sources to answer questions.
*NCTE #7:*   Students conduct research on issues and interests by generating ideas and questions, and by posing problems. They gather, evaluate, and synthesize data from a variety of sources to communicate their discoveries in ways that suit their purpose and audience.
*NETS #3b:*   The learner can interpret, use, and distinguish various representations of the earth, such as maps, globes, and photographs.

**Objectives:**

1. Students use the index of a primary atlas to locate maps.
2. Students understand that atlases are books of maps.

**Materials:**

- atlas sign
- 15 primary atlases (the atlas used for the lesson was the *National Geographic Beginner's World Atlas*)
- 15 copies of the work sheets from the CD

**Set:** Say, "I want to find a map of Canada. What would be the best way to do it?"

**Review:** Review that a table of contents is at the beginning of a book and lists topics in page order and that an index is at the end of a book and is in alphabetical order by subject. Also review that an atlas is a book of maps.

**Input:** Pair students and a primary atlas is distributed to each pair. Model looking in the table of contents for a map of Canada. (It probably won't be there.) Then show the students the index. Ask the students to respond chorally to the question, "What is the first letter of the word 'Canada'?" Guide the students to the page in the index that lists Canada, prompting them to identify the second letter of the word. Ask the students to respond chorally with the page number where the map of Canada can be found. Everyone turns to the page and identifies the map of Canada. Repeat the modeling for "Amazon River."

**Guided practice:** The work sheet is distributed, and the student pairs use the index to locate the page number of the map required. They write the page number of the map on the work sheet and then find the map in the atlas and locate the geographical feature required for the work sheet.

**Assessment:** Informally observe whether students use the index to find the maps and the geographical features required as well as understand that an atlas is a book of maps.

**Closure:** Ask the students to respond chorally to the question, "What did you use today to find a specific place?" (answers: "an atlas," "an index").

## SECOND-GRADE ATLAS LESSON 2: KEYS AND SYMBOLS ON MAPS

**Standards:**

*AASL #1:* Inquire, think critically, and gain knowledge. 1.1, Skills: 1.1.1, Follow an inquiry-based process in seeking knowledge in curricular subjects, and make the real-world connection for using this process in own life; 1.1.4, Find, evaluate, and select appropriate sources to answer questions.
*NCTE #7:* Students conduct research on issues and interests by generating ideas and questions, and by posing problems. They gather, evaluate, and synthesize data from a variety of sources to communicate their discoveries in ways that suit their purpose and audience.
*NETS #3b:* The learner can interpret, use, and distinguish various representations of the earth, such as maps, globes, and photographs.

**Objectives:**

1. Students use a key to read information from a map.
2. Students understand that atlases are books of maps.

**Materials:**

- atlas sign
- 15 primary atlases (the atlas used for the lesson was the *National Geographic Beginner's World Atlas*)
- 15 bookmarks

**Set:** Locate the physical map of South America in the primary atlas and show it to the students. Using think-pair-share, ask, "What do you think the different colors on this map mean?"

**Review:** Review that an atlas is a reference book of maps, showing the primary atlas.

**Input:** Pair students and give each pair a primary atlas. Explain that a "key" for a map is where the map-maker shows the readers how to find different features on a map. Use the table of contents or the index to find a physical map of South America. Give the page number of the map, and have the class turn to the page with the map of South America. Show the class the map key and use think-pair-share to have students identify the color and location of the mountains, deserts, rain forests, grasslands, and wetlands. Distribute bookmarks and ask the students to bookmark the map of South America.

**Guided practice:** The student pairs are directed to turn to the physical map of Africa by using the table of contents or index. The students take turns reading the map key and locating the mountains, deserts, rain forests, grasslands, and wetlands. Students as a whole group compare the physical features of South America and Africa, using think-pair share to answer questions such as "Which one has more desert? Which one has more rain forests? On which continent is it more likely that people can grow enough food to eat? Why?"

**Assessment:** Informally observe whether students read the map keys and identify the regions symbolized.

**Closure:** Use think-pair-share to answer the question, "What is the purpose of a key on a map?"

## THIRD-GRADE ATLAS LESSON 1: WHERE IN THE WORLD ARE WE?

**Standards:**

*AASL #1:* Inquire, think critically, and gain knowledge. 1.1, Skills: 1.1.1, Follow an inquiry-based process in seeking knowledge in curricular subjects, and make the real-world connection for using this process in own life; 1.1.4, Find, evaluate, and select appropriate sources to answer questions.

*NCTE #7:* Students conduct research on issues and interests by generating ideas and questions, and by posing problems. They gather, evaluate, and synthesize data from a variety of sources to communicate their discoveries in ways that suit their purpose and audience.

*NETS #3a:* The learner can construct and use mental maps of locales, regions, and the world that demonstrate understanding of relative location, direction, size, and shape.

**Objectives:**

1.  Students use the index of a primary atlas to locate maps.
2.  Students understand that atlases are books of maps.

**Materials:**

- atlas sign
- 15 primary atlases (the atlas used for the lesson was the *National Geographic Beginner's World Atlas*)
- 30 outline maps of the world, available from www.infoplease. com/statemaps.html (under continents)
- 30 work sheets from the CD
- board-ready outline map of the world
- 16 road maps of the state in which the lesson is taught
- box of colored pencils on each table

**Set:** Say, "I want to figure out where we are on a map of the world. What would be the best way to do it?"

**Review:** Review that a table of contents is at the beginning of a book and lists topics in page order and that an index is at the end of a book and is in alphabetical order by subject. Also review that an atlas is a book of maps.

**Input:** Pair students and distribute a primary atlas to each pair, along with an outline map of the world for each student. Model looking in the table of contents for a political map of the world. Give the page number of the map and ask the students to turn to that page in the atlas. Show the students that the map is the same as their outline maps. Show the students how to find the United States on the map in the atlas. Ask a student to come to the board and point to where the United States is on the outline map. The student outlines the United States with a colored pen. Ask the students to point to the United States on their outline maps. After checks for understanding, ask the students to outline the United States in colored pencil on their individual maps. Model looking in the table of contents for a political map of the United States. Guide the students to the page of the United States political map. Ask the students to find their state on the map. One student is asked to come to the board and pinpoint where the state is on the world outline map. This will have to be approximate. Draw the state outline on the world map while the students do the same on their maps. Distribute a road map to each pair and ask them to unfold it. Ask the students to respond chorally as to the beginning letter of their town or city. Model how to find this in the alphabetical index of cities and towns. Then record the coordinates and ask the students to find their town or city, modeling how to use coordinates. Everyone locates the town or city on the map. Guide the students in pinpointing where their town or city is in relation to the rest of the state. A student points to the location on the board-ready outline world map. Indicate the place by making a circle. The students do this on their own maps.

**Guided practice:** The student pairs use the index to find the geographical features listed on the work sheet. They write the page number of the map on the work sheet and then turn to that map in the atlas. They locate the required geographical feature on the map and then label it on their own world outline map. One student searches in the index of the atlas and finds the map and the location of the geographical feature, and the other student locates it on the outline map and labels it. Students switch roles after each item. Do the first item on the work sheet with the students to make sure everyone understands the procedure.

**Assessment:** Informally observe whether students use the table of contents and the index to find the maps required as well as understand that an atlas is a book of maps.

**Closure:** Ask the students to respond chorally to the question, "What did you use today to find a specific place?" (answers: "an atlas," an "index").

## THIRD-GRADE ATLAS LESSON 2:  THEMATIC MAPS

**Standards:**

*AASL #1:*   Inquire, think critically, and gain knowledge. 1.1, Skills: 1.1.1, Follow an inquiry-based process in seeking knowledge in curricular subjects, and make the real-world connection for using this process in own life; 1.1.4, Find, evaluate, and select appropriate sources to answer questions.

*NCTE #7:*   Students conduct research on issues and interests by generating ideas and questions, and by posing problems. They gather, evaluate, and synthesize data from a variety of sources to communicate their discoveries in ways that suit their purpose and audience.

*NETS #3c:*   The learner can use appropriate resources . . . to generate, manipulate, and interpret information.

**Objectives:**

1.   Students use a key to read information from a map.
2.   Students draw conclusions based on thematic maps.
3.   Students understand that atlases are books of maps.

**Materials:**

- atlas sign
- 15 primary atlases (the atlas used for the lesson was the *National Geographic Beginner's World Atlas*)
- 15 copies of a world population density map if the primary atlas does not contain one
- Internet site for the population density map: http://sedac. ciesin.columbia.edu/gpw/global.jsp# (click on "download map" and print)
- board-ready copy of the world population density map
- work sheets from the CD
- board-ready copy of the work sheet

**Set:** Use think-pair-share to elicit answers to the question, "What kinds of information can a thematic map give us?"

**Review:** Review that an atlas is a reference book of maps, and keys and symbols are used to "read" maps.

**Input:** Pair students and give each pair a primary atlas and a work sheet. Giving the students the page number in the atlas, ask everyone to look at the "Climate and Vegetation" map of the world. Explain the map key and use think-pair-share to have the students identify the color and location of the climates and the vegetation. With the students, write down the parts of the world with an arid (desert) land: northern Africa, southwestern North America, the middle of Australia, the southeast tip and the western strip of South America, most of the Arabian Peninsula, and northern Europe. The continents are identified by using a political map either on the wall or in the atlas. Then direct the students to turn to the population density map in the atlas or distribute the map from the Internet.

**Guided practice:** Each table of students is assigned a continent and asked to ascertain whether people live in the arid areas. Using think-pair-share, the students discuss why or why not. Direct the students' attention to the population density map and ask where most of the people in the world live, referring to the political map as well. Use think-pair-share to ask in which climates do most of the world's population live in and why? In pairs, the students write the answer for their continent on the work sheet. After the research is finished, the pairs at the table compare their conclusions.

**Assessment:** Informally observe whether students read the map keys and identify the regions symbolized.

**Closure:** Use think-pair-share to answer the question, "What kinds of information can be read from thematic maps?"

## FOURTH-GRADE ATLAS LESSON 1: MAP OF OUR STATE

**Standards:**

*AASL #1:*   Inquire, think critically, and gain knowledge. 1.1, Skills: 1.1.1, Follow an inquiry-based process in seeking knowledge in curricular subjects, and make the real-world connection for using this process in own life; 1.1.4, Find, evaluate, and select appropriate sources to answer questions.
*NCTE #7:*   Students conduct research on issues and interests by generating ideas and questions, and by posing problems. They gather, evaluate, and synthesize data from a variety of sources to communicate their discoveries in ways that suit their purpose and audience.
*NETS #3a:*   The learner can construct and use mental maps of locales, regions, and the world that demonstrate understanding of relative location, direction, size, and shape.

**Objectives:**

1.   Students use the table of contents or index of an atlas to locate a specific map.
2.   Students use several maps to find information to transfer to an outline map of their state.
3.   Students understand that atlases are books of maps.

**Materials:**

- atlas sign
- 15 intermediate atlases
- 30 outline maps of the state the students live in, available from www.infoplease.com/statemaps.html (under U.S. state maps)
- 30 copies of the work sheet personalized for the state in which the lesson is taught, with the requirements for the completed map from the CD
- board-ready copy of the outline map
- 30 bookmarks

**Set:** Say, "I want to find a map of our state. What would be the best way to do it?"

**Review:** Review that a table of contents is at the beginning of a book and lists topics in page order and that an index is at the end of a book and is in alphabetical order by subject. Also review that an atlas is a book of maps.

**Input:** Pair students and distribute an atlas to each pair. Model looking in the table of contents for a map of their state. Students turn to the map and bookmark it. Then show the students the index. Ask the students to respond chorally to the question, "What is the first letter of our state's name?" Guide the students to the page in the index that lists the state, prompting them to identify the second letter of the word. Ask the students to respond chorally with the page numbers where the map can be found. Everyone turns to the page(s) and identifies the map(s) that has their state. Outline maps of your state are distributed to each student. Put the board-ready copy of the same outline map on the projector and point out the list of items that must be found and transferred to the outline map. Start with mountains, if any, stating the name of the mountains. The students put their fingers on the mountains. Ask a student to pinpoint that location on the board-ready outline map and write the name of the mountains. The other students use "thumbs up" or "thumbs down" to agree or disagree with the placement. When there is agreement, all students label the mountains on the map. This strategy is repeated for the rivers.

**Guided practice:** The student pairs look up the geographical features on the work sheet, writing the locations on their outline maps. After the research is completed, have the students look at the map and locate the capital. Ask whether any mountains or rivers are nearby. Use think-pair-share to have students draw conclusions about why the city is so close to a river. Ask other questions designed to have students draw conclusions using the information on their maps. Some examples are:

- "Does our state have a border with another country? What are the advantages and disadvantages of that?"
- "Look at the rivers, lakes, and mountains. What are the advantages and disadvantages of these to our transportation system?"

**Assessment:** Informally observe whether students use the map information to locate geographical features and label them on the outline maps. Also informally observe whether students make conclusions based on map information.

**Closure:** Using think-pair-share, ask, "What kinds of information did we put on our state map today?"

---

## FOURTH-GRADE ATLAS LESSON 2: MAKING A NEIGHBORHOOD MAP

**Standards:**

*AASL #1:* Inquire, think critically, and gain knowledge. 1.1, Skills: 1.1.1, Follow an inquiry-based process in seeking knowledge in curricular subjects, and make the real-world connection for using this process in own life; 1.1.4, Find, evaluate, and select appropriate sources to answer questions.
*NCTE #7:* Students conduct research on issues and interests by generating ideas and questions, and by posing problems. They gather, evaluate, and synthesize data from a variety of sources to communicate their discoveries in ways that suit their purpose and audience.
*NETS #3a:* The learner can construct and use mental maps of locales, regions, and the world that demonstrate understanding of relative location, direction, size, and shape.

**Objectives:**

1. Students create a map of their school neighborhood.
2. Students create a key to read information from a map.

**Materials:**

- atlas sign
- blank copy paper
- 30 rulers
- blank, board-ready transparency to make the neighborhood map

**Set:** Use think-pair-share to elicit answers to the question, "What kinds of information can a map give us?"

**Review:** Review that an atlas is a reference book with maps, and use a map in the atlas to review that keys and symbols are used to "read" maps.

**Input:** Tell the students that today everyone will make a map of the school's neighborhood, including a key. The school will be in the center of the map. The students offer suggestions for a symbol for "school." Choose one of the suggestions, write it in the key section, and put the symbol in the middle of the page. Ask what street the school is on. With the students, use the ruler to put a line for the street and label it. This is repeated for the cross street. Students offer suggestions for a symbol for a stoplight. This is repeated for several streets away from the school.

**Guided practice:** Each student fills in more of the map and adds symbols to the key. The items to be added could include streets, shopping centers, places of worship, and so on. After the students have finished their maps, ask the students to give their map a title.

**Assessment:** Informally observe whether students fill in the map and create symbols for the new items.

**Closure:** Use think-pair-share to answer the question, "Why do maps have symbols and keys?"

## FOURTH-GRADE ATLAS LESSON 3: USING A MAP TO PLAN A TRIP

**Standards:**

*AASL #1:* Inquire, think critically, and gain knowledge. 1.1, Skills: 1.1.1, Follow an inquiry-based process in seeking knowledge in curricular subjects, and make the real-world connection for using this process in own life; 1.1.4, Find, evaluate, and select appropriate sources to answer questions.

*NCTE #7:* Students conduct research on issues and interests by generating ideas and questions, and by posing problems. They gather, evaluate, and synthesize data from a variety of sources to communicate their discoveries in ways that suit their purpose and audience.

*NETS #3d:* The learner can estimate distances and calculate scale.

**Objectives:**

1. Students use the table of contents or index of an atlas to locate a specific map.
2. Students use several maps to find information about the distance in planning a road trip.
3. Students understand that atlases are books of maps.

**Materials:**

- atlas sign
- 15 intermediate atlases
- 30 outline maps of the United States with a distance scale, available from www.eduplace.com/ss/maps/usa.html (United States—no labels)
- board-ready copy of the outline map
- 15 paper strips from the CD
- 15 bookmarks
- 15 rulers

**Set:** Say, "I want to go to Disneyland in Anaheim, California. Does anyone know how far it is from here?"

**Review:** Review that a table of contents is at the beginning of a book and lists topics in page order and that an index is at the end of a book and is in alphabetical order by subject. Also review that an atlas is a book of maps.

**Input:** Pair students and distribute an atlas to each pair along with an outline map for each student. Model looking in the table of contents or index for a map of the United States. Students turn to the map and bookmark it. Then ask the students to pinpoint their location on the map. Label this on the outline map of the United States. The students point to the location on their own maps and label it. Look up Anaheim, California, in the index and have the students turn to the page number of the map of California. Show the location of Anaheim on the map and guide the students in finding it on their individual maps and labeling it. Guide the students in drawing a route from their city or town to Anaheim. Show the key that shows the mileage scale on the map of the United States and demonstrate how to use a ruler to estimate the mileage from one place to another. Students record this number on the route.

**Guided practice:** Each pair is given a paper strip with two destinations. One student will locate the first destination, draw the route, and figure out the mileage of the trip from their home town or city to the assigned destination. The other person checks the answer. The number of miles is written on the route. These roles are reversed for the second destination.

**Assessment:** Informally observe whether students can use the map information to plan the routes and estimate the mileage of a trip.

**Closure:** Use think-pair-share to answer the question, "How did you figure out the miles from one place to another on a map?"

## FIFTH-GRADE ATLAS LESSON 1: MAP OF THE UNITED STATES

**Standards:**

*AASL #1:*   Inquire, think critically, and gain knowledge. 1.1, Skills: 1.1.1, Follow an inquiry-based process in seeking knowledge in curricular subjects, and make the real-world connection for using this process in own life; 1.1.4, Find, evaluate, and select appropriate sources to answer questions.
*NCTE #7:*   Students conduct research on issues and interests by generating ideas and questions, and by posing problems. They gather, evaluate, and synthesize data from a variety of sources to communicate their discoveries in ways that suit their purpose and audience.

*NETS #3a:*    The learner can construct and use mental maps of locales, regions, and the world that demonstrate understanding of relative location, direction, size, and shape.

**Objectives:**

1.  Students use the table of contents or index of an atlas to locate a specific map.
2.  Students use several maps to find information to transfer to an outline map of the United States.
3.  Students understand the difference between a physical and political map.
4.  Students understand that atlases are books of maps.

**Materials:**

- atlas sign
- 15 intermediate atlases
- 30 outline maps of the United States, available from www.eduplace.com/ss/maps/usa.html (United States—no labels)
- 30 copies of the work sheet with the requirements of the completed map from the CD
- board-ready copy of the outline map
- 30 bookmarks

**Set:** Say, "I want to find a map of the United States. What would be the best way to do it?"

**Review:** Review that a table of contents is at the beginning of a book and lists topics in page order and that an index is at the end of a book and is in alphabetical order by subject. Also review that an atlas is a book of maps.

**Input:** Pair students, and distribute an atlas and work sheet to each pair. Model looking in the table of contents for a political and physical map of the United States. Students turn to these maps and bookmark them. Then show the students the index (some atlases may have the page numbers to the maps in the index). Outline maps of the United States are distributed to each student. Project the board-ready outline map and point out the list of items on the work sheet that must be found and transferred to their individual outline map. Start with the Rocky Mountains and the Mississippi River. The students put their fingers on the mountains. Ask a student to pinpoint that location on the board-ready outline map and write the name of the mountains. The other students use "thumbs up" or "thumbs down" to agree or disagree with the placement. When there is agreement, all students label the Rocky Mountains on the map. This strategy is repeated for the Mississippi River.

**Guided practice:** Using the bookmarked physical and political maps of the United States, the student pairs locate the physical and political features required on the work sheet and label them on their individual outline map. After the research is completed, have the students look at their maps and use think-pair-share to have students draw conclusions. Some examples are:

- "Why isn't the capital, Washington, D.C., in the middle of the country? Why is it located in the eastern part of the country?"
- "Look at the Rocky Mountains. What were some of the problems these mountains would have given early transportation, postal service, and trade with states east and west of them?"
- "Why do you think some of the states' borders are straight and others are very curvy?"

**Assessment:** Informally observe whether students use the map information to locate specific items and place them on the correct place on the outline maps. Also informally observe whether students make conclusions based on map information.

**Closure:** Using think-pair-share, ask, "What is the difference in the information that a physical map provides compared to the information that a political map provides?"

## FIFTH-GRADE ATLAS LESSON 2:  GATHERING INFORMATION USING THEMATIC MAPS

**Standards:**

*AASL #1:*   Inquire, think critically, and gain knowledge. 1.1, Skills: 1.1.1, Follow an inquiry-based process in seeking knowledge in curricular subjects, and make the real-world connection for using this process in own life; 1.1.4, Find, evaluate, and select appropriate sources to answer questions.
*NCTE #7:*   Students conduct research on issues and interests by generating ideas and questions, and by posing problems. They gather, evaluate, and synthesize data from a variety of sources to communicate their discoveries in ways that suit their purpose and audience.
*NETS #3c:*   The learner can use . . . geographic tools such as atlases, data bases, grid systems, charts, graphs, and maps to generate, manipulate, and interpret information.

**Objectives:**

1.   Students generate information by using thematic maps and their keys.
2.   Students interpret information to make conclusions about the United States' geography and people.
3.   Students understand that atlases are books of maps.

**Materials:**

- atlas sign
- 15 copies each of a population density map, a vegetation map, and other thematic maps from the Internet, or 15 atlases with maps with the same information
- thematic map Web sites from the CD
- 15 copies of the work sheet from the CD
- board-ready copy of the work sheet and thematic maps (if needed)

**Set:** Use think-pair-share to elicit answers to the question, "What kinds of information can a thematic map give us?"

**Review:** Review that an atlas is a reference book with maps, and keys and symbols are used to "read" maps.

**Input:** Pair students and give each pair an atlas or a vegetation and population density map and a work sheet. Tell the students that today everyone will extract information from thematic maps and use that information to make conclusions about the United States' geography and people. Ask everyone to look at the vegetation map in the atlas or from the Internet and go over the key with the students. With the students, answer the questions on the work sheet about vegetation. Then guide the students in writing the bibliographic citation.

**Guided practice:** The students are directed to the population density map of the United States (or North America, or the world) from the atlas or from the Internet. The student pairs look at the map, read its key, and answer the questions on the work sheet. After the research is completed, assist the students in comparing other thematic maps and making conclusions. The subject of the map depends on the availability in the atlas being used, or which thematic maps have been printed from the Web sites.

**Assessment:** Informally observe whether the students read the maps by using the keys, whether they note the type of maps being used, and whether they make conclusions based on the maps.

**Closure:** Use think-pair-share to answer the question, "What kind of information can you find on a thematic map?"

## FIFTH-GRADE ATLAS LESSON 3:  USING HISTORICAL MAPS

**Standards:**

*AASL #1:*    Inquire, think critically, and gain knowledge. 1.1, Skills: 1.1.1, Follow an inquiry-based process in seeking knowledge in curricular subjects, and make the real-world connection for using this process in own life; 1.1.4, Find, evaluate, and select appropriate sources to answer questions.
*NCTE #7:*    Students conduct research on issues and interests by generating ideas and questions, and by posing problems. They gather, evaluate, and synthesize data from a variety of sources to communicate their discoveries in ways that suit their purpose and audience.
*NETS #3c:*    The learner can use . . . geographic tools such as atlases, data bases, grid systems, charts, graphs, and maps to generate, manipulate, and interpret information.

**Objectives:**

1.    Students generate information by using historical maps and their keys.
2.    Students interpret information to make conclusions about the history of the expansion of the United States.

**Materials:**

- atlas sign
- 15 copies each of historical maps of the "U.S. Territorial Map 1775," "U.S. Territorial Map 1810," "U.S. Territorial Map 1840," and "U.S. Territorial Map 1860," from Web sites from the CD
- 15 copies of the work sheet from the CD
- board-ready copy of the work sheet and historical maps

**Set:** Use think-pair-share to elicit answers to the question, "What kinds of information can a historical map give us?"

**Review:** Review that an atlas is a reference book with maps, and keys and symbols are used to "read" maps.

**Input:** Tell the students that today everyone will extract information from historical maps and use that information to make conclusions about the United States' expansion. Pair students and distribute the first map, "U.S. Territorial Map 1775," and the work sheets. Guide the students in understanding the key, and together answer the questions on the work sheet about the size of the original United States. Distribute the next map, "U.S. Territorial Map 1810," and, together with the students, compare the two maps and answer the questions on the work sheet.

**Guided practice:** Give the paired students the last two historical maps, "U.S. Territorial Map 1840" and "U.S. Territorial Map 1860." The student pairs look at the maps, read their keys, and answer questions on the work sheet. After the research is completed, assist the students in comparing all four maps and writing conclusions about the expansion of the United States from 1775 to 1860.

**Assessment:** Informally observe whether the students read the maps by using the keys, whether they note the type of maps being used, and whether they make conclusions based on the maps.

**Closure:** Use think-pair-share to answer the question, "What kind of information can you find on a historical map?"

## SIXTH-GRADE ATLAS LESSON 1: MAKING A MAP OF A COUNTRY

**Standards:**

*AASL #1:* Inquire, think critically, and gain knowledge. 1.1, Skills: 1.1.1, Follow an inquiry-based process in seeking knowledge in curricular subjects, and make the real-world connection for using this process in own life; 1.1.4, Find, evaluate, and select appropriate sources to answer questions.
*NCTE #7:* Students conduct research on issues and interests by generating ideas and questions, and by posing problems. They gather, evaluate, and synthesize data from a variety of sources to communicate their discoveries in ways that suit their purpose and audience.
*NETS #3a:* The learner can construct and use mental maps of locales, regions, and the world that demonstrate understanding of relative location, direction, size, and shape.

**Objectives:**

1. Students use the table of contents or index of an atlas to locate a specific map.
2. Students use several maps to find information to transfer to an outline map of a specific country.
3. Students understand that atlases are books of maps.

**Materials:**

- atlas sign
- 15 intermediate atlases
- paper strips with country names from the CD

- 30 outline maps, two each of 15 different countries (named on the paper strips from the CD), available from http://geography. about.com/library/blank/blxindex.htm
- 30 copies of the work sheet with the requirements of the completed map, from the CD
- board-ready copy of an outline map of Argentina
- 30 bookmarks

**Set:** Say, "I want to find a map of Argentina. What would be the best way to do it?"

**Review:** Review that a table of contents is at the beginning of a book and lists topics in page order and that an index is at the end of a book and is in alphabetical order by subject. Also review that an atlas is a book of maps.

**Input:** Pair students and distribute an atlas to each student pair as well as a work sheet for each student. With the students, peruse the work sheet to see the type of information that is required. Model looking in the table of contents for a map of Argentina. (Some atlases will show this in the table of contents; others will not.) Students turn to this map and put a bookmark there. Then show the students the index. Guide students in looking up "Argentina" in the index under "A." Ask the students to look at each page suggested by the index and figure out which one will give them the information needed. The students all turn to the correct map. Start with the mountains. The students put their fingers on the mountains, the Andes and the Patagonia Pampas. Ask a student to pinpoint that location on the board-projected outline map and write the name of the mountains. The other students use "thumbs up" or "thumbs down" to agree or disagree with the placement. This strategy is repeated for the rivers. Ask individual students to come up to draw on and label the board-ready map with the required information from the work sheet. After the labeling of the map is done, model writing the bibliographic citation.

**Guided practice:** Pair students and give each pair a paper strip and two maps of the country named on the paper strip. The student pairs use the atlas to find the required information on the work sheet. They label the physical and political information on their individual country's outline map.

**Assessment:** Informally observe whether students use the map information to locate specific items and place them on the outline maps.

**Closure:** Using think-pair-share, ask the students to verbalize their strategies in locating places to label on the outline map.

*Note: Collect the maps for the next lesson, making sure that the students' names and room numbers are on them.*

## SIXTH-GRADE ATLAS LESSON 2: NATIONS OF THE WORLD

**Standards:**

*AASL #1:*   Inquire, think critically, and gain knowledge. 1.1, Skills: 1.1.1, Follow an inquiry-based process in seeking knowledge in curricular subjects, and make the real-world connection for using this process in own life; 1.1.4, Find, evaluate, and select appropriate sources to answer questions.
*NCTE #7:*   Students conduct research on issues and interests by generating ideas and questions, and by posing problems. They gather, evaluate, and synthesize data from a variety of sources to communicate their discoveries in ways that suit their purpose and audience.

*NETS #3c:* The learner can use . . . geographic tools such as atlases, data bases, grid systems, charts, graphs, and maps to generate, manipulate, and interpret information.

**Objectives:**

1. Students generate information by using maps and their keys.
2. Students interpret information to make conclusions about nations of the world.
3. Students understand that atlases are books of maps.

**Materials:**

- atlas sign
- 15 copies of an intermediate atlas with information about population density, vegetation, life expectancy, gross national product, per capita income, and religion (if all these maps are not available in the atlas being used, either edit the work sheet or supplement the materials with maps from the Internet)
- work sheets from the CD
- board-ready copy of the work sheet
- per capita income signs geared to the key of the map being used
- maps from Sixth-Grade Lesson 1

**Set:** Use think-pair-share to elicit answers to the question, "What kinds of information can a thematic map give us?"

**Review:** Review that an atlas is a reference book with maps, and that keys and symbols are used to read maps.

**Input:** Pair students and give each pair an atlas and a work sheet. Tell the students that today everyone will extract information from thematic maps and use that information to make conclusions about the nation they researched during the last lesson. Ask everyone to look at the vegetation map, either world or continent, in the atlas and go over the key. Ask the students to pinpoint Argentina on the map as you do so. Ask the students to study the key of the map and tell their partner what kind of vegetation covers the greatest area of Argentina. Fill out the information on the work sheet. Students do *not* copy this, because they will answer the questions for the countries they studied in Lesson 1. This is repeated for each of the thematic maps for information on Argentina. Explain what the gross national product and per capita income map measures. The gross national (or domestic) product is the market value of all final goods and services produced within a country within a period, a year on most maps. The per capita figure is that number divided by the number of people in the country.

**Guided practice:** Have several students hand out the maps completed in the previous lesson. The maps remind students of the name and shape of their countries as well as the continent it is on. The student pairs look up the thematic maps in the atlas, find the required information, and record it on the work sheet.

**Assessment:** Informally observe whether the students read the maps by using the keys, whether they note the type of maps being used, and whether they make conclusions based on the maps.

**Closure:** After the research is completed, the students are asked to stand under the sign that represents the gross national product per capita in the country they researched. (Use the scale in the atlas used for the assignment.) Say the per capita income and have the students under that sign say the name of the country. Using think-pair-share, ask, "Which is the poorest country and which is the richest country?"

## SIXTH-GRADE ATLAS LESSON 3: MAPS ON THE INTERNET

**Standards:**

*AASL #1:*    Inquire, think critically, and gain knowledge. 1.1, Skills: 1.1.1, Follow an inquiry-based process in seeking knowledge in curricular subjects, and make the real-world connection for using this process in own life; 1.1.4, Find, evaluate, and select appropriate sources to answer questions.

*NCTE #7:*    Students conduct research on issues and interests by generating ideas and questions, and by posing problems. They gather, evaluate, and synthesize data from a variety of sources to communicate their discoveries in ways that suit their purpose and audience.

*NETS Technology #3: Research and Information Fluency:*    Students apply digital tools to gather, evaluate, and use information.

**Objectives:**

1.    Using the Internet, students locate information on countries.
2.    Students understand that the Internet provides information and images on many topics.
3.    Students understand that Web sites need to be evaluated for their reliability.

**Materials:**

- atlas sign
- projection of an Internet computer screen (must have access to computer, Internet, and means of projection)
- 15 computers with Internet access, or enough so that each pair can access the Web sites
- personalized start page or bookmarked Web sites from the CD
- 15 copies of the work sheet from the CD
- board-ready copy of the work sheet
- visual of Albania

**Set:** Show the visual of Albania and ask, "If you were doing your homework and you needed to know the capital of Albania, and your only atlas had been damaged when the kitchen flooded, where else could you look to find the answer?" The students guess. Then say, "Today we are going to explore several online atlases."

**Review:** Review that the Internet is a network of interconnected computers around the world and a source of information and images. A user must determine the reliability of a Web site.

**Input:** Click on the online atlas, Altapedia (www.atlapedia.com). Explain that the Web site is a combination atlas and encyclopedia of countries. Click on "Countries A to Z," then click on "A" and "Albania." Scroll down and briefly show the information that Altapedia provides. Explain that there are two ways to view a map of the country: political and physical. Click on both views of the map of Albania. Point out where the capital is on the political map. Then click on the next Web site, "World Factbook" (https://www.cia.gov/cia/ publications/factbook/ index.html), which is sponsored by the CIA. Pull down "select a country or location" to "Albania." Scroll down and briefly show all the information the "World Factbook" provides on Albania. Point out where the capital is on the map. Finally, click on the last Web site, "GeographyIQ" (www.geographyiq.com/ index.htm). Click on the "A" of the alphabet on the left-hand side of the Web site and find "Albania." Scroll down and briefly show the information the Web site provides on Albania. Point out where the capital is on the map. Project the board-ready copy of the work sheet and explain that the information required is the capitals of two countries. The work sheet shows the Web site to use to find the capitals of the countries. The students are instructed to use the personalized start page or bookmarked sites.

**Guided practice:** Pair students, give them a work sheet, and assign a computer. Circulate, offering assistance as necessary. After all students complete the assignment, they share the information with the other students at their table.

**Assessment:** Informally assess whether students can navigate, locate, and record the information from the assigned Web site.

**Closure:** Use think-pair-share to answer the question, "Did the Web site provide enough information to complete most homework assignments?"

# Chapter 5

# The Almanac

**Standards:**

*AASL #1:*    Inquire, think critically, and gain knowledge. 1.1, Skills: 1.1.1, Follow an inquiry-based process in seeking knowledge in curricular subjects, and make the real-world connection for using this process in own life; 1.1.4, Find, evaluate, and select appropriate sources to answer questions.
*NCTE #7:*    Students conduct research on issues and interests by generating ideas and questions, and by posing problems. They gather, evaluate, and synthesize data from a variety of sources to communicate their discoveries in ways that suit their purpose and audience.

**Objectives:**

1.    Students guess the speeds of selected animals.
2.    Students associate random information with *The World Almanac for Kids*.
3.    Students recognize that the use of an index is necessary in finding information in an almanac.

**Materials:**

- *The World Almanac for Kids*
- almanac sign
- visuals of the animals from the CD
- list of animals and their running speeds from the CD
- index cards

**Set:** Ask, "Which animal do you think runs faster, a cat or a wild turkey?"

**Input:** Show the almanac and discuss its features: it contains facts, is not arranged in any particular order, and comes out every year. Show the students where the index is located and how it is arranged. Model how to look up the heading "animals" in the index, and then find the subheading "fastest/largest/smallest," and turn to the appropriate page. Walk around and show the page to all the tables. Two students hold visuals of a cat and a wild turkey. Hold up two speeds each on an index card: 15 miles per hour and 30 miles per hour. Ask, "Which animal runs 15 miles per hour, and which animal runs 30 miles per hour?" After the students have guessed, read from the almanac how many miles per hour (mph) each one runs. (The turkey goes 15 miles per hour, while the cat goes 30 miles per hour.) Affix the numbers 15 mph and 30 mph to the correct visuals.

**Guided practice:** Give visuals of two more animals to two more students to display to the rest of the class. Show two numbers that represent how fast the two animals run. Students use think-pair-share to hypothesize which speed goes with which animal. Look in the almanac to affirm the correct or incorrect guesses and say, "*The World Almanac for Kids* says that a lion runs . . ." This is repeated for all the examples in the list provided in the CD.

**Assessment:** Informally observe whether students notice what's in an almanac and whether they are able to guess the speeds of the animals.

**Closure:** Close with the statement that almanacs have current information and statistics and are *not* in alphabetical order, so an index must be used.

## KINDERGARTEN ALMANAC LESSON 2: HOW LONG DO ANIMALS LIVE?

**Standards:**

*AASL #1:*   Inquire, think critically, and gain knowledge. 1.1, Skills: 1.1.1, Follow an inquiry-based process in seeking knowledge in curricular subjects, and make the real-world connection for using this process in own life; 1.1.4, Find, evaluate, and select appropriate sources to answer questions.
*NCTE #7:*   Students conduct research on issues and interests by generating ideas and questions, and by posing problems. They gather, evaluate, and synthesize data from a variety of sources to communicate their discoveries in ways that suit their purpose and audience.

**Objectives:**

1.    Students guess the life spans of selected animals.
2.    Students associate random information with *The World Almanac for Kids*.
3.    Students recognize that the use of an index is necessary for finding information in an almanac.

**Materials:**

- *The World Almanac for Kids*
- almanac sign
- visuals of the animals from the CD
- list of animals and their life spans from the CD
- index cards

**Set:** Ask, "Which animal do you think lives longer, a gorilla or a humpback whale?"

**Review:** Review that an almanac is a reference book with current facts that is not arranged alphabetically. An index is needed to find information.

**Input:** Show the almanac and model how to look up the heading "animals" in the index. Then find the subheading "life spans," and turn to the appropriate page. Explain that the term "life span" means how long, on average, an animal lives. Walk around and show the page to all the tables. Two students hold visuals of a gorilla and a humpback whale. Hold up two ages each on two index cards: 30 years and 50 years. Ask, "Which animal lives 30 years and which animal lives 50 years?" The students use think-pair-share to guess which animal lives longer. Read from the almanac how many years each animal lives. (The gorilla lives 30 years, while the humpback whale lives 50 years.) Affix the numbers 30 years and 50 years to the correct visuals. Reiterate that the whale lives longer and ask for reasons why.

**Guided practice:** Give visuals of two more animals to two more students to display. Show two numbers that represent the life spans of the two animals. Students use think-pair-share to hypothesize which animal lives longer. Look in the almanac to affirm the correct or incorrect guesses and say, *"The World Almanac for Kids* says that a cat lives . . ." This is repeated for all of the animals in the list provided in the CD.

**Assessment:** Informally observe whether students notice what's in an almanac, and whether they are able to guess the life spans of the animals.

**Closure:** Close with the statement that almanacs have current information and statistics and are *not* in alphabetical order, so an index must be used.

## FIRST-GRADE ALMANAC LESSON 1: WHAT ARE GROUPS OF ANIMALS CALLED?

**Standards:**

*AASL #1:* Inquire, think critically, and gain knowledge. 1.1, Skills: 1.1.1, Follow an inquiry-based process in seeking knowledge in curricular subjects, and make the real-world connection for using this process in own life; 1.1.4, Find, evaluate, and select appropriate sources to answer questions.
*NCTE #7:* Students conduct research on issues and interests by generating ideas and questions, and by posing problems. They gather, evaluate, and synthesize data from a variety of sources to communicate their discoveries in ways that suit their purpose and audience.

**Objectives:**

1. Students guess names for groups of selected animals.
2. Students associate random information with *The World Almanac for Kids*.
3. Students recognize that the use of an index is necessary in finding information in an almanac.

**Materials:**

- *The World Almanac for Kids*
- almanac sign
- visuals of groups of animals from the CD
- names of the groups of animals from the CD

**Set:** Say, "We call a group of students a class. We call a group of classes a school. Today we are going to investigate the names that zoologists, people who study animals, give to groups of animals."

**Review:** Review that an almanac is a reference book with current facts that is not arranged alphabetically. An index is needed to find information.

**Input:** Show the almanac and model how to look up the heading of "animals" in the index, find the subheading "names of groups," and turn to the appropriate page. Walk around and show the page to all the tables. Show a visual of a group of lions. The students use think-pair-share to guess what a group of lions might be called. Record the guesses on the board. Read the information from the almanac that a group of lions is called a "pride." Use think-pair-share for students to speculate on reasons why zoologists called the group a "pride."

**Guided practice:** Show visuals of groups of animals. The students use think-pair-share to guess the name of the group. After you record the guesses, read the correct information from the almanac. Students use think-pair share to reason why that name was given. This is repeated for all the examples in the list provided in the CD.

**Assessment:** Informally observe whether students notice that an almanac contains facts and that an index is needed to find information.

**Closure:** Close with the statement that almanacs have current information and statistics and are *not* in alphabetical order, so an index must be used.

## FIRST-GRADE ALMANAC LESSON 2:  WHAT'S YOUR FAVORITE CLASSIC TOY?

**Standards:**

*AASL #1:*    Inquire, think critically, and gain knowledge. 1.1, Skills: 1.1.1, Follow an inquiry-based process in seeking knowledge in curricular subjects, and make the real-world connection for using this process in own life; 1.1.4, Find, evaluate, and select appropriate sources to answer questions.

*NCTE #7:*    Students conduct research on issues and interests by generating ideas and questions, and by posing problems. They gather, evaluate, and synthesize data from a variety of sources to communicate their discoveries in ways that suit their purpose and audience.

**Objectives:**

1.    Students match the classic toys with the dates on which they were introduced.
2.    Students make a graph based on data collected about their favorite classic toys.
3.    Students recognize that the use of an index is necessary for finding information in *The World Almanac for Kids*.

**Materials:**

- *The World Almanac for Kids*
- almanac sign
- visuals of groups of classic toys: teddy bear, yo-yo, Barbie doll, Legos, Matchbox cars, and Crayola crayons
- list of the dates on which they were introduced, from the CD
- one box of erasable markers per table
- laminated chart with the name of each toy in a column

**Set:** Say, "Have you ever seen or played with a hula hoop? The hula hoop was invented when I was young" (or "before I was born"). "It was a huge craze. It is a 'classic' toy because it's still being sold and played with today."

**Review:** Review that an almanac is a reference book with current facts that is not arranged alphabetically. An index is needed to find information.

**Input:** Show the poster of the six classic toys and identify them. "Today we're going to guess the year when each toy was introduced." Put a year on each table. The students use think-pair-share to decide which toy was introduced in the year they were given. Ask each group what toy they chose and affix the year. (More than one table may choose the same toy.) Then look up the answers in the almanac by using the index. Look up "toys" first, and you will be directed to see "games and toys." Look that up and locate the subheading "classic toys." Turn to the appropriate page and read the correct information, changing the chart if necessary. Students are asked to choose which of the toys on the chart is their favorite. After think time, call up each table and have each student mark an "X" in the box under his or her favorite toy. Lead the students in analyzing the chart.

**Assessment:** Informally observe whether students relate the almanac to the facts on the chart.

**Closure:** The students chorally say which is the class's favorite toy. Close with the statement that almanacs have current information and statistics and are *not* in alphabetical order, so an index must be used.

## SECOND-GRADE ALMANAC LESSON 1: TO WHAT PARTY DO YOU BELONG?

**Standards:**

*AASL #1:*    Inquire, think critically, and gain knowledge. 1.1, Skills: 1.1.1, Follow an inquiry-based process in seeking knowledge in curricular subjects, and make the real-world connection for using this process in own life; 1.1.4, Find, evaluate, and select appropriate sources to answer questions.
*NCTE #7:*    Students conduct research on issues and interests by generating ideas and questions, and by posing problems. They gather, evaluate, and synthesize data from a variety of sources to communicate their discoveries in ways that suit their purpose and audience.
*Language Arts:*    Using an index to locate information.

**Objectives:**

1.    Students use the index in *The World Almanac for Kids* to find a specific topic.
2.    Students categorize the president they researched as either a Democrat or a Republican.

**Materials:**

- 16 copies of *The World Almanac for Kids*
- almanac sign
- chart with two columns, one labeled "Democratic Party," one labeled "Republican Party"
- visual of Woodrow Wilson
- visuals of a Republican elephant and a Democratic donkey
- 15 president paper strips from the CD
- board-ready copy of input paper strip from the CD

**Set:** Say, "In the United States there are two major political parties, the Democrats and the Republicans. The symbol of the Republican Party is the elephant. The symbol of the Democratic Party is the donkey. I wonder how many of the most recent presidents have been from the Republican Party and how many from the Democratic Party."

**Review:** Review that an almanac is a reference book with current facts that is not arranged alphabetically. An index is needed to find information.

**Input:** Show the students where the index is in *The World Almanac for Kids* and state that an index is arranged alphabetically and is useful when a book is not arranged alphabetically. Pair students and give each pair a copy of *The World Almanac for Kids*. Take a paper strip with the name "Woodrow Wilson" and show it to the students. Think aloud about looking up a person by his last name and the first letter of the last name. Find the name in the index and instruct all the students to turn to that page number. Guide them to find Wilson's name and the page number on which his information is found. All students turn to that page number. Physically put your finger on the information about Woodrow Wilson, and direct the students to do the same. Then point out where the political party information is. Write "Democratic Party" on the paper strip with Woodrow Wilson's name. Ask the students under which category on the chart you should put Woodrow Wilson. Affix the paper strip to the column with the heading "Democratic Party."

**Guided practice:** Each student pair is given a paper strip with a president's name. The students use the index to look up the president by his last name and to find the page with his information. They find the political party to which he is or was a member and write it on the paper strip. After the student pairs have finished the research, call the pairs, by tables, to affix the strips to the correct category on the chart.

**Assessment:** Informally observe whether students are able to access the almanac by using the index, find the required information, and correctly place the president's party on the chart.

**Closure:** Use think-pair-share to ascertain which party had the most recent presidents.

## SECOND-GRADE ALMANAC LESSON 2:  NICKNAMES OF THE STATES

**Standards:**

*AASL #1:*   Inquire, think critically, and gain knowledge. 1.1, Skills: 1.1.1, Follow an inquiry-based process in seeking knowledge in curricular subjects, and make the real-world connection for using this process in own life; 1.1.4, Find, evaluate, and select appropriate sources to answer questions.
*NCTE #7:*   Students conduct research on issues and interests by generating ideas and questions, and by posing problems. They gather, evaluate, and synthesize data from a variety of sources to communicate their discoveries in ways that suit their purpose and audience.
*Language Arts:*   Students use an index to locate information.

**Objectives:**

1.   Students use the index of *The World Almanac for Kids* to find specific information.
2.   Students locate the nickname of a state and hypothesize the meaning and origin of the nickname.

**Materials:**

- 16 copies of *The World Almanac for Kids*
- almanac sign

- 15 paper strips from the CD
- board-ready input paper strip
- visual of New Jersey

**Set:** Say, "My name is _____, but when I was a kid, my nickname was _____. Today we're going to find out the nicknames and abbreviations of some of the states of the United States."

**Review:** Review that an almanac is a reference book with current facts that is not arranged alphabetically. It is necessary to use an index to locate information.

**Input:** Pair students and distribute a copy of *The World Almanac for Kids* to each pair. Project the board-ready input paper strip. Model how to find "New Jersey" in the index, with the students following along as they go to the correct pages. Read the beginning of the information about New Jersey, asking the students to place their fingers on the abbreviation and nickname of the state. Write this information on the paper strip. Speculate aloud why New Jersey is nicknamed The Garden State.

**Guided practice:** Each student pair is given a paper strip with the name of a state on it. They look it up in the index and write the abbreviation and nickname of the state on the paper strip. The student pairs at each table share their information. They imagine why the states were given their nicknames. Call for each pair to report the name of their state and its nickname.

**Assessment:** Informally observe whether students access the almanac by using the index and whether they find and record the required information.

**Closure:** Use think-pair-share to have students discuss how many letters are in each abbreviation, and where the two letters are located in the name of the state.

## THIRD-GRADE ALMANAC LESSON 1: COUNTING ON COUNTRIES

**Standards:**

*AASL #1:*  Inquire, think critically, and gain knowledge. 1.1, Skills: 1.1.1, Follow an inquiry-based process in seeking knowledge in curricular subjects, and make the real-world connection for using this process in own life; 1.1.4, Find, evaluate, and select appropriate sources to answer questions.
*NCTE #7:*  Students conduct research on issues and interests by generating ideas and questions, and by posing problems. They gather, evaluate, and synthesize data from a variety of sources to communicate their discoveries in ways that suit their purpose and audience.
*Language Arts:*  Students use an index to locate information.

**Objective:**
Students use the index of *The World Almanac for Kids* to find specific information.

**Materials:**

- 16 copies of *The World Almanac for Kids*
- two boxes of crayons on each table

- two rulers on each table
- almanac sign
- 15 paper strips from the CD
- 30 copies of the work sheet from the CD
- visual of China and a handmade picture of the flag
- board-ready work sheet
- board-ready copy of a page of the almanac with enlarged information on China (optional)
- 30 copies of the almanac brochure from the CD

**Set:** Say, "China is a country almost on the opposite side of the world from the United States. When I was a youngster, there was a saying that if you dug far enough, you would reach China. Let's find out what information the almanac has on China."

**Review:** Review that an almanac is a reference book with current facts that is not arranged alphabetically. It is necessary to use an index to locate information.

**Input:** Pair students and distribute a copy of *The World Almanac for Kids* to each pair. Show a paper strip with "China "written on it. Model how to find "China" in the index, with the students following along as they go to the correct pages. It is important that you use the first page number after the country's name, but point out that the subheadings have additional information. With the students, turn to the page on China and look at the chart. You may choose to enlarge the information on China and make it board ready. The students place their fingers on the capital and population of China in their almanacs. Write the required information on the board-ready work sheet. Show the hand-drawn flag to the students. Point out the color key, which indicates the continent of the country.

**Guided practice:** Give each student pair a paper strip with the name of a country on it and two copies of the work sheet. They will look for their country in the index, find the correct page of facts, and write the capital and population on their work sheet. Each student uses the crayons to color in the flag of their country. Early finishers can read and take notes on the "Did You Know" section. After the research, the students are directed to get in a line in order, according to the populations of their countries, from the smallest to the largest. As students get in order, they present the information on the capital and the population and show the flag.

**Assessment:** Informally observe whether students access the almanac by using the index and whether they find the required information.

**Closure:** Ask the students which country that they researched has the most people and which has the least. Encourage the students to take the work sheets home and share them with their families. Distribute the Almanac brochure from the CD-ROM, go over it, and ask the students to share it with their families.

## THIRD-GRADE ALMANAC LESSON 2:  MAKE YOUR OWN TRIVIA GAME

**Standards:**

*AASL #1:*    Inquire, think critically, and gain knowledge. 1.1, Skills: 1.1.1, Follow an inquiry-based process in seeking knowledge in curricular subjects, and make the real-world connection for using this process in own life; 1.1.4, Find, evaluate, and select appropriate sources to answer questions.

*NCTE #7:* Students conduct research on issues and interests by generating ideas and questions, and by posing problems. They gather, evaluate, and synthesize data from a variety of sources to communicate their discoveries in ways that suit their purpose and audience.

**Objective:**
Students use *The World Almanac for Kids* to find unusual and interesting facts to stump their friends.

**Materials:**

- 30 copies of *The World Almanac for Kids*
- almanac sign
- 30 copies of the work sheet from the CD
- index cards on the tables
- visual of the Great Wall of China
- board-ready work sheet
- board-ready page of the almanac with the Great Wall of China enlarged (optional)

**Set:** Ask, "What is the longest humanmade structure built before modern times?" After the students guess, inform the students that it's the Great Wall of China.

**Review:** Review that an almanac is a reference book with current facts that is not arranged alphabetically. It is necessary to use an index to locate information.

**Input:** Distribute a copy of *The World Almanac for Kids* to each student. Model how to find "China" in the index, with the students following along as they go to the correct pages. It is important that you use the first page number after the country's name, but point out that the subheadings have additional information. With the students, turn to the page or pages on "China" and look at the information. You may choose to enlarge the information on China and make it board ready. The students place their fingers on the "Did You Know" section of the entry on China in their almanacs. Think aloud about how to word a question around the information. Example: How long is the Great Wall of China? Write this question in the question section of the work sheet. Model where to write the answer. Take an index card and write the question in large print, reminding yourself aloud to write a large "Q" on the upper left corner of the index card, to capitalize the first letter of the sentence, and to use the correct punctuation. Flip the card over and write a large "A" in the upper left corner and write the answer in the middle of the card in large print, not necessarily using a complete sentence.

**Guided practice:** Each student is given a "Trivia Game Cards" work sheet. Point out the index cards on each table. The students search their almanacs, looking for unusual facts and statistics. They fill out the work sheet and make a flashcard for each question. The students try to make as many flashcards as they can in the time allotted.

**Assessment:** Informally observe whether students find facts for the trivia questions in the almanac by using the index.

**Closure:** Ask several students to read their questions and have the class guess the answers. (The flashcards can either be used as a class set for a trivia game or be sent home with the students to amaze their parents.)

## FOURTH-GRADE ALMANAC LESSON 1: THE ARRANGEMENT OF *THE WORLD ALMANAC AND BOOK OF FACTS*

**Standards:**

*AASL #1:* Inquire, think critically, and gain knowledge. 1.1, Skills: 1.1.1, Follow an inquiry-based process in seeking knowledge in curricular subjects, and make the real-world connection for using this process in own life; 1.1.4, Find, evaluate, and select appropriate sources to answer questions.

*NCTE #7:* Students conduct research on issues and interests by generating ideas and questions, and by posing problems. They gather, evaluate, and synthesize data from a variety of sources to communicate their discoveries in ways that suit their purpose and audience.

**Objective:**

Students use the index to find specific information in *The World Almanac and Book of Facts*.

**Materials:**

- 30 copies of *The World Almanac and Book of Facts*
- almanac sign
- board-ready pages of the almanac: table of contents, the quick thumb index, the quick reference index, and the index pages with the "Super Bowl"

**Set:** Ask, "What team has won the most Super Bowls since the year 2000?" Students guess. After the students guess, ask, "Where could I find that information?"

**Review:** Review that an almanac is a reference book with current facts that is not arranged alphabetically. It is necessary to use an index to locate information.

**Input:** State, "The best place to find the information is the almanac, because it comes out every year and it is easy to locate the most current information." Explain that previously the students had used *The World Almanac for Kids*, but now they will be using *The World Almanac and Book of Facts*, which is used by adults. Distribute a copy of *The World Almanac and Book of Facts* to each student. Direct them to look at the one-page "table of contents" at the front of the book as you project it on a board. Point out the current nature of the first part of the book, that it contains information about last year such as "The Top Ten News Stories" and "The Year in Review." Point out the "quick reference index" on the last page of the almanac, which is in alphabetical order and has specific subjects. Note that there is a separate index on the bottom for "sports," and ask students whether the answer to the original question, "Who won the most Super Bowls since 2000?" could be found by using this quick reference. Students should suggest it would be under "Football, professional." Everyone turns to the first page listed and sees that the information wanted is not there. They look at succeeding pages until the chart of the Super Bowl winners is found. Students then answer the question.

Then point out the extended index and ask, "How old do you have to be to get a learner's permit and a driver's license in our state?" Imagine aloud what subject to look up in the index and come up with "automobiles." All students look up "automobiles" in the index. With the students, look at the subheadings and eliminate them alphabetically up to "drivers." The students look on the first page cited to see whether it will give them the answer. The answer is found on the chart "Selected Motor Vehicle Statistics." Students will examine the chart to find the answers. Give students some time to look through the almanac and see what types of information it contains.

**Assessment:** Informally observe whether students are able to follow along with you.

**Closure:** The students use "table talk" to share the information they found.

## FOURTH-GRADE ALMANAC LESSON 2: HOW HOT, HOW COLD?

**Standards:**

*AASL #1:* Inquire, think critically, and gain knowledge. 1.1, Skills: 1.1.1, Follow an inquiry-based process in seeking knowledge in curricular subjects, and make the real-world connection for using this process in own life; 1.1.4, Find, evaluate, and select appropriate sources to answer questions.
*NCTE #7:* Students conduct research on issues and interests by generating ideas and questions, and by posing problems. They gather, evaluate, and synthesize data from a variety of sources to communicate their discoveries in ways that suit their purpose and audience.

**Objectives:**

1. Students use the index to find specific information in *The World Almanac and Book of Facts*.
2. Students read a chart to find information.

**Materials:**

- 30 copies of *The World Almanac and Book of Facts*
- almanac sign
- board-ready enlarged page of the index page with "temperatures" and its subheadings
- paper strips with names of states and weather stations from the CD
- 30 copies of the work sheet from the CD
- chart with two columns, one labeled "Winter Vacations" and one "Summer Vacations"
- transparent tape at the tables

**Set:** Say, "I have relatives in both Phoenix, Arizona, and Buffalo, New York. I get two vacations: one in January and one in July. Which city should I visit in the winter and which in the summer, to have the most comfortable weather while visiting my relatives?"

**Review:** Review that an almanac is a reference book with current facts that is not arranged alphabetically. It is necessary to use an index to locate information.

**Input:** Say, "The best place to find the information is the almanac because it comes out every year and it is easy to locate the most current information. We need to use the index for the question about where to spend my vacations. Under what subject should we look?" (The students make suggestions. If they don't mention temperature, mention it.) Model looking up "temperature" in the general index. All students turn to the correct page in the index. Show the subheadings on the projected and enlarged page. Discuss whether each subheading is relevant, and select "U.S. normal highs and lows. All students turn to the page indicated and find the chart "Normal High and Low Temperatures, Precipitation, U.S. Cities." Model while the students follow along, finding Arizona and Phoenix. Note that the state column is first followed by a city, which has a weather station in it. Everyone reads across the chart and finds out that the January maximum temperature is 65 degrees, and the minimum is 43 degrees. In July, the maximum temperature is 104 degrees, and the minimum 81 degrees. Model finding New York and Buffalo and read across to find that the maximum temperature in January is 31 degrees, and the minimum is 18 degrees. In July, the maximum temperature is 80 degrees, and the minimum is 62 degrees. Use think-pair-share to ask the students which city would be best to visit in January and which city in July. Write out a work sheet for Phoenix in January with an average maximum of 65 degrees and an average minimum of 43 degrees. Place the work sheet under "Winter Vacations." Do the same with Buffalo under "Summer Vacations."

**Guided practice:** Pair students and give each pair a paper strip with two cities on it and two work sheets. They must look up the maximum and minimum temperatures in January and July and decide which city is best to visit in which month. They write on each work sheet the name of the state and station and the maximum and minimum temperatures for the most comfortable month. Each student pair tapes their work sheet onto the chart under the appropriate vacation and announces the temperatures during that month.

**Assessment:** Informally observe whether students read the chart, record the information, and make a decision based on the information.

**Closure:** Read the cities under "Summer Vacations" and the cities under "Winter Vacations."

## FOURTH-GRADE ALMANAC LESSON 3: WHERE ARE ALL THE PEOPLE?

**Standards:**

*AASL #1:*   Inquire, think critically, and gain knowledge. 1.1, Skills: 1.1.1, Follow an inquiry-based process in seeking knowledge in curricular subjects, and make the real-world connection for using this process in own life; 1.1.4, Find, evaluate, and select appropriate sources to answer questions.
*NCTE #7:*   Students conduct research on issues and interests by generating ideas and questions, and by posing problems. They gather, evaluate, and synthesize data from a variety of sources to communicate their discoveries in ways that suit their purpose and audience.

**Objectives:**

1.   Students use the index to find specific information in *The World Almanac and Book of Facts*.
2.   Students read a chart to find information.

**Materials:**

- 30 copies of *The World Almanac and Book of Facts*
- almanac sign
- board-ready enlarged index pages of "Arkansas" and "Oregon" and their subheadings
- work sheet from the CD
- visuals of Arkansas and Oregon
- board-ready outline map of the United States with the states labeled, available from www.infoplease.com/statemaps.html (under U.S. regions)

**Set:** Ask, "What state is the most crowded? What state is the least crowded?" Record the students' guesses.

**Review:** Review that an almanac is a reference book with current facts that is not arranged alphabetically. It is necessary to use an index to locate information.

**Input:** Show the visuals of Arkansas and Oregon and model how to look in the index for "Arkansas." Note the page on the same line in bold print. With the students, turn to that page and look up the heading "People" and then the subheading "Pop. Density." Record the name of the state and the population density on a board-ready work sheet. Follow the same procedures to find the population density of Oregon.

**Guided practice:** Give each student a paper strip with the names of two states and a work sheet. Students use the index to locate the population density of each state. Students write the name of the state and the population density on the work sheet. After the research is done, ask, "Who has a state with a population density between 0 and 25 people per square mile?" Record the population density on a board-ready outline map of the United States. After several students have reported their low-density states, use think-pair-share to draw conclusions about why these states are not crowded. Then ask, "Who has a state with a population density between 700 and 1,200 people per square mile? Record the population density on the board-ready map. Use think-pair-share to draw conclusions about why these states are so crowded. Students do "table talk" to share the densities of the states not placed on the map.

**Assessment:** Informally observe whether students are able to use the index to locate the information.

**Closure:** Ask, "Who has the information for our state?" The student gives the information. The students use think-pair-share to decide whether it's not crowded, very crowded, or in the middle.

## FIFTH-GRADE ALMANAC LESSON 1: THE U.S. PRESIDENT

**Standards:**

*AASL #1:* Inquire, think critically, and gain knowledge. 1.1, Skills: 1.1.1, Follow an inquiry-based process in seeking knowledge in curricular subjects, and make the real-world connection for using this process in own life; 1.1.4, Find, evaluate, and select appropriate sources to answer questions.
*NCTE #7:* Students conduct research on issues and interests by generating ideas and questions, and by posing problems. They gather, evaluate, and synthesize data from a variety of sources to communicate their discoveries in ways that suit their purpose and audience.

**Objectives:**

1. Students use the index to find specific information in *The World Almanac and Book of Facts*.
2. Students read a chart to find information.
3. Students write a bibliographic entry.

**Materials:**

- 30 copies of *The World Almanac and Book of Facts*
- almanac sign

- board-ready enlarged page of the chart with "Presidents of the United States" that shows birth and death dates from *The World Almanac and Book of Facts*
- work sheet from the CD
- board-ready work sheet
- visual of the seal of the president of the United States

**Set:** Show the visual and ask, "Which president lived the longest? Which president lived the shortest?" Record the students' guesses.

**Review:** Review that an almanac is a reference book with current facts that is not arranged alphabetically. It is necessary to use an index to locate information and to use headings and subheadings to find the correct page for information.

**Input:** Model how to look in the index for "Presidents of the United States," with the students following along in their almanacs. Together, discuss the subheadings and decide which one will answer the question. Everyone turns to the page indicated by the subheading "birth, death dates." Ask students to examine the chart and find the president who was the youngest when he died. After having time to find the answer, students orally answer the question. Ask the students to examine the chart and find the president who was the oldest when he died. After having think time, the students chorally answer. Repeat the procedure for the question of what president was the youngest when inaugurated and what president was the oldest when inaugurated. Project the board-ready work sheet and go over what information is required. Model how to record the information needed for a bibliographic entry and its correct format. Sample:

McGeveran, William A. *The World Almanac and Book of Facts 2006*. New York: World Almanac Books, 2006.

**Guided practice:** Each student is given a work sheet with questions about the president's and vice president's taxable salary, the presidential oath of office, and the official greeting for a president. Students use the index to locate the answers to the questions on the work sheet. The students note the information needed for the bibliographic entry and format it correctly. After the research is done, the students check their answers with their table mates. Ask for a choral response to each of the questions.

**Assessment:** Informally observe whether students use the index to locate the information and whether they have correctly written a bibliographic entry.

**Closure:** Students use think-pair-share to review the step-by-step procedure used in finding information in *The World Almanac and Book of Facts*.

## FIFTH-GRADE ALMANAC LESSON 2: OLYMPIC RECORDS

**Standards:**

*AASL #1:*    Inquire, think critically, and gain knowledge. 1.1, Skills: 1.1.1, Follow an inquiry-based process in seeking knowledge in curricular subjects, and make the real-world connection for using this process in own life; 1.1.4, Find, evaluate, and select appropriate sources to answer questions.

*NCTE #7:* Students conduct research on issues and interests by generating ideas and questions, and by posing problems. They gather, evaluate, and synthesize data from a variety of sources to communicate their discoveries in ways that suit their purpose and audience.

**Objectives:**

1. Students use the index to find specific information in *The World Almanac and Book of Facts*.
2. Students read a chart to find information.
3. Students write a bibliographic entry.

**Materials:**

- 15 copies of the *World Almanac and Book of Facts*
- 15 paper strips from the CD
- board-ready copy of the input paper strip
- almanac sign

**Set:** Say, "The life span of American adults changed from 1900 to 2002, from an average of 47.3 years to 77.4 years. People live almost 30 years longer today. What do you think are the reasons for this?" Students use think-pair-share to discuss the question.

**Review:** Review that an almanac is a reference book with current facts that is not arranged alphabetically. It is necessary to use an index to locate information and to use headings and subheadings to find the correct page for information.

**Input:** Pair students and distribute a copy of *The World Almanac and Book of Facts* to each pair. Project the board-ready input paper strip and ask, "What was the Olympic record for the discus throw for women in 1928 and in the latest Olympics?" Model by reading the question and by thinking aloud which of the words in the question are key and should be the ones to be looked up in the index. Then look up "discus throw" in the index and look up the first page cited. This will be for men, so look up the next two pages cited, which are for women. The answer is that in 1928 it was 130 feet. In 2004, it was 219 feet 9 inches. Record this on the work sheet. Model how to find the difference between the two records: 88 feet 3 inches. Students should be reminded that the answer is to be given in time (hours, minutes, and seconds) or in distance in feet (the number in parentheses). Model how to record the information needed for a bibliographic entry and its correct format. Sample:

McGeveran, William A. *The World Almanac and Book of Facts 2006*. New York: World Almanac Books, 2006.

**Guided practice:** Each student pair is given a paper strip. They identify the key words in the sentences in order to find the information in the index. They look up the required information and determine the differences in Olympic records. Have some of the student pairs report the differences in the Olympic records.

**Assessment:** Informally observe whether students use the index to locate the information.

**Closure:** Students use think-pair-share to answer the question "Why have the Olympic records improved over the years?"

## FIFTH-GRADE ALMANAC LESSON 3: DEADLY DISASTERS

**Standards:**

*AASL #1:*    Inquire, think critically, and gain knowledge. 1.1, Skills: 1.1.1, Follow an inquiry-based process in seeking knowledge in curricular subjects, and make the real-world connection for using this process in own life; 1.1.4, Find, evaluate, and select appropriate sources to answer questions.
*NCTE #7:*    Students conduct research on issues and interests by generating ideas and questions, and by posing problems. They gather, evaluate, and synthesize data from a variety of sources to communicate their discoveries in ways that suit their purpose and audience.

**Objectives:**

1.    Students use the index to find specific information in *The World Almanac and Book of Facts*.
2.    Students read a chart to find information.
3.    Students write a bibliographic entry.

**Materials:**

- 30 copies of *The World Almanac and Book of Facts*
- almanac sign
- board-ready chart from the CD
- paper strip with disaster on it, from the CD
- 30 copies of the work sheet from the CD
- board-ready work sheet
- visual of a train wreck

**Set:** Show the visual and ask, "How many people died in the worst railroad disaster since 1925?" Record the students' guesses.

**Review:** Review that an almanac is a reference book with current facts that is not arranged alphabetically. It is necessary to use an index to locate information and to use headings and subheadings to find the correct page for information.

**Input:** Distribute a copy of *The World Almanac and Book of Facts* to each student. Model how to look for the answer to the question in the set. Project the work sheet and model how to look in the index under the heading "Railroads, World." Then look at the subheadings and choose the first one, "Accidents, Deaths." Together, look at the pages cited until the correct chart is found, "Some notable railroad disasters since 1925." Students examine the chart to find the answer, which is June 6, 1981, in Bihar, India, when 800+ people died. Fill out the required information on the work sheet. Model how to record the information needed for a bibliographic entry and its correct format. Sample:

McGeveran, William A. *The World Almanac and Book of Facts 2006*. New York: World Almanac Books, 2006.

**Guided practice:** Give each student a paper strip and a work sheet about the deaths from a particular disaster. Students use the index to locate the information necessary to fill out the work sheet. The students note the information needed for the bibliographic entry and format it correctly. After the research is done, the students use their answers to make a board-ready chart to show the most people killed in each category of disaster.

**Assessment:** Informally observe whether students are able to use the index to locate the information.

**Closure:** Using think-pair-share, students examine the results and conclude which type of disaster kills the most people.

## SIXTH-GRADE ALMANAC LESSON 1: COMPARING COUNTRIES

**Standards:**

*AASL #1:* Inquire, think critically, and gain knowledge. 1.1, Skills: 1.1.1, Follow an inquiry-based process in seeking knowledge in curricular subjects, and make the real-world connection for using this process in own life; 1.1.4, Find, evaluate, and select appropriate sources to answer questions.
*NCTE #7:* Students conduct research on issues and interests by generating ideas and questions, and by posing problems. They gather, evaluate, and synthesize data from a variety of sources to communicate their discoveries in ways that suit their purpose and audience.

**Objectives:**

1.  Students use the index to find specific information in *The World Almanac and Book of Facts*.
2.  Students write a bibliographic entry.

**Materials:**

*   30 copies of *The World Almanac and Book of Facts*
*   almanac sign
*   15 copies of the work sheet from the CD
*   board-ready copy of the work sheet
*   paper strips with two countries on them, from the CD
*   visuals: maps of the United States and Haiti

**Set:** Show the visuals and ask, "If we compare the countries of Haiti and the United States, which one has more television sets per 1000 people? In which one do men and women live longer? Which country has the highest literacy rate (people who can read and write)?" Record the students' guesses.

**Review:** Review that an almanac is a reference book with current facts that is not arranged alphabetically. It is necessary to use an index to locate information and to use headings and subheadings to find the correct page for information.

**Input:** Pair students and distribute an almanac to each pair. Project the board-ready work sheet. Model how to look for the answer to the questions in the set. Model how to look in the index for each country and to look for the page or pages that are in bold print. Together, find the page with the information on the United

States. Model how to use the headings and subheadings in the entry to find the answers to the questions and record them on the chart on the work sheet. This will be repeated for the country of Haiti. Model how to record the information needed for a bibliographic entry and its correct format. Sample:

McGeveran, William A. *The World Almanac and Book of Facts 2006.* New York: World Almanac Books, 2006.

**Guided practice:** Each pair is given a paper strip with two countries to research and a work sheet with a chart. Students use the index to locate the information necessary to fill out the chart. Each student does a country and gives his or her partner the necessary information to complete the chart. The students note the information needed for the bibliographic entry and format it correctly. After the research is done, the students discuss with their partners whether there is a correlation between the number of television sets, literacy, and life expectancy.

**Assessment:** Informally observe whether students use the index to locate the information.

**Closure:** Students use "table talk" to compare their inferences. Monitor whether the inferences are the same, and make a closing statement about that.

## SIXTH-GRADE ALMANAC LESSON 2:  PER CAPITA INCOME

**Standards:**

*AASL #1:*    Inquire, think critically, and gain knowledge. 1.1, Skills: 1.1.1, Follow an inquiry-based process in seeking knowledge in curricular subjects, and make the real-world connection for using this process in own life; 1.1.4, Find, evaluate, and select appropriate sources to answer questions.
*NCTE #7:*    Students conduct research on issues and interests by generating ideas and questions, and by posing problems. They gather, evaluate, and synthesize data from a variety of sources to communicate their discoveries in ways that suit their purpose and audience.

**Objectives:**

1.    Students use a chart to find specific information in *The World Almanac and Book of Facts.*
2.    Students write a bibliographic entry.

**Materials:**

- 30 copies of *The World Almanac and Book of Facts*
- almanac sign
- board-ready enlarged page of the pages with the information on per capita income of Las Vegas, Nevada
- paper strips, each with the name of a city on it, from the CD
- 30 copies of the work sheet from the CD
- board-ready work sheet

- map of the United States
- chart from the CD

**Set:** Ask, "If I wanted to live in a city where I would have a good chance of making the most money, which city in the United States should I move to?" Record the students' guesses.

**Review:** Review that an almanac is a reference book with current facts that is not arranged alphabetically. It is necessary to use an index to locate information and to use headings and subheadings to find the correct page for information.

**Input:** Distribute an almanac to each student. Explain that per capita income is the yearly money a person earns in a particular area. This is calculated by taking the whole area's income and dividing it by the population. This means that a couple would earn twice the per capita income. Project the board-ready work sheet and model how to look in the index under "Cities, U.S." and the pages cited in bold print. The several pages of information, "The 100 Most Populous U.S. Cities," are listed alphabetically by city. Write the information on the work sheet. Model how to record the information needed for a bibliographic entry and its correct format. Sample:

McGeveran, William A. *The World Almanac and Book of Facts 2006.* New York: World Almanac Books, 2006.

**Guided practice:** Each student is given a paper strip with the name of a city and state on it and a work sheet to fill out. Students look up their city in the index, locate the per capita income of the city, and record it on the work sheet. Students write a bibliographic entry for the almanac. After the research is done, assist the students in making a chart of the per capita incomes, from the smallest to the largest. The students pinpoint the cities with the three highest per capita incomes on the map of the United States and note their location. The same is done for the three cities with the lowest per capita incomes.

**Assessment:** Informally observe whether students find the information and use the index to locate the information.

**Closure:** Students use "table talk" to discuss the reasons for the physical placements of the cities of the highest and lowest per capita incomes.

## SIXTH-GRADE ALMANAC LESSON 3: MAKE YOUR OWN TRIVIA GAME

**Standards:**

*AASL #1:* Inquire, think critically, and gain knowledge. 1.1, Skills: 1.1.1, Follow an inquiry-based process in seeking knowledge in curricular subjects, and make the real-world connection for using this process in own life; 1.1.4, Find, evaluate, and select appropriate sources to answer questions.
*NCTE #7:* Students conduct research on issues and interests by generating ideas and questions, and by posing problems. They gather, evaluate, and synthesize data from a variety of sources to communicate their discoveries in ways that suit their purpose and audience.

**Objective:**
Students use *The World Almanac and Book of Facts* to find unusual and interesting facts.

**Materials:**

- 30 copies of *The World Almanac and Book of Facts*
- almanac sign
- work sheets for each student from the CD
- index cards on the tables
- board-ready work sheet

**Set:** Ask, "What was the life expectancy for humans at the beginning of the twentieth century (1900) and what is it today, at the beginning of the twenty-first century? Let's use *The World Almanac and Book of Facts* to find out."

**Review:** Review that an almanac is a reference book with current facts that is not arranged alphabetically. It is necessary to use an index to locate information.

**Input:** Distribute a copy of *The World Almanac and Book of Facts* to each student. Model how to find "life expectancy" in the index, with the students following along as they go to the correct page. With the students, turn to the page on "life expectancy" and look at the information. You may choose to enlarge the information on the page and make it board ready. Think aloud about how to word a question around the information. Example: What was the life expectancy for humans in 1900? Project the board-ready work sheet. Write the question in the question section. Model where to write the answer. Take an index card and write the question in large print, reminding yourself aloud to write a large "Q" on the upper left corner of the index card, to capitalize the first letter of the sentence, and to use the correct punctuation. Flip the card over, write a large "A" in the upper left corner, and write the answer in the middle of the card in large print, not necessarily using a complete sentence.

**Guided practice:** Give each student a "Trivia Game Cards" work sheet and point out the index cards on each table. The students search their almanacs, looking for interesting facts and statistics. They fill out the work sheet and make a flashcard for each question. The students try to make as many flashcards as they can in the time allotted.

**Assessment:** Informally observe whether students find facts and write complete sentences for the questions from the information searched for in the almanac by using the index, and whether they find and record the required information.

**Closure:** Ask several students to read their questions and have the class guess the answers. (The flashcards can either be used as a class set for a trivia game or be sent home with the students to amaze their parents.)

# Chapter 6

# The Online Catalog

## KINDERGARTEN THROUGH SECOND-GRADE ONLINE CATALOG LESSON 1: THE VISUAL ONLINE CATALOG

**Standards:**

*AASL #1:* Inquire, think critically, and gain knowledge. 1.1, Skills: 1.1.1 Follow an inquiry-based process in seeking knowledge in curricular subjects, and make the real-world connection for using this process in own life; 1.1.6, Read, view, and listen for information in any format (e.g., textual, visual, media, digital) in order to make inferences and gather meaning; 1.1.8, Demonstrate mastery of technology tools for accessing information and pursuing inquiry.
*NETS Technology #3: Research and Information Fluency:* Students apply digital tools to gather, evaluate, and use information.

**Objective:**
Students understand that the visual online catalog can assist them in locating books in the library.

**Materials:**

- online catalog sign
- projection of an Internet computer screen (must have access to computer, Internet, and means of projection)
- library software program that includes a visual online catalog (the Follett Destiny library software was used for the lesson)

**Set:** Ask, "What are some of the ways that you have used to find a book in the library?" Using think-pair-share, the students report on some of their strategies.

**Review:** Review that every book in the library has its own address on the library shelves.

**Input:** Using a projection of a computer screen, demonstrate how to access and use the Visual Search Online Catalog to locate a book.

1. Click on the Online Catalog icon on the computer.
2. Click on the school name (if the district has a union catalog system).
3. Click on the Visual Search part of the online catalog.

4.  Point out the picture next to each category and ask the students to guess what kinds of books they represent.
5.  Click on a category and have the students identify each subject within that category by the picture.
6.  Click on a subject and use a mouse or a pointer to identify the parts of a book entry: picture of book, title, call number, number of copies, and whether the book is available.
7.  Repeat the procedure several more times with other categories.

**Assessment:** Informally observe whether the students follow along as you model the procedure for finding books by using the Visual Search Online Catalog.

**Closure:** Using think-pair-share, ask, "How can a computer help you find a book in our library?"

## KINDERGARTEN THROUGH SECOND-GRADE ONLINE CATALOG LESSON 2: USING THE VISUAL SEARCH

**Standards:**

*AASL #1:*   Inquire, think critically, and gain knowledge. 1.1, Skills: 1.1.1 Follow an inquiry-based process in seeking knowledge in curricular subjects, and make the real-world connection for using this process in own life; 1.1.6, Read, view, and listen for information in any format (e.g., textual, visual, media, digital) in order to make inferences and gather meaning; 1.1.8, Demonstrate mastery of technology tools for accessing information and pursuing inquiry.
*NETS Technology #3: Research and Information Fluency:*   Students apply digital tools to gather, evaluate, and use information.

**Objective:**
Students access and use the Visual Search Online Catalog to find a book.

**Materials:**

*   online catalog sign
*   projection of an Internet computer screen (must have access to computer, Internet, and means of projection)
*   library software program that includes a visual online catalog (the Follett Destiny library software was used for the lesson)
*   "Look for a Book" form from the CD

**Set:** Ask, "How can you use a computer to find a book in the library?" Using think-pair-share, the students report.

**Review:** Say, "You can find a book by using the Visual Search part of the online catalog."

**Input:** Pair students and assign each pair to a computer. Instruct the pairs to click on the online catalog icon, click on their school name (if a district has a union catalog), and then click on the visual search.

**Guided practice:** The pairs explore the visual search catalog by clicking on the categories. They take turns with the mouse. If a student finds a book he or she is interested in, model filling out the "Look for a Book" form and using it to find the book on the shelf.

**Assessment:** Informally observe whether the students are able to access the visual search.

**Closure:** Use think-pair-share and ask, "How can a computer help you find a book in our library?"

### Repeating These Lessons in First and Second Grade

These lessons should be repeated for first grade and second grade. The review for first and second grade is:

**Review:** Library books are arranged into three sections: easy, fiction, and nonfiction. The easy and fiction sections are arranged alphabetically by the author's last name. The nonfiction section is arranged by the subject of the book. Computers are tools that can help students find information. The online catalog is a software program that helps students find books in the library.

## THIRD- THROUGH SIXTH-GRADE ONLINE CATALOG LESSON 1: ACCESSING AND USING THE ONLINE CATALOG

**Standards:**

*AASL #1:*    Inquire, think critically, and gain knowledge. 1.1, Skills: 1.1.1 Follow an inquiry-based process in seeking knowledge in curricular subjects, and make the real-world connection for using this process in own life; 1.1.6, Read, view, and listen for information in any format (e.g., textual, visual, media, digital) in order to make inferences and gather meaning; 1.1.8, Demonstrate mastery of technology tools for accessing information and pursuing inquiry.
*NETS Technology #3: Research and Information Fluency:*    Students apply digital tools to gather, evaluate, and use information.

**Objective:**
Students understand the procedure for accessing and using the online catalog.

**Materials:**

- online catalog sign
- projection of an Internet computer screen (must have access to computer, Internet, and means of projection)
- library software program that includes an online catalog (the Follett Destiny library software was used for the lesson)
- "Look for a Book" form from the CD
- 30 copies of the customized Online Catalog brochure from the CD

**Set:** Ask, "What are some of the ways that you have used to find a book in the library?" Using think-pair-share, the students report some of their strategies.

**Review:** Library books are arranged into three sections: easy, fiction, and nonfiction. The easy and fiction sections are arranged alphabetically by the author's last name. The nonfiction section is arranged by the subject of the book. Computers are tools that can help students find information. The online catalog is a software program that helps students find books in the library.

**Input:** Using a projection of a computer screen, demonstrate how to access and use the online catalog to locate a book.

1.   Click on the Online Catalog icon on the computer.
2.   Click on the school name if the district has a union catalog system.
3.   Click on the Library Search part of the online catalog.
4.   Point out the five ways that a book can be searched for: keyword, author, title, subject, and series.
5.   Ask the students for some suggestions of books to search for in each of the five categories.
6.   When the first book entry appears on the screen, point out that the title, author, call number, and copyright date are provided. Model finding the publisher, number of pages, and list of subject headings, by clicking on the "details" icon next to the title. Point out that this is the screen that will be useful when getting information for a bibliography. Point out that clicking on the "find it" icon next to a subject heading will send the user to other books with that subject heading.
7.   Model using the "Look for a Book" form (writing the call number and title) to locate a book on the shelf.

**Assessment:** Informally observe whether the students follow along as you model the procedure for finding books by using the online catalog.

**Closure:** Using think-pair-share, ask, "Using the online catalog, what are the five ways you can search for a book in our library?" Distribute the Online Catalog brochure, go over it, and ask the students to share it with their families.

## THIRD- THROUGH SIXTH-GRADE ONLINE CATALOG LESSON 2: FINDING A BOOK BY THE AUTHOR'S LAST NAME

**Standards:**

*AASL #1:*   Inquire, think critically, and gain knowledge. 1.1, Skills: 1.1.1 Follow an inquiry-based process in seeking knowledge in curricular subjects, and make the real-world connection for using this process in own life; 1.1.6, Read, view, and listen for information in any format (e.g., textual, visual, media, digital) in order to make inferences and gather meaning; 1.1.8, Demonstrate mastery of technology tools for accessing information and pursuing inquiry.
*NETS Technology #3: Research and Information Fluency:*   Students apply digital tools to gather, evaluate, and use information.

**Objective:**
Students use the online catalog to search for a book by author and locate it on the library shelf.

**Materials:**

*   online catalog sign
*   projection of an Internet computer screen (must have access to computer, Internet, and means of projection)

- library software program that includes an online catalog (the Follett Destiny library software was used for the lesson)
- 15 copies of the "Online Catalog: Author" work sheet from the CD (must be customized for a specific school's library)
- 15 authors whose books are in the library (if prolific authors are chosen, it is more likely the students will find their books on the shelves)
- 15 shelf markers or rulers

**Set:** Ask, "What are some of the ways that you have used to find a book in the library?" Using think-pair-share, the students report some of their strategies.

**Review:** Library books are arranged into three sections: easy, fiction, and nonfiction. The easy and fiction sections are arranged alphabetically by the author's last name. The nonfiction section is arranged by the subject of the book. Computers are tools that can help students find information. The online catalog is a software program that allows the user to search for a book by keyword, title, author, and subject.

**Input:** Using a projection of a computer screen, demonstrate how to access and use the online catalog to locate a book by the author's last name.

1. Click on the Online Catalog icon on the computer.
2. Click on the school name if the district has a union catalog system.
3. Click on Library Search.
4. Point out that to find a book by a particular author, you have to type in the author's last name, a comma, and then first name (if known) in the Find box and then click on Author.
5. Type "Cleary, Beverly" in the Find box, click on Author, and scroll down the list, pointing out where the call number and title are located on each entry.
6. Model using the "Online Catalog: Author" work sheet to write the call number and title and to locate a Beverly Cleary book on the shelf.
7. Model taking a shelf marker and the "Online Catalog: Author" work sheet and going to the fiction section to find a Beverly Cleary book. Remind the students that the fiction section is arranged alphabetically by the author's last name.
8. Model pulling a Bevery Cleary book off the library shelf and putting the shelf marker in its place.
9. Show the book to the students and then put the book back and take the shelf marker off the library shelf and put it away.

**Guided practice:** Pair students and give them an "Online Catalog: Author" work sheet (with an author's name on the sheet) and a shelf marker. Assign each pair to a computer. Tell the pairs that they are to use the online catalog to find a book by their assigned author, fill out the "Online Catalog: Author" work sheet, and locate the book on the shelf. They are to use the shelf marker so that they will know where to return the book on the shelf. The pair locates the book on the library shelf and brings the book to you so that you can see that they have completed the assignment. The students return the book to the shelf, remove the shelf marker, and put it away. One way to increase access is to have half of the students check out books while the other half completes the assignment at the computers.

**Assessment:** Informally observe whether the students bring you a book by their assigned author and return it to the correct library shelf.

**Closure:** Using think-pair-share, ask, "How are fiction and easy books arranged on the shelf?"

## THIRD- THROUGH SIXTH-GRADE ONLINE CATALOG LESSON 3: FINDING A BOOK BY THE TITLE

**Standards:**

*AASL #1:*   Inquire, think critically, and gain knowledge. 1.1, Skills: 1.1.1 Follow an inquiry-based process in seeking knowledge in curricular subjects, and make the real-world connection for using this process in own life; 1.1.6, Read, view, and listen for information in any format (e.g., textual, visual, media, digital) in order to make inferences and gather meaning; 1.1.8, Demonstrate mastery of technology tools for accessing information and pursuing inquiry.

*NETS Technology #3: Research and Information Fluency:*   Students apply digital tools to gather, evaluate, and use information.

**Objective:**
Students use the online catalog to search for a book by its title and locate it on the library shelf.

**Materials:**

- online catalog sign
- projection of an Internet computer screen (must have access to computer, Internet, and means of projection)
- library software program that includes an online catalog (the Follett Destiny library software was used for the lesson)
- 15 copies of the "Online Catalog: Title" work sheet from the CD (must be customized for a specific school's library)
- 15 titles of books in the library (*Hint:* If the books chosen are books that are hardly ever checked out, the students would be able to find the titles on the library shelves)
- 15 shelf markers or rulers

**Set:** Ask, "What are some of the ways that you have used to find a book in the library?" Using think-pair-share, the students report some of their strategies.

**Review:** Library books are arranged into three sections: easy, fiction, and nonfiction. The easy and fiction sections are arranged alphabetically by the author's last name. The nonfiction section is arranged by the subject of the book. Computers are tools that can help students find information. The online catalog is a software program that allows the user to search for a book by keyword, title, author, and subject.

**Input:** Using a projection of a computer screen, demonstrate how to access and use the online catalog to locate a book by its title.

1.   Click on the Online Catalog icon on the computer.
2.   Click on the school name if the district has a union catalog system.
3.   Click on Library Search.
4.   Point out that to find a book by its title, you have to type the title in the Find box and click on Title.
5.   Type in "A Single Shard" (or another title that the library has) in the Find box, click on Title, and point out where the call number and title are located in the entry.

6. Model using the "Online Catalog: Title" work sheet to write the call number and title to locate the book on the shelf.
7. Model taking a shelf marker and the "Online Catalog: Title" work sheet and going to the fiction section to find the book.
8. Model pulling the book off the library shelf and putting the shelf marker in its place.
9. Show the book to the students and then put the book back and take the shelf marker off the library shelf and put it away.

**Guided practice:** Pair students and give them a "Online Catalog: Title" work sheet (with a title on the sheet) and a shelf marker. Assign the pairs to a computer. Tell the pairs that they are to use the online catalog to find a book by their assigned title, fill out the "Online Catalog: Title" work sheet, and locate the book on the shelf. They are to use the shelf marker so that they will know where to return the book on the shelf. The pair locates the book on the library shelf and brings it to you, so that you can see that they have completed the assignment. The students return the book to the shelf, remove the shelf marker, and put it away. One way to increase access is to have half of the students check out books while the other half completes the assignment at the computers.

**Assessment:** Informally observe whether the students bring you their assigned title and then return it to the correct library shelf.

**Closure:** Using think-pair-share, ask, "How are fiction and easy books arranged on the shelf?"

## THIRD- THROUGH SIXTH-GRADE ONLINE CATALOG LESSON 4: FINDING A BOOK BY ITS SUBJECT

**Standards:**

*AASL #1:* Inquire, think critically, and gain knowledge. 1.1, Skills: 1.1.1 Follow an inquiry-based process in seeking knowledge in curricular subjects, and make the real-world connection for using this process in own life; 1.1.6, Read, view, and listen for information in any format (e.g., textual, visual, media, digital) in order to make inferences and gather meaning; 1.1.8, Demonstrate mastery of technology tools for accessing information and pursuing inquiry.
*NETS Technology #3: Research and Information Fluency:* Students apply digital tools to gather, evaluate, and use information.

**Objective:**
Students use the online catalog to search for a book by its subject and locate it on the library shelf.

**Materials:**

- online catalog sign
- projection of an Internet computer screen (must have access to computer, Internet, and means of projection)
- library software program that includes an online catalog (the Follett Destiny library software was used for the lesson)

- 15 copies of the "Online Catalog: Subject" work sheet from the CD (must be customized for a specific school's library)
- 15 subjects of books in the library (choose subjects that would be of interest to most students)
- 15 shelf markers or rulers

**Set:** Ask, "What are some of the ways that you have used to find a book in the library?" Using think-pair-share, the students report some of their strategies.

**Review:** Library books are arranged into three sections: easy, fiction, and nonfiction. The easy and fiction sections are arranged alphabetically by the author's last name. The nonfiction section is arranged by the subject of the book. Computers are tools that can help students find information. The online catalog is a software program that allows the user to search for a book by keyword, title, author, and subject.

**Input:** Using a projection of a computer screen, demonstrate how to access and use the online catalog to locate a book by its subject.

1. Click on the Online Catalog icon on the computer.
2. Click on the school name if the district has a union catalog system.
3. Click on Library Search.
4. Point out that to find a book by its subject, you have to type in the subject in the Find box and click on Subject.
5. Type in "dinosaurs" in the Find box, click on Subject, and scroll down the list, pointing out where the call number and title are located on each entry.
6. Model using the "Online Catalog: Subject" work sheet to write the call number and title of one of the books in order to locate the book on the shelf.
7. Model taking a shelf marker and the "Online Catalog: Subject" work sheet and going to the nonfiction section to find the book.
8. Model pulling the book off the library shelf and putting the shelf marker in its place.
9. Show the book to the students and then put the book back and take the shelf marker off the library shelf and put it away.

**Guided practice:** Pair students and give them an "Online Catalog: Subject" work sheet with a subject on the sheet and a shelf marker. Assign the pairs to a computer. Tell the pairs that they are to use the online catalog to find a book on their assigned subject, fill out the "Online Catalog: Subject" work sheet, and locate the book on the shelf. They use the shelf marker so that they will know where to return the book on the shelf. The pair locates the book on the library shelf and brings it to you, so that you can see that they have completed the assignment. The students return the book to the shelf, remove the shelf marker, and put it away. One way to increase access is to have half of the students check out books while the other half completes the assignment at the computers.

**Assessment:** Informally observe whether the students bring you a book from their assigned subject and then return it to the correct library shelf.

**Closure:** Using think-pair-share, ask, "How are nonfiction books arranged on the shelf?"

### Repeating These Lessons in Fourth through Sixth Grade

The four lessons should be repeated for fourth, fifth, and sixth grade. The only changes would be the specific authors, titles, and subjects of the books.

# Chapter 7

# The Internet

---

**KINDERGARTEN INTERNET LESSON 1: THE WONDERS OF SNOWFLAKES**

---

**Standards:**

*AASL #1:* Inquire, think critically, and gain knowledge. 1.1, Skills: 1.1.1 Follow an inquiry-based process in seeking knowledge in curricular subjects, and make the real-world connection for using this process in own life; 1.1.6, Read, view, and listen for information in any format (e.g., textual, visual, media, digital) in order to make inferences and gather meaning; 1.1.8, Demonstrate mastery of technology tools for accessing information and pursuing inquiry.

*NCTE #8:* Students use a variety of technological and information resources (e.g., libraries, databases, computer networks, video) to gather and synthesize information and to create and communicate knowledge.

*NETS Technology #3: Research and Information Fluency:* Students apply digital tools to gather, evaluate, and use information.

**Objective:**
Students understand that the Internet is a tool to locate specific information and images.

**Materials:**

- Internet sign
- projection of an Internet computer screen (must have access to computer, Internet, and means of projection)
- personalized start page or bookmarked Internet sites from the CD
- *Snowflake Bentley* by Jacqueline Briggs, 1999 Caldecott Winner
- 30 copies of the Letter to Parents with the list of Web sites for Lesson K.1 from the CD
- 30 pieces of paper and scissors for optional activity
- visual of a snowflake from www.its.caltech.edu/~atomic/snowcrystals/photos/photos.htm

**Set:** Conduct a short informal survey to assess students' familiarity with the Internet with questions such as "How many of you have a computer at home? How many of you have computers that are connected to the Internet? How many of you have ever looked for something on the Internet?"

**Review:** Review that computers are tools for information and leisure.

**Input:** Explain that the Internet is a way for anyone with a computer to get information stored on Web sites on other computers all over the world. This has completely changed the way information is shared and stored. It is easier to find many kinds of information, pictures, and games for all ages than it ever was in the past. Show the book *Snowflake Bentley* and summarize the story and his accomplishments. Ask the students whether they have noticed differences in snowflakes. (In areas where it doesn't snow, some students may have visited the snow.) Then use a personalized start page or bookmarked sites to show students more information about Wilson A. Bentley and ice crystal photos. On the first site, http://snowflakebentley.com, read the quote at the top of the page and point out the photo of Mr. Bentley photographing snowflakes. Then read the first three paragraphs and ask students to restate important facts, such as that he was the first person to photograph a snow crystal, and that he photographed more than 5,000 snowflakes and never found two that were alike. Then navigate to the second site, www.its.caltech.edu/~atomic/snowcrystals/photos/photos.htm, and click on the various photos of snow crystals. Point out that the snow crystals are symmetrical, meaning a line can be drawn through the middle and both sides will match.

**Optional activity:** With the students, make symmetrical paper snowflakes by folding white paper and cutting designs.

**Assessment:** Informally observe whether students follow and can restate information as requested.

**Closure:** Distribute the Letter to Parents with the list of Web sites for Lesson K.1. Ask the students where they looked for information and images on snowflakes and have the students chorally respond "the Internet."

## FIRST-GRADE INTERNET LESSON 1:  WOLVES AREN'T ALL BAD

**Standards:**

*AASL #1:*    Inquire, think critically, and gain knowledge. 1.1, Skills: 1.1.1 Follow an inquiry-based process in seeking knowledge in curricular subjects, and make the real-world connection for using this process in own life; 1.1.6, Read, view, and listen for information in any format (e.g., textual, visual, media, digital) in order to make inferences and gather meaning; 1.1.8, Demonstrate mastery of technology tools for accessing information and pursuing inquiry.
*NCTE #8:*    Students use a variety of technological and information resources (e.g., libraries, databases, computer networks, video) to gather and synthesize information and to create and communicate knowledge.
*NETS Technology #3: Research and Information Fluency:*    Students apply digital tools to gather, evaluate, and use information.

**Objectives:**

1.    Students discover that wolves have positive attributes.
2.    Students understand that the Internet provides information and images on many topics.
3.    Students understand that stereotypes can be eliminated with information.

**Materials:**

- •   Internet sign
- •   projection of an Internet computer screen (must have access to computer, Internet, and means of projection)

- personalized start page or bookmarked Internet sites from the CD
- *Little Red Riding Hood* retold and illustrated by Trina Schart Hyman, a 1984 Caldecott honor book
- 30 copies of the Letter to Parents from the CD with the list of Web sites for Lesson 1.1
- visual of a wolf

**Set:** Show a visual of a wolf. Using think-pair-share, ask the students whether wolves are good or bad and why.

**Review:** Review that the Internet is a network of interconnected computers around the world and a source of information and images.

**Input:** Show *Little Red Riding Hood,* summarize the story, and focus on the illustrations of the wolf. Using think-pair-share, ask the students for words to describe the wolf and his actions and record the words. Navigate to the first of the Web sites about wolves from a personalized start page or bookmarked Web sites.

The following sites and facts are suggested:

1. Go to www.boomerwolf.com and click on "All About Wolves" and then "Gray Wolf Short Course" to read some facts and ask students to restate. Look at "The Wolf Pack" for information about wolf family life, "Wolves Talk" for audios of vocalizations, and "The BoomerWolf Gets Funky" for very short videos of wolves in action.
2. The International Wolf Center "just for Kids" at www.wolf.org/wolves/learn/justkids/kids.asp has facts, masks, puzzles, and coloring books.
3. "Wolves of the World" at www.cosmosmith.com/wolfpage.html has excellent pictures of all types of wolves.
4. *"National Geographic* Geoguide/Wolves" at www.nationalgeographic.com/resources/ngo/education/geoguide/wolves/index.html has classroom ideas and family activities.

**Guided practice:** After showing the Web sites and reading the pertinent information, use think-pair share and ask the students to tell at least three facts they've learned. Read the words from the input and using think-pair-share, ask the students to ponder whether their ideas about wolves are the same as they had been before or have changed, and how.

**Assessment:** Informally assess whether the students can restate the information presented by the Web sites and whether their initial poor impressions of wolves have changed.

**Closure:** Distribute to the students the Letter to Parents with the list of Web sites for Lesson 1.1 and encourage the students to visit the sites at home with their parents.

## SECOND-GRADE INTERNET LESSON 1:  ANANSI SPINS TALES ON THE WEB

**Standards:**

*AASL #1:*   Inquire, think critically, and gain knowledge. 1.1, Skills: 1.1.1 Follow an inquiry-based process in seeking knowledge in curricular subjects, and make the real-world connection for using this process in own life; 1.1.6, Read, view, and listen for information in any format (e.g., textual, visual, media, digital) in order to make inferences and gather meaning; 1.1.8, Demonstrate mastery of technology tools for accessing information and pursuing inquiry.

*NCTE #8:*    Students use a variety of technological and information resources (e.g., libraries, databases, computer networks, video) to gather and synthesize information and to create and communicate knowledge.

*NETS Technology #3: Research and Information Fluency:*    Students apply digital tools to gather, evaluate, and use information.

**Objectives:**

1.    Students discover that there are many folktales about Anansi the Spider, a folk hero, from the Ashanti people of Ghana.
2.    Students discover other folktale Web sites on the Internet.
3.    Students understand that the Internet provides information and images on many topics.

**Materials:**

- Internet sign
- projection of an Internet computer screen (must have access to computer, Internet, and means of projection)
- personalized start page or bookmarked Internet sites from the CD
- *Anansi the Spider: A Tale from the Ashanti* retold and illustrated by Gerald McDermott, a 1973 Caldecott honor book
- 30 copies of the Letter to Parents from the CD with the list of Web sites for Lesson 2.1
- display of Anansi folktales books

**Set:** Introduce "Anansi the Spider" by showing the visual. Read the preface of *Anansi the Spider: A Tale from the Ashanti* and note the map that shows where the story originated.

**Review:** Review that the Internet is a network of interconnected computers around the world and a source of information and images.

**Input:** Read *Anansi the Spider: A Tale from the Ashanti* by Gerald McDermott. Mention afterward that Anansi is a folktale character who has many adventures. These can be found in books and on the Internet. Show the display of Anansi books. Click on two pages of Anansi folktales:

www.motherlandnigeria.com/stories/anansi_and_turtle.html
www.motherlandnigeria.com/stories/anansi_and_firefly.html

Read the beginning of each story. Then click on "Tales of Wonder" Web site, www.darsie.net/talesofwonder; "Aesop's Fables" Web site, www.aesopfables.com; "Gullah Net" Web site, www.knowitall.org/gullahnet; and "Myths, Folktales & Fairy Tales" Web site, http://teacher.scholastic.com/writewit/mff/index.htm, and explain the features and the information of each Web site.

**Assessment:** Informally observe whether students are following the search and understand that many more Anansi stories and other folktales are available on the Internet.

**Closure:** Distribute to the students the Letter to Parents with the list of Web sites for Lesson 2.1 and encourage the students to visit the sites at home with their parents.

## THIRD-GRADE INTERNET LESSON 1: EARTHQUAKE RISKS

**Standards:**

*AASL #1:*   Inquire, think critically, and gain knowledge. 1.1, Skills: 1.1.1 Follow an inquiry-based process in seeking knowledge in curricular subjects, and make the real-world connection for using this process in own life; 1.1.6, Read, view, and listen for information in any format (e.g., textual, visual, media, digital) in order to make inferences and gather meaning; 1.1.8, Demonstrate mastery of technology tools for accessing information and pursuing inquiry.

*NCTE #8:*   Students use a variety of technological and information resources (e.g., libraries, databases, computer networks, video) to gather and synthesize information and to create and communicate knowledge.

*NETS Technology #3: Research and Information Fluency:*   Students apply digital tools to gather, evaluate, and use information.

**Objectives:**

1.   Students identify the risk of an earthquake occurring in their area.
2.   Students read and discuss facts and fiction about earthquakes.
3.   Students understand that the Internet provides information and images on many topics.
4.   Students understand that Web sites need to be evaluated for their reliability.

**Materials:**

- Internet sign
- projection of an Internet computer screen (must have access to computer, Internet, and means of projection)
- personalized start page or bookmarked Internet sites from the CD
- 15 copies of the "Earthquake – Modified Mercalli Scale and The Richter Scale" from the "Disaster Intensity Scales" page on the Federal Emergency Management Agency (FEMA) Web site, www.fema.gov/kids/intense.htm, which must be printed on the Landscape preference of a printer and cut and pasted before copying
- 15 copies of the "History of Big Earthquakes" page on the FEMA Web site, www.fema.gov/kids/eqhist.htm
- 30 copies of the "Earthquakes: Facts and Fiction" page on the FEMA Web site, www.fema.gov/kids/eqfact.htm
- 30 copies of the Letter to the Parents from the CD
- 30 copies of the Internet brochure from the CD
- display of nonfiction books about earthquakes

**Set:** Show the visual of earthquake damage. Read the titles and show pictures from several of the earthquake books. Then say, "Where else could we find information about earthquakes? Today we are going to find information about earthquakes on the Internet."

**Review:** Review that the Internet is a network of interconnected computers around the world and a source of information and images.

**Input:** Go to the FEMA Web site, www.fema.gov, and navigate the Web site by clicking on "kids" on the left side of the page, then clicking on "The Disaster Area" when the next window appears. Read the links and ask the students which link should be followed. After the students decide on the correct link, "earthquakes," go to the next window and click on "map of earthquake risk states." Explain that the key shows that the pink or very shaded portions of the map are the most likely areas to have an earthquake. Using the computer mouse, point to your state on the map. Using think-pair-share, the students evaluate the probability of an earthquake occurring in the near future in their area. Navigate back to "earthquakes" and click on "Disaster Intensity Scales" and scroll down to "earthquakes." Distribute copies of the scales to the pairs and then discuss the Modified Mercalli and the Richter scale, asking students to compare them. Navigate back to "Earthquakes" and click on "Historic Earthquakes." Distribute copies of the "History of Big Earthquakes" page to the pairs and discuss the information. Navigate back to "Earthquakes," click on "Earthquake Facts and Fiction," and distribute a copy of the text to every student. Divide the class into two groups. One group reads the fiction text, and the other group answers with the fact text. Click back to the original FEMA site and ask the students whether they know what FEMA is. Click on "About Us" at the top of the webpage and read "Federal Emergency Management Agency" and its mission. The fact that the Web site is designed and maintained by a governmental agency lets users know that it is a very reliable site, and the information found on it can be trusted.

**Assessment:** Informally assess whether students can read and interpret the disaster scale.

**Closure:** Distribute the letter to the parents and ask the students to test their families on the Facts and Fiction earthquake page. Distribute the Internet brochure, go over it, and ask the students to share it with their families.

## THIRD-GRADE INTERNET LESSON 2:  COMPARING DINOSAURS

**Standards:**

*AASL #1:*  Inquire, think critically, and gain knowledge. 1.1, Skills: 1.1.1 Follow an inquiry-based process in seeking knowledge in curricular subjects, and make the real-world connection for using this process in own life; 1.1.6, Read, view, and listen for information in any format (e.g., textual, visual, media, digital) in order to make inferences and gather meaning; 1.1.8, Demonstrate mastery of technology tools for accessing information and pursuing inquiry.

*NCTE #8:*  Students use a variety of technological and information resources (e.g., libraries, databases, computer networks, video) to gather and synthesize information and to create and communicate knowledge.

*NETS Technology #3: Research and Information Fluency:*  Students apply digital tools to gather, evaluate, and use information.

**Objectives:**

1.  Using an Internet site, students locate information on two dinosaurs.
2.  Students use the information to group themselves into length categories.
3.  Students understand that the Internet provides information and images on many topics.
4.  Students understand that Web sites need to be evaluated for their reliability.

**Materials:**

- Internet sign
- projection of an Internet computer screen (must have access to computer, Internet, and means of projection)
- 15 computers with Internet access, or enough so that each pair can access the Web site
- personalized start page or bookmarked Web site from the CD
- paper strips for each pair with the names of dinosaurs from a list from the CD
- board-ready copy of the paper strip input from the CD
- visuals of a *Nanosaurus* and a *Hadrosaurus*
- four length categories signs from the CD
- 30 copies of the Letter to Parents and the list of Web sites for Lesson 3.2 from the CD

**Set:** Show the visuals of two dinosaurs, *Hadrosaurus* and *Nanosaurus*, and ask which is longer.

**Review:** Review that the Internet is a network of interconnected computers around the world and a source of information and images. A user must determine the reliability of a site.

**Input:** Go to the Web site "DinoDictionary" (www.dinodictionary.com/index.asp). Ask what letter "*Nanosaurus*" begins with, click on the letter "N," and locate the information on the *Nanosaurus*. Read the translation of the scientific name ("dwarf lizard") and locate the length (4 feet). Project the board-ready paper strip, record the information, and repeat the modeling for the *Hadrosaurus*. Ask the students to respond chorally as to which of the dinosaurs is longer.

**Guided practice:** Pair students, give them paper strips with the names of two dinosaurs, and assign a computer. They go to the bookmarked DinoDictionary Web site and locate the information needed: the length of the dinosaur and the translation of the scientific name. One student locates the information for the first dinosaur, while the other student records it on the paper strip. The students switch seats and jobs for the second dinosaur. Post the category signs around the room. After the students have completed the research, each pair tears the paper strip apart so that each student has information on one dinosaur. Ask the students to stand under the signs that include the length of their dinosaur. Under each category, the students tell the names of their dinosaurs, the translation of the scientific name, and the length. The students decide which dinosaur is the shortest and longest in their category.

**Assessment:** Informally assess whether students can navigate, locate, and record the information from the Web site.

**Closure:** Ask each group to report which is the shortest and longest dinosaur in their category. Distribute the Letter to Parents with the list of Web sites for Lesson 3.2 and ask the students to explore with their parents the dinosaur Web sites on the list.

## FOURTH-GRADE INTERNET LESSON 1: FACTS ABOUT OUR STATE

**Standards:**

*AASL #1:* Inquire, think critically, and gain knowledge. 1.1, Skills: 1.1.1 Follow an inquiry-based process in seeking knowledge in curricular subjects, and make the real-world connection for using this process in own life; 1.1.6, Read, view, and listen for information in any format (e.g., textual, visual, media, digital) in order to make inferences and gather meaning; 1.1.8, Demonstrate mastery of technology tools for accessing information and pursuing inquiry.

*NCTE #8:*    Students use a variety of technological and information resources (e.g., libraries, databases, computer networks, video) to gather and synthesize information and to create and communicate knowledge.

*NETS Technology #3: Research and Information Fluency:*    Students apply digital tools to gather, evaluate, and use information.

**Objectives:**

1. Using the Internet, students locate a Web site with information on their state.
2. Students use the information from the Web site to make bookmarks on specific topics.

**Materials:**

- Internet sign
- projection of an Internet computer screen (must have access to computer, Internet, and means of projection)
- 10 to 15 computers with Internet access, or enough so that each pair can access the Web site
- personalized start page or bookmarked Web site from the CD
- paper strips for each pair with questions from the CD
- board-ready paper strip for input modeling question from the CD
- tag board cut into bookmark-sized strips
- boxes of crayons on the table
- teacher-made bookmark of the state flower
- 30 copies of the "state map/quiz" printout from the Web site (optional) (the Web site is a user-supported site and site members can get printer-friendly information)

**Set:** Ask the students whether they know the state flower for the state in which they live. Answer the question by showing the bookmark you have made with information about the state flower.

**Review:** Review that the Internet is a network of interconnected computers around the world and a source of information and images. A user must determine the reliability of a site.

**Input:** Show a board-ready copy of the paper strip and say that you and the students are going to make bookmarks by taking notes from a Web site. Review with the students the information that is required and state that each pair will be searching for different required information. Go to the bookmarked Web site www.enchantedlearning.com/usa/states; scroll down and find the state in which you live, and click on the state name. Scroll down and find the state flower and write it in the space on the paper strip. Model how you made the bookmark.

**Guided practice:** Pair students, give them a paper strip with a question about their state, and assign a computer. After the pair has answered the question, each student is given a bookmark-sized piece of tag board on which he or she prints the researched information and then illustrates the bookmark.

**Optional activity or homework:** Distribute copies of the "state map/quiz" printout from the Web site and have the students complete the work sheet in class or at home with their parents.

**Assessment:** Informally assess whether students can navigate, locate, and record the information on the Web site and create an appropriate bookmark.

**Closure:** Ask each pair to share the information they have found.

## FOURTH-GRADE INTERNET LESSON 2: LOCATING INFORMATION ABOUT PETS

**Standards:**

*AASL #1:* Inquire, think critically, and gain knowledge. 1.1, Skills: 1.1.1 Follow an inquiry-based process in seeking knowledge in curricular subjects, and make the real-world connection for using this process in own life; 1.1.6, Read, view, and listen for information in any format (e.g., textual, visual, media, digital) in order to make inferences and gather meaning; 1.1.8, Demonstrate mastery of technology tools for accessing information and pursuing inquiry.

*NCTE #8:* Students use a variety of technological and information resources (e.g., libraries, databases, computer networks, video) to gather and synthesize information and to create and communicate knowledge.

*NETS Technology #3: Research and Information Fluency:* Students apply digital tools to gather, evaluate, and use information.

**Objectives:**

1. Using a search engine, students locate a site with information on a specific pet.
2. Students find the answers to specific questions about a specific pet.

**Materials:**

- Internet sign
- projection of an Internet computer screen (must have access to computer, Internet, and means of projection)
- 10 to 15 computers with Internet access, or enough so that each pair can access the Web sites
- bookmarked search engines: Google (www.google.com), Ask for Kids (www.askforkids.com), and Dogpile (www.dogpile.com/info.dogpl)
- paper strips for each student from the CD
- visual of a corn snake
- board-ready paper strip for the input from the CD

**Set:** Show the visual of a corn snake and ask the students, "Do you know what food to feed a pet corn snake and how big they grow?" Students guess. Tell them that they are going to research information about corn snakes and other pets on the Internet using one of three search engines: Google, Ask for Kids, and Dogpile.

**Review:** Review that the Internet is a network of interconnected computers around the world and a source of information and images. A user must determine the reliability of a site.

**Input:** Model how to use the bookmarked search engines. Type "corn snake" in all three of the search engines and click on the first Web site that comes up in the list of Web sites, commenting that it usually is the most on target to answer questions. Explain that Dogpile is a meta-search engine that is a compilation of several other search engines: Google, Yahoo! search, MSN search, and Ask. Find the answer to the set questions. While reading information on one of the sites, write that corn snakes eat mice and they grow to five feet long. Write the name and URL of the Web site where the information has been found.

**Guided practice:** Give each student a separate paper strip with the name of a pet and two questions to answer. The paper strip also has the search engine that the student should use to find the information and a place for the URL. One way to increase access is to have half of the students check out books while the other half completes the assignment at the computer. After all students complete the assignment, they share their information with the others at their table.

**Assessment:** Informally assess whether students can navigate, locate, and record the information from the Web site and correctly cite the URL.

**Closure:** Use think-pair-share to ask the students how hard was it to find the information on the pet they researched.

*Note: Collect the papers in order to have the URL information for the next lesson.*

## FOURTH-GRADE INTERNET LESSON 3: EVALUATING WEB SITES

**Standards:**

*AASL #1:*   Inquire, think critically, and gain knowledge. 1.1, Skills: 1.1.1 Follow an inquiry-based process in seeking knowledge in curricular subjects, and make the real-world connection for using this process in own life; 1.1.6, Read, view, and listen for information in any format (e.g., textual, visual, media, digital) in order to make inferences and gather meaning; 1.1.8, Demonstrate mastery of technology tools for accessing information and pursuing inquiry.
*NCTE #8:*   Students use a variety of technological and information resources (e.g., libraries, databases, computer networks, video) to gather and synthesize information and to create and communicate knowledge.
*NETS Technology #3: Research and Information Fluency:*   Students apply digital tools to gather, evaluate, and use information.

**Objective:**
   Students locate the Web site they used in a prior lesson and evaluate it based on authorship, sponsorship, reliability, accuracy, and currency.

**Materials:**

   • Internet sign
   • projection of an Internet computer screen (must have access to computer, Internet, and means of projection)
   • 10 to 15 computers with Internet access, or enough so that each pair can access the Web sites
   • bookmarked Web sites or a personalized start page from the CD
   • board-ready copy of the work sheet from the CD
   • board-ready copy of the list of variables from the CD
   • 15 copies of the work sheet for Lessons 4.3, 5.3, and 6.3 from the CD

**Set:** Using think-pair-share, ask students, "Is something true just because you found it on the Internet?"

**Review:** Review that the Internet is a network of interconnected computers around the world and a source of information and images. A user must determine the reliability of a site.

**Input:** State that there are specific questions to answer to determine whether a Web site can be trusted. Present the variables: Who wrote the information on the Web site? When was the last date that the information was revised or updated? Is the information biased in any way? Is the Web site useful for my search? Present the idea of "domain" and show four Web sites with the different domains, "gov," "edu," "org," and "com": www.loc.gov/index.html, www.princeton.edu/main, http://kids.nypl.org, and www.louissachar.com. Discuss the variables that determine the trustworthiness of a Web site. Use the list of variables work sheet and determine the trustworthiness of two of the sites by answering the questions. Model how to evaluate a Web site by showing the board-ready work sheet and clicking on the Web site used for the last Internet lesson's input. Answer the questions on the board-ready work sheet and determine whether the Web site is trustworthy and why.

**Guided practice:** Pair students and assign each pair to a computer. Give them the Web site evaluation work sheet and the work sheet from the last Internet lesson. The students navigate to the Web site used in the last Internet lesson and answer the questions about the Web site. Each pair determines whether the Web site is trustworthy. Circulate, offering assistance as necessary. One way to increase access is to have half of the students check out books while the other half completes the assignment at the computer. After all students complete the assignment, they share their information with the entire class.

**Assessment:** Informally assess whether students can navigate, locate, and record the information from the Web site and correctly enter the URL.

**Closure:** Use think-pair-share to ask the students which variable (authorship, etc.) was the most important part of determining trustworthiness of a Web site. Expect divergent answers.

## FIFTH-GRADE INTERNET LESSON 1: WHO FOUGHT THE AMERICAN REVOLUTION?

**Standards:**

*AASL #1:* Inquire, think critically, and gain knowledge. 1.1, Skills: 1.1.1 Follow an inquiry-based process in seeking knowledge in curricular subjects, and make the real-world connection for using this process in own life; 1.1.6, Read, view, and listen for information in any format (e.g., textual, visual, media, digital) in order to make inferences and gather meaning; 1.1.8, Demonstrate mastery of technology tools for accessing information and pursuing inquiry.
*NCTE #8:* Students use a variety of technological and information resources (e.g., libraries, databases, computer networks, video) to gather and synthesize information and to create and communicate knowledge.
*NETS Technology #3: Research and Information Fluency:* Students apply digital tools to gather, evaluate, and use information.

**Objectives:**

1. Using a bookmarked site or personalized start page, students locate a Web site with information on a specific group during the American Revolution.

2. Students answer specific questions about how that group participated in the Revolutionary War.
3. Students write a paragraph based on their research notes.

**Materials:**

- Internet sign
- projection of an Internet computer screen (must have access to computer, Internet, and means of projection)
- 10 to 15 computers with Internet access, or enough so that each pair can access the Web sites
- bookmarked Web sites or a personalized start page from the CD
- 15 copies of the work sheet from the CD
- visual of a Continental Army soldier

**Set:** Ask whether anyone knows of any other groups who fought in the American Revolution, aside from the Revolutionary Army. State that today the class will be investigating the Minutemen, the loyalists, the Hessians, the French, free blacks and slaves, Native Americans, women, and spies.

**Review:** Review that the Internet is a network of interconnected computers around the world and a source of information and images. A user must determine the reliability of a site.

**Input:** State that many groups participated in the American Revolution and model how to research one by using the Continental Army as an example. Show the visual of the Continental Army soldier and the work sheet and explain what information must be found by looking at different Web sites. Then navigate to the input Web sites and read the Internet information, modeling how to take notes using your own words. Write the URL and title of one of the Web site on the work sheet. Explain that on Wikipedia, if you click on "cite this article" on the left side of the Web page, you can find the bibliographic entry.

Wikipedia contributors, "Continental Army," *Wikipedia, The Free Encyclopedia,* http://en.wikipedia.org/w/index.php?title=Continental_Army&oldid=106062668 (accessed February 8, 2007).

Then model how to write a short paragraph based on the notes.

**Guided practice:** Pair students and assign each pair a computer. Give them a work sheet with a specific group of the Revolutionary War circled. The pair navigates to the appropriate Web sites and reads for information, taking notes in their own words. Circulate, offering assistance as necessary. The pair collaborates on a paragraph based on their notes, as well as writing a bibliographic entry for one of the Web sites they used. One way to increase access is to have half of the students check out books while the other half completes the assignment at the computer. After all students complete the assignment, have them share their information with the entire class.

**Assessment:** Informally assess whether students can navigate, locate, and record the information from the Web site, and correctly cite the URL.

**Closure:** Using think-pair-share, ask, "What contributions did each group make in the Revolutionary War?"

*Note: This lesson can be split into two lessons. The research is done during one period and the paragraph and bibliographic citations are written in the next period.*

## FIFTH-GRADE INTERNET LESSON 2: DIVERSITY MAKES AMERICA GREAT

**Standards:**

*AASL #1:* Inquire, think critically, and gain knowledge. 1.1, Skills: 1.1.1 Follow an inquiry-based process in seeking knowledge in curricular subjects, and make the real-world connection for using this process in own life; 1.1.6, Read, view, and listen for information in any format (e.g., textual, visual, media, digital) in order to make inferences and gather meaning; 1.1.8, Demonstrate mastery of technology tools for accessing information and pursuing inquiry.

*NCTE #8:* Students use a variety of technological and information resources (e.g., libraries, databases, computer networks, video) to gather and synthesize information and to create and communicate knowledge.

*NETS Technology #3: Research and Information Fluency:* Students apply digital tools to gather, evaluate, and use information.

**Objectives:**

1. Using a bookmarked site or personalized start page, students locate a Web site with information on a specific immigrant group.
2. Students take notes on how, why, and when their group came to America and where they settled.
3. Students write a paragraph based on their research notes.

**Materials:**

- Internet sign
- projection of an Internet computer screen (must have access to computer, Internet, and means of projection)
- 10 to 15 computers with Internet access, or enough so that each pair can access the Web sites
- bookmarked Web sites or a personalized start page from the CD
- board-ready copy of the work sheet
- 15 copies of the work sheet from the CD
- visual of a Scandinavian in native costume

**Set:** Using think-pair-share, ask the students to identify the countries that their families or ancestors came from.

**Review:** Review that the Internet is a network of interconnected computers around the world and a source of information and images. A user must determine the reliability of a site.

**Input:** State that many groups immigrated to the United States and all have made contributions to our history and culture. Model how to research the topics by using the Scandinavians as an example. Show the visual and the work sheet and read the questions that must be answered by looking at the Web site. Then navigate to the bookmarked Web site, http://memory.loc.gov/learn/features/immig/scandinavian.html. Click on the globe on the left side of the Web page. A window will open up. The needed information is available at this location. Model how to take notes using your own words. Write the URL and title of the Web site on the work sheet. Then model how to write a short paragraph based on the information, and write a bibliographic entry for the Web site. Example: Donlan, Leni, "Scandinavian Immigration," *Library of Congress*, http://memory.loc.gov/learn/features/immig/scandinavian.html (accessed February 8, 2007).

**Guided practice:** Pair students and assign each pair a computer. Give each pair a work sheet on which a specific immigrant group is circled. The students navigate to the appropriate Web site, click on the globe, and read for information, taking notes in their own words. Circulate, offering assistance as necessary. The pair collaborates on a paragraph based on their notes, as well as writing a bibliographic entry for the Web site they used. After all students complete the assignment, they share their information with the entire class.

**Assessment:** Informally assess whether students can navigate, locate, and record the information from the Web site and correctly cite the URL.

**Closure:** Using think-pair-share, ask, "Why is America such a magnet for immigrants?"

*Note: Collect the papers in order to have the URL information for the next lesson.*

## FIFTH-GRADE INTERNET LESSON 3: EVALUATING WEB SITES

**Standards:**

*AASL #1:* Inquire, think critically, and gain knowledge. 1.1, Skills: 1.1.1 Follow an inquiry-based process in seeking knowledge in curricular subjects, and make the real-world connection for using this process in own life; 1.1.6, Read, view, and listen for information in any format (e.g., textual, visual, media, digital) in order to make inferences and gather meaning; 1.1.8, Demonstrate mastery of technology tools for accessing information and pursuing inquiry.
*NCTE #8:* Students use a variety of technological and information resources (e.g., libraries, databases, computer networks, video) to gather and synthesize information and to create and communicate knowledge.
*NETS Technology #3: Research and Information Fluency:* Students apply digital tools to gather, evaluate, and use information.

**Objective:**
Students locate the Web sites they used for a prior lesson, and evaluate them based on authorship, sponsorship, reliability, accuracy, and currency.

**Materials:**

- Internet sign
- projection of an Internet computer screen (must have access to computer, Internet, and means of projection)
- 10 to 15 computers with Internet access, or enough so that each pair can access the Web sites
- bookmarked Web sites or a personalized start page from the CD
- board-ready copy of the work sheet
- board-ready copy of the list of variables
- 15 copies of the work sheet for Lessons 4.3, 5.3, and 6.3 from the CD

**Set:** Using think-pair-share, ask students, "Is something true just because you found it on the Internet?"

**Review:** Review that the Internet is a network of interconnected computers around the world and a source of information and images. A user must determine the reliability of a site.

**Input:** State that there are specific questions to answer to determine whether a Web site can be trusted. Present the variables: Who wrote the information on the Web site? When was the last date that the information was revised or updated? Is the information biased in any way? Is the Web site useful for my search? Present the idea of "domain" and show four Web sites with the different domains, "gov," "edu," "org," and "com": www.fbi.gov, www.yale.edu, www.democrats.org, and www.gop.com. Discuss the variables that determine the trustworthiness of a Web site. Use the list of variables work sheet and determine the trustworthiness of two of the sites by answering the questions. Model how to evaluate a Web site by showing the board-ready work sheet and clicking on the Web site used for the last Internet lesson's input. Answer the questions on the board-ready work sheet and determine whether the Web site is trustworthy and why.

**Guided practice:** Pair students and assign each pair to a computer. Give each pair the Web site evaluation work sheet and the work sheet from the last Internet lesson. The students navigate to the Web sites used in the last Internet lesson and answer the questions about the Web sites. Each pair determines whether the Web sites are trustworthy. Circulate, offering assistance as necessary. After all students complete the assignment, they share their information with the entire class.

**Assessment:** Informally assess whether students can navigate, locate, and record the information from the Web site, and correctly enter the URLs.

**Closure:** Use think-pair-share to ask the students which variable (authorship, etc.) was the most important part of determining trustworthiness of a site. Expect divergent answers.

## SIXTH-GRADE INTERNET LESSON 1: COMPARING COUNTRIES

**Standards:**

*AASL #1:* Inquire, think critically, and gain knowledge. 1.1, Skills: 1.1.1 Follow an inquiry-based process in seeking knowledge in curricular subjects, and make the real-world connection for using this process in own life; 1.1.6, Read, view, and listen for information in any format (e.g., textual, visual, media, digital) in order to make inferences and gather meaning; 1.1.8, Demonstrate mastery of technology tools for accessing information and pursuing inquiry.

*NCTE #8:* Students use a variety of technological and information resources (e.g., libraries, databases, computer networks, video) to gather and synthesize information and to create and communicate knowledge.

*NETS Technology #3: Research and Information Fluency:* Students apply digital tools to gather, evaluate, and use information.

**Objectives:**

1. Students locate a Web site using a bookmark or personalized start pad.
2. Students locate the answers to specific questions about two countries and take notes on the required information.
3. Students compare and contrast two countries using the information found on the Internet.

**Materials:**

- Internet sign
- projection of an Internet computer screen (must have access to computer, Internet, and means of projection)
- 10 to 15 computers with Internet access, or enough so that each pair can access the Web sites
- bookmarked search engines or a personalized start page from the CD
- board-ready copy of the Internet Input Work Sheet 6.1 from the CD
- 15 copies of the Internet Guided Practice Work Sheet 6.1 from the CD
- chart for each pair
- visuals of France and Botswana
- bookmark for CIA *World Factbook*, www.cia.gov/cia/publications/factbook/index.html

**Set:** Ask the students what the CIA is. After students respond, tell the students that the CIA is an information-gathering agency for the United States.

**Review:** Review that the Internet is a network of interconnected computers around the world and a source of information and images. A user must determine the reliability of a site.

**Input:** Go to "CIA World Factbook" Web site www.cia.gov/cia/publications/factbook/index.html. Say, "Today we are going to compare specific information on two countries. I will show you how to gather the information and fill out the chart." Show the visuals of France and Botswana. Model how to navigate to each section and do an overview of the information available. Show the work sheet and read the questions that must be answered by looking at a particular section of the Web site. Then navigate to the appropriate sections of the Web site, "Geography," "People," and "Economy," which contain the information necessary to answer the specific questions. Demonstrate that the students will have to scroll down on the pages to find some of the information. Model how to transfer the information onto the chart. After the chart is complete, model how to compare and contrast the information to come up with conclusions about importance of the factors. The answers are:

| Country | Location | Area | Median Age | Life Expectancy | Literacy | GDP Per Capita | GPD Composite by Sector |
|---------|----------|------|------------|-----------------|----------|----------------|-------------------------|
| France | Western Europe | 643,427 | 39.1 | 79.73 | 99% | $30,100 | Agr. 2.2%<br>Ind. 20.6%<br>Ser. 77.2% |
| Botswana | Southern Africa | 600,370 | 19.4 | 33.74 | 79.8% | $11,400 | Agr. 2.4%<br>Ind. 46.9%<br>Ser. 50.7% |

**Conclusion:** Both countries have about the same area, and only 2.4% of their economies are in agriculture. However, age is quite different, with Botswana's median age being 19 and France's median age being 39 years. The life expectancy of people in Botswana is less than half that of the people who live in France. Almost all the people in France can read and write, while only 79.8% can in Botswana. People in Botswana make one-third of the money that people in France make. Botswana has half of its jobs in the service industry, while France has more than three-fourths.

**Guided practice:** Pair students and assign each pair to a computer. Give each pair a work sheet and a paper strip with two countries. The students navigate to the "CIA World Factbook" Web site and read for information to answer the questions on the work sheet. Circulate, offering assistance as necessary. The pair fills in the chart based on their notes, then compares and contrasts the information on the countries. The pair collaborates in writing a few sentences to sum up their conclusions about the two countries.

**Assessment:** Informally assess whether students can navigate, locate, and record the information from the Web site.

**Closure:** The student pairs share their conclusions with the other pair at their table. Circulate and recap the important conclusions, giving the students credit for their thinking.

## SIXTH-GRADE INTERNET LESSON 2: GETTING TO KNOW AUTHORS

**Standards:**

*AASL #1:* Inquire, think critically, and gain knowledge. 1.1, Skills: 1.1.1 Follow an inquiry-based process in seeking knowledge in curricular subjects, and make the real-world connection for using this process in own life; 1.1.6, Read, view, and listen for information in any format (e.g., textual, visual, media, digital) in order to make inferences and gather meaning; 1.1.8, Demonstrate mastery of technology tools for accessing information and pursuing inquiry.

*NCTE #8:* Students use a variety of technological and information resources (e.g., libraries, databases, computer networks, video) to gather and synthesize information and to create and communicate knowledge.

*NETS Technology #3: Research and Information Fluency:* Students apply digital tools to gather, evaluate, and use information.

**Objectives:**

1. Students locate a Web site with information on a specific author.
2. Students locate the answers to specific questions about that author and take notes on the required information.

**Materials:**

- Internet sign
- projection of an Internet computer screen (must have access to computer, Internet, and means of projection)
- 10 to 15 computers with Internet access, or enough so that each pair can access the Web sites
- board-ready copy of the work sheet
- 15 copies of the work sheet from the CD
- list of authors from the CD
- visual of Gary Paulsen
- bookmark for Gary Paulsen site, www.randomhouse.com/features/garypaulsen/about.html

**Set:** Using think-pair-share, ask students to identify the kinds of book a particular author writes after being given clues. *Clues:* The author ran away to join a carnival at 14. He worked many different jobs. He competed in two Iditarods, the 1180-mile dog sled race from Canada to Alaska. The students should come up with "adventure stories." Show the visual and reveal that you were talking about Gary Paulsen, the author of *Hatchet* and many other adventure stories.

**Review:** Review that the Internet is a network of interconnected computers around the world and a source of information and images. A user must determine the reliability of a site.

**Input:** Go to one of the bookmark or personalized start page search engines and input "Gary Paulsen" in quotation marks, explaining that the quotation marks make the search engine keep the two words together, so the results will be for Gary Paulsen only, not every site that has "Gary" or "Paulsen." Click on the Random House site, show the Web site cited in the materials, and do an overview of the information available. Show the work sheet and read the questions that must be answered by looking at a Web site. Then navigate to the appropriate part of the Web site, "About Gary Paulsen," which contains the information necessary to answer the specific questions. Model how to answer the questions on the work sheet. Then write the URL and title of the Web site on the work sheet. Close the Web site and then model how to write a bibliographic entry for the Web site. Example: Paulsen, Gary, "About Gary," *Random House*, www.randomhouse.com/features/garypaulsen/about.html (accessed February 8, 2007).

**Guided practice:** Pair students, assign each pair to a computer, and give each pair a work sheet. Each pair chooses an author from the paper strips displayed. The students navigate to an appropriate search engine and type in the author's name using quotation marks. They find a Web site that provides the necessary information and answer the questions on the work sheet. The pair collaborates on writing a bibliographic entry for the Web site they used. Circulate, offering assistance as necessary. After all students complete the assignment, they share their information with the entire class.

**Assessment:** Informally assess whether students can navigate, locate, and record the information from the Web site, and correctly cite the URL.

**Closure:** Using think-pair share, the students discuss whether the author's life experiences are reflected in the books the author writes.

*Note: Collect the papers in order to have the URL information for the next lesson.*

## SIXTH-GRADE INTERNET LESSON 3: EVALUATING WEB SITES

**Standards:**

*AASL #1:* Inquire, think critically, and gain knowledge. 1.1, Skills: 1.1.1 Follow an inquiry-based process in seeking knowledge in curricular subjects, and make the real-world connection for using this process in own life; 1.1.6, Read, view, and listen for information in any format (e.g., textual, visual, media, digital) in order to make inferences and gather meaning; 1.1.8, Demonstrate mastery of technology tools for accessing information and pursuing inquiry.

*NCTE #8:* Students use a variety of technological and information resources (e.g., libraries, databases, computer networks, video) to gather and synthesize information and to create and communicate knowledge.

*NETS Technology #3: Research and Information Fluency:* Students apply digital tools to gather, evaluate, and use information.

**Objective:**
  Students locate the Web sites they used for a prior lesson, and evaluate them based on authorship, sponsorship, reliability, accuracy, and currency.

**Materials:**

- Internet sign
- projection of an Internet computer screen (must have access to computer, Internet, and means of projection)
- 10 to 15 computers with Internet access, or enough so that each pair can access the Web sites
- bookmarked sites or a personalized start page from the CD
- board-ready copy of the work sheet
- board-ready copy of the list of variables
- 15 copies of Work Sheet 4.3, 5.3, and 6.3 from the CD

**Set:** Using think-pair-share, ask students "Is something true just because you found it on the Internet?"

**Review:** Review that the Internet is a network of interconnected computers around the world and a source of information and images. A user must determine the reliability of a site.

**Input:** State that there are specific questions to answer to determine whether a Web site can be trusted. Present the variables: Who is the sponsor of the domain? Who wrote the information on the Web site? How can I check whether the information is correct? When was the last date that the information was revised or updated? Is the information biased in anyway? Is the Web site useful for my search? Present the idea of "domain" and show four Web sites with the different domains, "gov," "edu," "org," and "com": www.fema.gov, www.ucla.edu, www.un.org/english, and www.lemonysnicket.com/index.cfm. Discuss the variables that determine the trustworthiness of a Web site. Use the list of variables work sheet and determine the trustworthiness of two of the sites by answering the questions. Model how to evaluate a Web site by showing the board-ready work sheet and clicking on the Web site used for the last Internet lesson's input. Answer the questions on the board-ready work sheet and determine whether the Web site is trustworthy and why.

**Guided practice:** Pair students, assign each pair to a computer, and give them the Web site evaluation work sheet and the work sheet from the last Internet lesson. The students navigate to the Web sites used in the last Internet lesson and answer the questions about the Web sites. Each pair determines whether each Web site they used is trustworthy. Circulate, offering assistance as necessary. After all students complete the assignment, they share their information with the entire class.

**Assessment:** Informally assess whether students can navigate, locate, and record the information from the Web sites, and correctly enter the URLs.

**Closure:** Use think-pair-share to ask the students which variable (authorship, etc.) was the most important part of determining trustworthiness of a site. Expect divergent answers.

# PART II

# CURRICULUM UNITS USING REFERENCE SOURCES

# Introduction to Unit Design

## DESIGN

The units that follow were written to give students practice in using the reference sources to which they have been introduced. Not all reference sources are used in every unit. The units have been created to capture student interest and integrated with the national standards for either the social studies or the science curriculum. Different products were chosen for each unit: a simple book for kindergarten, a picture dictionary of animal defenses and a card game for first grade, a model and a museum presentation for second grade, a transportation dictionary and timeline for third grade, a brochure for fourth grade, an emergency flyer for fifth grade, and a PowerPoint presentation and chart for sixth grade.

The units would be excellent collaborative projects for the librarian and the classroom teacher. If the school library has not done collaborative units, we might suggest trying one with the most cooperative teacher on the faculty.

The units were planned using the understanding by design template found in *Understanding by Design* by Grant Wiggins and Jay McTigue (Association for Supervision and Curriculum Development, 2005). In the first stage, the planner identifies the desired results by first basing the unit on established goals. These are either national, state, or district content standards. Next, the planner decides on the essential questions. What is it that makes this unit worth studying? These questions are broad in nature but have specific answers. This is where the words of Bloom's Taxonomy, especially "why" and "how," are used. The next step is to write down what understandings the students will learn. These are also broad statements. The final step of stage one is to break down the understandings into key knowledge and skills the students will learn from the unit.

The second stage is to decide what evidence will show that the students have acquired the understandings and key knowledge and skills. The units of this book concentrate on performance tasks. Each of the performance tasks should mirror the understandings, knowledge, and skills that have been targeted for the unit. Work sheets can also be collected for formative assessments. Part of this stage is student self-assessment and reflection. The rubrics can be used either by librarians or teachers to assess performance tasks or by the students to assess their performance tasks. The rubrics in the units were created on RubiStar (http://rubistar.4teachers. org/index.php). This is a free Web site at which all kinds of rubrics can be designed.

The third and last stage is planning the learning experiences. These are summarized in the beginning of each unit in this book and are made specific with the lesson plans that follow. Some units have a dictionary lesson to build background information, not for a particular product.

## SCHEDULING

Ideally, these units would be taught to a class every day for 30 to 40 minutes for a week or two, depending on the unit. If a flexible schedule is already in place in the school library, this is relatively easy to plan. For school libraries with fixed schedules, it may take some creativity to find a time when the class and the library are both available. The units can be done on a regular fixed schedule, but the time needed to complete the unit may be unwieldy.

## MATERIALS

The Web sites used for the units are listed in the CD. Specific books are listed for the opening sets. There is no list of books for the nonfiction lessons, as this will vary greatly from library to library, depending on the availability of interlibrary loan and the budget. It is strongly suggested that you gather the nonfiction books for the unit and consider purchasing some if the unit will be taught to many classes for several years. Both Bound to Stay Bound and Follett Books have excellent Web sites for finding books by subject. Also consider using the public library to fill in areas where the school library does not have enough books.

There are Internet lessons in all of the units. If no Internet access is available or if access is limited, these lessons can be deleted for some of the units, but the products will be different. For some schools, these lessons might be better done in the computer lab.

A cooperative group chart is recommended for these units. This is merely a piece of chart paper with student numbers, usually one to four, in one column and tasks that need to be done in the next column. The chart might list the tasks generally such as materials director, reader, recorder, and presenter. The chart may also have tasks specific to a particular lesson. If it is laminated, it can be used over and over.

## ADDITIONAL HELP

Several of the primary units require additional help for the students. This additional help can be a class of older students, parents, volunteers, or university interns. The training for the additional help is minimal and can be done in 10 minutes or less.

## CONCLUSION

These units were created to include authentic learning. Students can show their skills in using reference books best when using them for a greater purpose than individual lessons. The lessons on each of the reference books is background for the real task: researching.

## REFERENCE

Wiggins, Grant, and Jay McTigue. 2005. *Understanding by Design*. Alexandria, VA: ASCD.

# Chapter 8

# Kindergarten: Who Am I?

---

## PLANNING

### Stage One: Identify Desired Results

**Established goals:**

*National Science Education Content Standard A: Science as Inquiry:*   Ask a question about objects, organisms, and events in the environment.
*National Science Content Standard C: Life Sciences:*   Characteristics of Organisms: Each animal has different structures that serve different functions in growth, survival, and reproduction.

**Essential questions:**

1. What are the defining characteristics of a specific animal?
2. Can one guess an animal when presented with important clues?

**Understandings:**

1. Students understand the salient characteristics of a specific animal.
2. Students understand that clues help them puzzle out an answer to a riddle. What key knowledge and skills will the students acquire?
3. Students use a dictionary and encyclopedia to extract information.
4. Students determine the salient characteristics of a specific animal.
5. Students learn how to put together a riddle that can be solved reasonably and easily by another person.

### Stage Two: Determine Acceptable Evidence

**Performance task:**

- Each student creates a riddle book, *Who Am I?*, that uses salient characteristics of an animal as clues to the animal's identity.

**Student self-assessment and reflection:**

Can other people guess the animal in my book?

### Stage Three:  Plan Learning Experiences

- Read *The Alphabet Tale* by Jan Garten or *It Began with A* by Stephanie Calmenson and brainstorm what made it easy to guess the correct animal.
- Students do research with the help of a third-grade student helper.
- Students choose an animal and look in the dictionary for information.
- Students look up information on the animal in the encyclopedia.
- With assistance, students make the product. Each student makes a *Who Am I?* book using an animal's characteristics as clues to the identity of the animal.
- Students present their books to partners and to the third-grade helpers.

## LESSON 1:  RIDDLES

**Standards:**

*National Science Education Content Standard A: Science as Inquiry:*   Ask a question about objects, organisms, and events in the environment.
*National Science Content Standard C: Life Sciences:*   Characteristics of Organisms: Each animal has different structures that serve different functions in growth, survival, and reproduction.

**Objective:**
Students understand that important clues need to be given to solve a riddle.

**Materials:**

- a model of a *Who Am I?* book. Make the book about a skunk. The template for the book is available on the CD
- *The Alphabet Tale* by Jan Garten (Greenwillow, 1994) or *It Began with an A* by Stephanie Calmenson (Scholastic, 1993) (These books may be hard to find new.)

**Set:** Say, "I have a riddle for you. See if you can figure it out. When you know the answer, raise your hand. Let's see how many clues I need to give until everyone has figured out the answer." (Pause between clues.) "I'm thinking of an animal. It lives in a barn. It's usually pink or white. It has a curly tail. It says, "Oink!"

**Input:** Read one of the books listed in the materials, using the cloze method of pausing for the students to give a choral answer to each riddle. After reading the book, go back over a few of the riddles and the clues, emphasizing what in the clues made it hard or easy to solve the riddle. Review the riddle from the set. Together you and the class make up a riddle for "cow." Show the students a model of the *Who Am I?* book that each will make after doing research with an older student helper.

**Assessment:** Informally observe whether the students can solve the riddles in the book and understand the importance of meaningful clues.

**Closure:** Using think-pair-share, name a barn animal and ask the students to come up with clues.

## LESSON 2: RESEARCHING AN ANIMAL IN THE PRIMARY DICTIONARY

**Standards:**

*National Science Education Content Standard A: Science as Inquiry:* Ask a question about objects, organisms, and events in the environment.

*National Science Content Standard C: Life Sciences:* Characteristics of Organisms: Each animal has different structures that serve different functions in growth, survival, and reproduction.

*AASL #2:* Draw conclusions, make informed decisions, apply knowledge to new situations, and create new knowledge. 2.1, Skills: 2.1.1, Continue an inquiry-based research process by applying critical-thinking skills (analysis, synthesis, evaluation, organization) to information and knowledge in order to construct new understandings, draw conclusions, and create new knowledge; 2.1.4, Use technology and other information tools to analyze and organize information.

**Objectives:**

1. Students choose an animal to research.
2. Students, with assistance, look up the animal in a dictionary and dictate information.

**Materials:**

- a model of a *Who Am I?* book
- 30 primary dictionaries
- 30 laminated index cards with the name of animal and its picture from the dictionary laid out on a flat source (there can be many duplicates, because it doesn't matter how many students do the same animal; the list in the CD was based on Scholastic's *First Dictionary*)
- 30 copies of the work sheet from the CD
- board-ready copy of the work sheet
- a class of third-grade or older students to act as research assistants, who receive training (the input) for 10 minutes before the kindergarten class arrives; parents or volunteers may be substituted for the students

**Set:** Show the model *Who Am I?* book based on a skunk and ask the students to guess the animal.

**Review:** Dictionaries are reference books that give definitions of words and are arranged in alphabetical order.

**Input:** Show an index card with the picture and word "skunk." Ask a student helper to look up the word in the dictionary. The student helper should find the word and show the entry to you. The student helper reads the definition, then asks you to tell him or her the important information, assisting as necessary. For example, "What two colors was the skunk? What kind of tail? When it's in danger, what does it do?" Answer the questions. The student helper will take notes on the board-ready work sheet.

**Guided practice:** Each student picks an animal from the table. The student helpers get a primary dictionary and work one-on-one with the kindergarteners. The student helper asks the kindergarten student what letter the animal starts with. The student helper then follows the example of the input and fills out as much of the work sheet as there are answers. *Note:* Some of the information will be collected during the second lesson using the encyclopedia.

**Assessment:** Informally assess whether the kindergarten students are able to repeat the important information.

**Closure:** The student helpers at each table read the information gleaned so far. A few of them present to the entire class while you point out how the information was gathered.

*Note: Have the students hand all work sheets in, as they will be needed in another lesson.*

## LESSON 3: GATHERING INFORMATION FROM AN ENCYCLOPEDIA

**Standards:**

*National Science Education Content Standard A: Science as Inquiry:*  Ask a question about objects, organisms, and events in the environment.
*National Science Content Standard C: Life Sciences:*  Characteristics of Organisms: Each animal has different structures that serve different functions in growth, survival, and reproduction.
*AASL #2:*  Draw conclusions, make informed decisions, apply knowledge to new situations, and create new knowledge. 2.1, Skills: 2.1.1, Continue an inquiry-based research process by applying critical-thinking skills (analysis, synthesis, evaluation, organization) to information and knowledge in order to construct new understandings, draw conclusions, and create new knowledge; 2.1.4, Use technology and other information tools to analyze and organize information.

**Objective:**
Kindergarten students repeat important information on a specific animal that a student helper locates in an encyclopedia.

**Materials:**

- two sets of *The World Book Encyclopedia* or sets of animal encyclopedias
- 30 copies of the work sheet available from the CD
- board-ready copy of the work sheet
- a class of third-grade or older students to act as research assistants, who will receive training (the input) for 10 minutes before the kindergarten class arrives; parents or volunteers may be substituted for the students
- a model of a *Who Am I?* book

**Set:** Show the model of a *Who Am I?* book and tell the students they are gathering information for a similar book.

**Review:** Encyclopedias have information about people, places, and things and are arranged in alphabetical order.

**Input:** Project the board-ready encyclopedia work sheet. Ask a student helper to look up "skunk" in the encyclopedia. The student helper asks what letter the name of the animal begins with, finds the entry, and shows the entry to you. The student helper silently reads the first and second paragraph and facts in brief. The student helper consults the work sheet to see what information is still needed. The student helper reads the pertinent information to you, posing questions as necessary. "What does the skunk eat? What is the most outstanding fact about the skunk?" Answer the questions as the student helper finishes the sentences on the work sheet.

**Guided practice:** Distribute the work sheets. The student helpers work one-on-one with the kindergarteners. The student helpers follow the example of the input and fill out the work sheet as the kindergarteners give the answers.

**Assessment:** Informally assess whether the kindergarten students are able to repeat the important information.

**Closure:** The student helpers at each table read the information gleaned so far. A few of them present to the entire class while you point out how the information was gathered.

## LESSON 4: MAKING THE BOOK

**Standards:**

*National Science Education Content Standard A: Science as Inquiry:* Ask a question about objects, organisms, and events in the environment.

*National Science Content Standard C: Life Sciences:* Characteristics of Organisms: Each animal has different structures that serve different functions in growth, survival, and reproduction.

*AASL #2:* Draw conclusions, make informed decisions, apply knowledge to new situations, and create new knowledge. 2.1, Skills: 2.1.1, Continue an inquiry-based research process by applying critical-thinking skills (analysis, synthesis, evaluation, organization) to information and knowledge in order to construct new understandings, draw conclusions, and create new knowledge; 2.1.4, Use technology and other information tools to analyze and organize information.

**Objectives:**

1.  Students identify which information goes with each clue.
2.  Students illustrate their individual *Who Am I?* books.

**Materials:**

*   30 blank books made of six pieces of $8\frac{1}{2}'' \times 11''$ copy paper. Each book is stapled on the left side of the paper.
*   30 blank rectangles $3'' \times 5''$ for the last page of the book
*   pencils and boxes of crayons placed on the tables

- a class of third-grade or older students to act as research assistants, who receive training (the input) for 10 minutes before the kindergarten class arrives; parents or volunteers may be substituted for the students
- board-ready copy of the work sheet
- a model of a *Who Am I?* book

**Set:** Show a model of a *Who Am I?* book and tell the students that today they are making and illustrating their own *Who Am I?* book.

**Review:** The information for the *Who Am I?* book came from the dictionary and the encyclopedia.

**Input:** Use the board-ready work sheet to model how to figure out the clues to write on each page. First, write the name of the book (*Who Am I?*) and your name as the author on the cover. Model how to find the information and write it on each page. After the writing is complete, draw the illustrations to match each page. Tape a blank piece of paper over the name of the animal on the last page of the book.

**Guided practice:** Distribute the blank books and work sheets along with the work sheets from the prior lessons. The student helpers work one-on-one with the kindergarteners. The student helper reads what goes on each page and writes it, unless the kindergartner can do the writing. The student helper also rereads the clues and makes sure that the kindergartners illustrate each clue. The kindergartener tapes the blank piece of paper over the name of the animal on the last page of the book. After the books are completed, the kindergarteners are paired, with their student helpers accompanying them. The kindergarteners or the student helpers read the books, with the other pair guessing the animal.

**Assessment:** Informally assess whether the kindergarten students are able to create the specific clues and illustrate them.

**Closure:** Using think-pair-share, the students evaluate whether the clues were sufficient for others to guess the animal.

*Note: The books can also be presented to another class or to parents.*

# Chapter 9

# First Grade:  Animal Defenses

## PLANNING

### Stage 1:  Identify Desired Results

**Established goals:**

*National Science Education Content Standard A: Science as Inquiry:*    Communicate investigations and explanations.
*National Science Content Standard C: Life Sciences:*    Characteristics of Organisms: Each animal has different structures that serve different functions in growth, survival, and reproduction.

**Essential questions:**

1.    Why do animals need protection?
2.    How do animals defend themselves?

**Understandings:**

1.    Students understand the varied defenses animals use against their enemies.
2.    Students understand that some animals are predators and some animals are prey.

**What key knowledge and skills will the students acquire?**

1.    Students use a dictionary to define the key vocabulary: camouflage, predator, prey, chemical, armor, mimicry, defense, speed, quills, claws, talons, horns, and fangs.
2.    Students use an encyclopedia, the Internet, and nonfiction books to research animals and their defenses.
3.    By creating and playing an animal defense card game, students match the defense with the animal.

### Stage 2:  Determine Acceptable Evidence

**Performance tasks:**

1.    Students make a picture dictionary of the key vocabulary words.

2. Students make cards that show the defenses of specific animals.
3. Students successfully play the defense game to demonstrate understanding of specific animals and their defenses.

**Student self-assessment and reflection:**

Summative assessment: Students assess their final product. Students use the following rubric to assess their performance task:

### Rubric for Animal Defenses Dictionary

| Category | 4 Great | 3 Very Good | 2 Okay | 1 Needs More Work |
|---|---|---|---|---|
| Is it easy to understand? | Each entry has a clear meaning. | Almost all the entries have clear meanings. | Most entries have clear meanings. | Less than half of the entries have clear meanings. |
| Are the facts correct? | All facts in the dictionary are correct. | Almost all facts in the dictionary are correct. | Most facts in the dictionary are correct. | Less than half of the facts in the dictionary are correct. |
| Does everyone understand the information? | All students in the group can correctly answer questions related to the dictionary. | Almost all of students in the group can correctly answer questions related to the dictionary. | Most students in the group can correctly answer questions related to the dictionary. | Less than half of students in the group can correctly answer questions related to the dictionary. |
| Grammar | There are no mistakes in spelling or the use of uppercase and lowercase letters. | There are no mistakes in spelling or the use of uppercase and lowercase letters after it was checked by an adult. | There are a few mistakes in spelling or the use of uppercase and lowercase letters after it was checked by an adult. | There are quite a few mistakes in spelling or the use of uppercase and lowercase letters after it was checked by an adult. |

## Stage 3: Plan Learning Experiences

- Read a book and the students brainstorm why and how animals protect themselves. Introduce the performance tasks and rubric of the unit.
- Students use a dictionary to research key vocabulary.
- Each group is assigned a defense and several animals to research in the encyclopedia, nonfiction books, and the Internet.
- Students create a dictionary of animal defense vocabulary.
- Each group makes five sets of cards, writing the name of an animal on one side and means of defense on the other side.
- Using the cooperative learning jigsaw strategy, students share information with the rest of the class.
- Students play the animal defense game several times.
- Students evaluate the picture dictionary according to the rubric.

## LESSON 1: BRAINSTORMING ANIMAL DEFENSES

**Standards:**

*National Science Education Content Standard A: Science as Inquiry:* Communicate investigations and explanations.
*National Science Content Standard C: Life Sciences:* Characteristics of Organisms: Each animal has different structures that serve different functions in growth, survival, and reproduction.

**Objective:**
Students understand the different ways animals defend themselves.

**Materials:**

- chart or empty board-ready paper
- visuals of a lion and antelopes
- one of the following books:
    Dahl, Michael. 2004. *Do Salamanders Spit? A Book about How Animals Protect Themselves* (Animals All Around). Minneapolis, MN: Picture Window Books. 24 pp.
    Dell, Pamela. 2007. *Why Do Tigers Have Stripes? A Book about Camouflage.* Mankato, MN: Capstone. 24 pp.
    Kaner, Etta. 1997. *How Animals Defend Themselves.* Toronto: Kids Can Press. 40 pp.
    O'Sullivan, Robyn. 2006. *Science Chapters: Weedy Sea Dragons, Spitting Cobras, and Other Wild and Amazing Animals (Science Chapters).* Washington, DC: National Geographic. 40 pp.
    Stockland, Patricia. 2005. *Red Eyes or Blue Feathers: A Book about Animal Colors.* Minneapolis, MN: Picture Window Books. 24 pp.

**Set:** Using think-pair-share, ask, "Let's make believe that I am a lion and you are antelopes. I'm lying in the grass, watching you, just waiting for my chance to pounce on one of you for dinner. What would be the best thing to do to save yourself?" Give the answer (run away) if no one guesses it.

**Input:** Read one of the books cited in the materials list. *Do Salamanders Spit: A Book about How Animals Protect Themselves* (Animals All Around) is the recommended title. Using think-pair-share, ask the students to think of defenses that animals use in the book. Write these on the chart or board. If the students do not come up with all of them, suggests scenarios to elicit them, such as "How does a rattlesnake defend itself?" (poison). The defense categories are: camouflage, flight, armor, hiding, mimicry, fighting with weapons (claws, talons, fangs, horns, and quills), chemical defense, and playing dead. Giving up a body part will be the defense to use for modeling. Explain the unit, performance tasks, and rubric.

**Assessment:** Informally observe whether the students are able to understand the concept of defenses.

**Closure:** Using think-pair-share, ask the students:

- What does defense mean?
- What are some examples of animal defenses?

## LESSON 2: USING THE DICTIONARY TO UNDERSTAND THE VOCABULARY OF ANIMAL DEFENSES

**Standards:**

*National Science Education Content Standard A: Science as Inquiry:* Communicate investigations and explanations.

*National Science Content Standard C: Life Sciences:* Characteristics of Organisms: Each animal has different structures that serve different functions in growth, survival, and reproduction.

*AASL #2:* Draw conclusions, make informed decisions, apply knowledge to new situations, and create new knowledge. 2.1, Skills: 2.1.1, Continue an inquiry-based research process by applying critical-thinking skills (analysis, synthesis, evaluation, organization) to information and knowledge in order to construct new understandings, draw conclusions, and create new knowledge; 2.1.4, Use technology and other information tools to analyze and organize information; 2.1.5, Collaborate with others to exchange ideas, develop new understandings, make decisions, and solve problems.

*NCTE #8:* Students use a variety of technological and information resources to gather and synthesize information and to create and communicate knowledge.

**Objective:**
Students research and explain a term of animal defense.

**Materials:**

- chart with the students' ideas on animal defenses from the previous lesson
- visual of a bird and a small lizard, such as a gecko
- 30 elementary dictionaries
- copies of the paper strips from the CD, at least two students per strip
- board-ready copy of input paper strip in the CD
- a class of fourth-grade or older students to act as research assistants, who receive training (the input) for 10 minutes before the first-grade class arrives; parents or volunteers may be substituted for the students

**Set:** Using think-pair-share, ask, "Let's make believe that I am a bird who needs to feed her hungry babies. You are geckos. What would be the best way to defend yourself from me, the bird?" Give the answer—giving up a body part, the tail—if no one guesses it. The tail will flop about and distract the bird from the fleeing gecko.

**Review:** Review the meaning of the words "defense" and "defend" as well as the chart listing the defenses the students brainstormed at the previous lesson.

**Input:** Project the board-ready copy of the paper strip and choose a student helper. Say the word "camouflage." Model, thinking aloud, how to look up a word in the dictionary (beginning letter, next letter, etc.). With the student helper, find the word. Have the student helper read the definition aloud. Put the definition in your own words, with input from the student helper. The student helper writes the paraphrased definition in the space on the paper strip. With the students, read the definition chorally.

**Guided practice:** Each first-grade student is paired with a student helper. Give each pair an elementary dictionary and a paper strip. Each word should be given to at least two students to look up. After the students find the word in the dictionary and read the entry, they write the paraphrased definition on the paper strip. After the research is complete, break the class into two large groups. Call a word and place the two students who had that word in separate locations in the library. This process continues until all the words have been called and two large groups have been formed. Go to each group and select a student to start explaining his or her word to the rest of the group.

**Assessment:** Informally observe whether the students are able to find the word in the dictionary and write it in their own words. If a formal assessment is desired, the work sheets may be assessed.

**Closure:** Using think-pair-share, ask the students how they found the word in the dictionary.

## LESSON 3:　RESEARCHING A SPECIFIC ANIMAL'S DEFENSE IN THE ENCYCLOPEDIA

**Standards:**

*National Science Education Content Standard A: Science as Inquiry:*　Communicate investigations and explanations.
*National Science Content Standard C: Life Sciences:*　Characteristics of Organisms: Each animal has different structures that serve different functions in growth, survival, and reproduction.
*AASL #2:*　Draw conclusions, make informed decisions, apply knowledge to new situations, and create new knowledge. 2.1, Skills: 2.1.1, Continue an inquiry-based research process by applying critical-thinking skills (analysis, synthesis, evaluation, organization) to information and knowledge in order to construct new understandings, draw conclusions, and create new knowledge; 2.1.4, Use technology and other information tools to analyze and organize information; 2.1.5, Collaborate with others to exchange ideas, develop new understandings, make decisions, and solve problems.
*NCTE #8:*　Students use a variety of technological and information resources to gather and synthesize information and to create and communicate knowledge.

**Objective:**
Students research the defense of an animal using the encyclopedia.

**Materials:**

- chart with the students' ideas on animal defenses from the first lesson
- two sets of encyclopedias with articles on specific animals bookmarked
- visuals of a fox and a turtle
- visual of a glass lizard
- board-ready copy of the work sheet in the CD
- 30 paper strips with an animal and its defense circled for the student (from the CD)
- eight group folders with the name of the animal defense on the cover
- a class of fourth-grade or older students to act as research assistants who receive training (the input) for 10 minutes before the first-grade class arrives; parents or volunteers may be substituted for the students

**Set:** Using think-pair-share, ask, "Let's make believe that I am a fox and you are turtles. What would be the best way to defend yourself?" Give the answer—pull into your shell (the armor defense)—if no one guesses it.

**Review:** Review the meaning of the words "defense" and "defend" as well as the chart listing the defenses the students brainstormed at a previous lesson.

**Input:** Choose the defense of "giving up a body part," and tell the class you are going to find information on an animal that uses that defense. Tell them that the glass lizard uses this type of defense. Model how to look up an animal in the encyclopedia: deciding on the first letter, getting that book, looking for the bookmark, finding the article, and asking for help in reading if it's too hard. Find the "G" encyclopedia. The student helper locates the bookmarked page for "glass lizard" and skims the article, looking for the information on the animal's defense. She or he reads that part of the article aloud. Repeat the information in your own words: "The defense the glass lizard uses is losing a body part. Its tail breaks off when a predator attacks. Later, the glass lizard grows another tail." Direct the student helper to write his or her notes in the appropriate place on the work sheet. With the students, chorally read the notes.

**Guided practice:** The students work in the groups of three or four, with each group assigned a type of animal defense. Distribute the group folders, the work sheets, and the paper strips with the animals to be researched. Each student within the group is given a paper strip with an animal circled that uses their assigned defense. The students fill out the letter on the work sheet for what encyclopedia they will use. Table by table, send the student helpers to get the encyclopedia volumes. The student helpers find the article on the assigned animal. They skim it, looking for the information on the animal's defense. The student helper reads, in a whisper, the pertinent part of the article. The first-grader restates the information in his or her words. The student helpers write the words on the work sheet. The students at each table share their information with each other, noting the similarities and differences. The work sheets and paper strips are put into the group folders. Collect the folders.

**Assessment:** Informally observe whether the students are able to find the information and write it in their own words. If a formal assessment is desired, the work sheets should be assessed.

**Closure:** Using think-pair-share, ask the students how they located the animal in the encyclopedia.

*Note: Make sure the students have put their names on their work sheets when you collect them.*

## LESSON 4: USING NONFICTION BOOKS TO FIND FURTHER INFORMATION

**Standards:**

*National Science Education Content Standard A: Science as Inquiry:* Communicate investigations and explanations.

*National Science Content Standard C: Life Sciences:* Characteristics of Organisms: Each animal has different structures that serve different functions in growth, survival, and reproduction.

*AASL #2:* Draw conclusions, make informed decisions, apply knowledge to new situations, and create new knowledge. 2.1, Skills: 2.1.1, Continue an inquiry-based research process by applying critical-thinking skills (analysis, synthesis, evaluation, organization) to information and knowledge in order to construct new understandings, draw conclusions, and create new knowledge; 2.1.4, Use technology and other information tools to analyze and organize information; 2.1.5, Collaborate with others to exchange ideas, develop new understandings, make decisions, and solve problems.

*NCTE #8:* Students use a variety of technological and information resources to gather and synthesize information and to create and communicate knowledge.

**Objectives:**

1. Students use nonfiction books to find out more information about their assigned animal and its defense.
2. Students teach that information to the other students at their table.

**Materials:**

- easy nonfiction books on the animals the students researched
- 30 work sheets available from the CD
- board-ready copy of the work sheet
- visual of a glass lizard
- eight group folders
- a class of fourth-grade or older students to act as research assistants, who receive training (the input) for 10 minutes before the first-grade class arrives; parents or volunteers may be substituted for the students

**Set:** Using think-pair-share, say, "I used the encyclopedia to look up information about what kind of defense a glass lizard used. Now I'm curious about glass lizards and want to learn more. Where can I look for more information about glass lizards?"

**Review:** Review the meaning of the words "defense" and "defend" as well as the chart listing the defenses the students brainstormed at the first lesson.

**Input:** Explain that the library has many resources. One of them is nonfiction books. Show the students where the animal books are on the shelves, in the 590s. Tell the students that you have pulled books for them on the animals they studied and they are going to look for some interesting facts about the animal assigned. Model this using a primary nonfiction book about lizards. Look at the pictures and read some of the captions and a few sentences to find some interesting facts. Elicit help from the students in reiterating some of the facts. Write these in your own words on the work sheet, modeling at least two sentences. Write the title of the book where the information was found.

**Guided practice:** The students get into their assigned groups with their student helpers. Distribute the group folders and the work sheets. By tables, the students with their student helpers go to the display table and find a book on the animal they have been researching. They go back to their group, look at the pictures, read a bit, and write one or two facts about the animal on the work sheet. They write the name of the book where the information was found. In the meantime, circulate around the room, offering assistance when necessary.

**Assessment:** Informally observe whether the students are able to find the information and write it in their own words. If a formal assessment is desired, the work sheets may be collected.

**Closure:** Students teach the others members of their group the new information they have acquired on the animal.

## LESSON 5:  FINDING FURTHER INFORMATION ON THE INTERNET

**Standards:**

*National Science Education Content Standard A: Science as Inquiry:*    Communicate investigations and explanations.

*National Science Content Standard C: Life Sciences:*    Characteristics of Organisms: Each animal has different structures that serve different functions in growth, survival, and reproduction.

*AASL #2:*    Draw conclusions, make informed decisions, apply knowledge to new situations, and create new knowledge. 2.1, Skills: 2.1.1, Continue an inquiry-based research process by applying critical-thinking skills (analysis, synthesis, evaluation, organization) to information and knowledge in order to construct new understandings, draw conclusions, and create new knowledge; 2.1.4, Use technology and other information tools to analyze and organize information; 2.1.5, Collaborate with others to exchange ideas, develop new understandings, make decisions, and solve problems.

*NCTE #8:*    Students use a variety of technological and information resources (e.g., libraries, databases, computer networks, video) to gather and synthesize information and to create and communicate knowledge.

*NETS Technology #3: Research and Information Fluency:*    Students apply digital tools to gather, evaluate, and use information.

**Objective:**
Students assist in reading and gathering interesting facts about their animals using the Internet.

**Materials:**

- projection of an Internet computer screen (must have accesses to computer, Internet, and means of projection)
- personalized start page or bookmarked Internet sites available from the CD
- 30 copies of the "letter to parents" with the Web sites, available on the CD
- visual of a glass lizard

**Set:** Say, "So far we've looked for information in the dictionary, the encyclopedia, and nonfiction books. Where else could we find information about the animals?"

**Review:** Review the meaning of the words "defense" and "defend" as well as the chart listing the defenses the students brainstormed at the first lesson.

**Input:** Explain that the library has many resources. One of them is the Internet. Show the students a Web page on glass lizards, www.dnr.state.wi.us/org/caer/ce/eek/critter/reptile/glasslizard.htm. Tell the students that you have bookmarked sites on the animals they studied and they are going to look for some interesting facts about the animal assigned. Model this by using the Web site to find information about glass lizards. Look at the pictures and choose one to print. Read captions and a few sentences to find some interesting facts. Elicit help from the students in reiterating some of the facts. Repeat this for as many of the animals as there is time for.

**Assessment:** Informally assess whether the students can restate the information presented by the Web sites.

**Closure:** Distribute to the students the letter to the parents with the Web sites and encourage the students to visit the sites at home with their parents.

*Note: This lesson may take several sessions to complete because each animal that the students are researching needs to have a picture printed and information found.*

## LESSON 6: MAKING THE ANIMAL DEFENSES DICTIONARY

**Standards:**

*National Science Education Content Standard A: Science as Inquiry:* Communicate investigations and explanations.

*National Science Content Standard C: Life Sciences:* Characteristics of Organisms: Each animal has different structures that serve different functions in growth, survival, and reproduction.

*AASL #2:* Draw conclusions, make informed decisions, apply knowledge to new situations, and create new knowledge. 2.1, Skills: 2.1.1, Continue an inquiry-based research process by applying critical-thinking skills (analysis, synthesis, evaluation, organization) to information and knowledge in order to construct new understandings, draw conclusions, and create new knowledge; 2.1.4, Use technology and other information tools to analyze and organize information; 2.1.5, Collaborate with others to exchange ideas, develop new understandings, make decisions, and solve problems.

*NCTE #8:* Students use a variety of technological and information resources to gather and synthesize information and to create and communicate knowledge.

**Objective:**

Students will use their research to make a class dictionary of animal defenses.

**Materials:**

- chart with the students' ideas on animal defenses from the first lesson
- students' work sheets from lessons 3 through 5
- board-ready work sheet
- one copy of work sheet per group from the CD
- eight group folders
- a class of fourth-grade or older students to act as research assistants, who receive training (the input) for 10 minutes before the first-grade class arrives; parents or volunteers may be substituted for the students

**Set:** State that the students are going to make an animal defenses dictionary. Using think-pair-share, ask in what order the information should be put.

**Review:** Review the meaning of the words "defense" and "defend" as well as the chart listing the defenses the students brainstormed at the previous lesson.

**Input:** Model the making of a page of the animal defenses dictionary. Write "losing a body part" on the part of the work sheet that says "defense." Model writing the explanation of the defense in the correct place on the work sheet. Remind the students that an example of an animal using that defense is the glass lizard. Write that under "example."

**Guided practice:** The students get into their assigned groups with their student helpers. Distribute the group folders with the work sheets from lessons 3 through 5. The students in the groups are numbered 1, 2, 3, and 4, if necessary. Assign the jobs to students according to number. The jobs are recorder, explainer, example finder, and presenter. The students complete one dictionary work sheet per group. Circulate around the room, offering assistance when necessary. After the pages are completed, ask the students to look at the first word of the animal defense and circle that letter. As you say a letter of the alphabet, the group whose animal defense starts with that word raises their hands. Collect that page. This is repeated until all the defenses are in alphabetical order.

**Assessment:** Informally observe whether the students are able to find the information and write it in their own words.

**Closure:** Using think-pair-share, ask the students how they organized their dictionary.

*Note: Input the dictionary into a computer, with one defense on each page. The animal defenses dictionary is printed and assembled into individual books for the students to use in the next lesson and to take home and share with their parents.*

## LESSON 7: READING AND RATING THE ANIMAL DEFENSES DICTIONARY

**Standards:**

*AASL #3:* Share knowledge and participate ethically and productively as members of our democratic society. 3.1, Skills: 3.1.1, Conclude an inquiry-based research process by sharing new understandings and reflecting on the learning; 3.1.3, Use writing and speaking skills to communicate new understandings effectively.

**Objectives:**

1.  Students read their dictionary of animal defenses.
2.  Students rate their dictionary based on a rubric.

**Materials:**

- 30 copies of typed animal defenses dictionary
- board-ready copy of the rubric, available from the CD
- 30 copies of the rubric

**Set:** Using think-pair-share, ask, "How can we tell what kind of job we did in making our dictionary of animal defenses?"

**Review:** Review where and how the students looked up the information they put in the animal defenses dictionary.

**Input:** Distribute the copies of the class's animal defense dictionary. After giving the students several minutes to peruse the dictionary, lead the students in choral reading of the dictionary. If the students' skill level does not permit this, use "echo" reading: read a sentence and then have the students read it after you. Put the rubric for the dictionary on the board, distribute copies to the students, and explain it. Take one category of the rubric and apply it to the dictionary, deciding how they did on that category. Circle the rating the class has decided on. This procedure is repeated for all categories of the dictionary rubric.

**Assessment:** Informally observe whether the students are able to assess the animal defenses dictionary using the rubric.

**Closure:** Lead the students through a summary of their evaluation.

## LESSON 8: MAKING CARDS FOR THE ANIMAL DEFENSES GAME

**Standards:**

*National Science Education Content Standard A: Science as Inquiry:* Communicate investigations and explanations.

*National Science Content Standard C: Life Sciences:* Characteristics of Organisms: Each animal has different structures that serve different functions in growth, survival, and reproduction.

*AASL #2:* Draw conclusions, make informed decisions, apply knowledge to new situations, and create new knowledge. 2.1, Skills: 2.1.1, Continue an inquiry-based research process by applying critical-thinking skills (analysis, synthesis, evaluation, organization) to information and knowledge in order to construct new understandings, draw conclusions, and create new knowledge; 2.1.4, Use technology and other information tools to analyze and organize information; 2.1.5, Collaborate with others to exchange ideas, develop new understandings, make decisions, and solve problems.

**Objective:**
Students create cards that show an animal and its defense.

**Materials:**

- work sheets on the research the students did in lessons 3 to 5
- board-ready work sheet on the glass lizard that you have filled out
- board-ready copy of a model of the card for the animal defenses game
- five copies of each animal picture, which was printed from a Web site in lesson 5
- white, unlined index cards on each table, enough so that each child has five
- glue sticks and black markers on each table
- eight group folders
- a class of fourth-grade or older students to act as research assistants, who receive training (the input) for 10 minutes before the first-grade class arrives; parents or volunteers may be substituted for the students

**Set:** Using think-pair-share, ask, "What games have you played?"

**Review:** Review the meaning of the words "defense" and "defend" as well as the chart listing the defenses the students brainstormed at the first lesson.

**Input:** Show the students their board-ready work sheets from the encyclopedia and nonfiction lessons and the picture from the Internet lesson. State that the students will be making cards based on that information. The cards will be used to play a game. Read the name of the animal, glass lizard, and the defense it uses, losing a body part. Project the board-ready blank card, write "glass lizard" on one side, and attach its picture under its name. Write "losing a body part" on the other side of the card.

**Guided practice:** The students get into their assigned groups with their student helpers. Distribute the group folders, which have five pictures of each animal and five index cards for each student. The work sheets from the research lessons are distributed to each student. The students and their helper use the information on the work sheet to write the name of their assigned animal on one side of the card and attach its picture, and then the name of its defense on the other side of the card. All five cards should be identical so there will be five copies of the game. After the cards are finished, students make five sets of cards at their table, with each set having one each of the animals. Students of each of the eight groups are numbered 1, 2, 3, and 4. All of the ones go to a table, bringing a set of the cards; all the 2s go to a table, bringing a set of the cards, and so on. There should be three to four new groups formed according to how many students are in the class. Each student in the new group shows their animal cards for their defense and teaches the names of the animals to the rest of the group. The activity is repeated, but this time each student shows the animal side of the card and asks which defense that animal uses.

**Assessment:** Informally observe whether the students are able to make the cards and teach the information to other students.

**Closure:** Ask the students to chorally respond to the question, "Do you think you now know all of the defenses and some examples of the animals that use that defense?"

*Note: Collect the cards from each of the teaching groups and the extra set left on the table to make five sets, each containing one card on an animal. These may be further divided into 10 sets if you want the groups playing the game to be smaller.*

## LESSON 9: PLAYING THE ANIMAL DEFENSES GAME

**Standards:**

*National Science Education Content Standard A: Science as Inquiry:* Communicate investigations and explanations.
*National Science Content Standard C: Life Sciences:* Characteristics of Organisms: Each animal has different structures that serve different functions in growth, survival, and reproduction.

**Objective:**
Students demonstrate an understanding of specific animals and their defenses.

**Materials:**

- five or ten sets of animal cards from the previous lesson

**Set:** Ask, "How many of you think you can name the defenses of at least five of the animals we've covered?"

**Review:** Review the meaning of the words "defense" and "defend" as well as the chart listing the defenses the students brainstormed at the first lesson.

**Input:** Choose four students to model the game with you. The jobs are dealer, recorder, and shuffler. The dealer gives each of the five players an equal number of cards onto the table top, with the defense side *not* showing. If the number is not equal, some cards are not used. The person to the right of the dealer is first.

Say the animal, and then guess the defense. The card is turned over to see the answer. If the student has answered correctly, the recorder puts a point, a tally mark, next to that person's name. If the student is incorrect, no point is given. The play continues clockwise until all the cards have been used. The student with the most points wins that round. The shuffler collects and shuffles all the cards and hands them to the dealer. Tell the students that the game continues for as many rounds as there is time.

**Guided practice:** Students are divided into five or ten groups, depending on the size of the class, number of sets of cards, and your inclination. Each student in the group counts out a number. Tell the students which number is the dealer, which is the recorder, and which is the shuffler. The students play the game for as many rounds as time permits while you circulate. Collect the card games. Lead the class to make conclusions based on their research. Do this by using think-pair-share and asking key questions and concluding questions.

Examples of key questions:

- Why do animals need protection?
- How do animals defend themselves?
- Can you name some predators?
- Can you name some animals that are prey for other animals?

Examples of concluding questions:

- Why do you think there are more antelopes than lions on the African plains?
- What would happen if all the animals' defenses worked all the time?
- As an animal gets older, do you think the animal has a better or worse chance of escaping from predators or catching prey?

**Assessment:** Informally observe whether the students are able to answer the key and concluding questions.

**Closure:** Using think-pair-share, ask the students to identify their favorite part of the unit.

*Note: The animal defenses card game can be played in the classroom as time and opportunity permit.*

# Chapter 10

# Second Grade: Shelter

## PLANNING

### Stage 1: Identify Desired Results

**Established goal:**

*National Council for the Social Studies Standard III: People, Places, and Environments G:* Describe how people create places that reflect ideas, personality, culture, and wants and needs as they design homes.

**Essential questions:**

1. Why do people make shelters?
2. What types of shelter do people use?
3. What are the factors that determine the type of shelter?

**Understandings:**

1. Shelters are made to guard against bad weather, danger, and pests.
2. Climate, building methods, and building materials make shelters different.
3. Students are able to show and tell the difference among structures that meet specific environmental needs.
4. Today people build structures in cities that control environment, building materials, and methods through technological advances. In cities worldwide, peoples' shelters are more the same than different.

**What key knowledge and skills will the students acquire?**

1. Students identify the different structures and materials used in early American shelters.
2. Students use dictionaries, encyclopedias, atlases, nonfiction books, and the Internet to extract information.
3. Students understand and use the key vocabulary: shelter, climate, adobe, pueblo, dugout, wigwam, tepee, log, cabin, sod, house, longhouse, hogan, igloo, plank house, and wickiup.

## Stage 2: Determine Acceptable Evidence

**Performance tasks:**

1. Students locate on a map the area where an assigned shelter was built.
2. Students create a model of their assigned shelter.
3. Students make a presentation to another class by setting up a museum exhibit and acting as guides.

**Student self-assessment and reflection:**

Summative assessment: Students assess their final product. Students use the following rubric to assess their performance task:

### Rubric for Model of Historic Shelters

| Category | 4 Great | 3 Very Good | 2 Okay | 1 Needs More Work |
|---|---|---|---|---|
| Function | Structure functions extraordinarily well, holding up under atypical stresses. | Structure functions well, holding up under typical stresses. | Structure functions pretty well, but deteriorates under typical stresses. | Fatal flaws in function with complete failure under typical stresses. |
| Information gathering | Accurate information taken from several sources in a systematic manner. | Accurate information taken from a couple of sources in a systematic manner. | Accurate information taken from a couple of sources but not systematically. | Information taken from only one source and/or information not accurate. |
| Construction: materials | Appropriate materials were selected and creatively modified in ways that made them even better. | Appropriate materials were selected and there was an attempt at creative modification to make them even better. | Appropriate materials were selected. | Inappropriate materials were selected and contributed to a product that performed poorly. |
| Construction: care taken | Great care taken in construction process so that the structure is neat, attractive, and follows plans accurately. | Construction was careful and accurate for the most part, but one or two details could have been refined for a more attractive product. | Construction accurately followed the plans, but three or four details could have been refined for amore attractive product. | Construction appears careless or haphazard. Many details need refinement for a strong or attractive product. |

## Stage 3: Plan Learning Experiences

- Read a book about a shelter and brainstorm why people need shelters and how they decided on the building materials they used in the past and today.
- Discuss the unit, performance tasks, and rubric.
- Using a dictionary, the students look up the key vocabulary of shelters.
- Groups are formed to study a specific shelter: adobe pueblo, dugout, wigwam, tipi (tepee), log cabin, sod house, longhouse, hogan, igloo, plank house, and wickiup. Model the input with the chickee shelter of the Seminole Indians.
- Students research their assigned shelter using the encyclopedia, nonfiction books, and Web sites.
- Students use outline maps of the United States to locate where their assigned shelter was located.

- Students make models of their assigned shelters (may be done in the art class, the classroom, or at home).
- Students set up and share the information on their model shelter based on a museum format. This could involve other classes, parents, and the community.
- Students evaluate the museum presentation based on the rubric.
- Lead a class discussion using key and concluding questions.

## LESSON 1: BRAINSTORMING

**Standards:**

*National Council for the Social Studies Standard III: People, Places, and Environments G:* Describe how people create places that reflect ideas, personality, culture, and wants and needs as they design homes.

**Objectives:**

1. Students understand that people need shelter because of climate, danger, and pests.
2. Students understand that shelters were different long ago due to climate, building materials, and building methods.
3. Students understand that today people control some of these factors so that houses in many places now look the same.
4. Students understand the performance tasks and rubric required for the unit.

**Materials:**

- chart or empty board-ready paper
- visual of houses in cities worldwide now
- visual of a chickee, an early Seminole house
- photo of the front of your house
- one of the following books:
    Gustafson, Angela. 2003. *Imagine a House: A Journey to Fascinating Houses around the World.* Minneapolis, MN: Out of the Box. 32 pp.
    Hall, Margaret. 2001. *Homes.* Chicago: Heinemann Library. 32 pp.
    Jeunesse, Gallimard. 1995. *House.* New York: Scholastic. Read from "igloo" to "houses on stilts."
    Petty, Kate. 2006. *Homes.* Minnetonka, MN: Two-Can. unpaged.
- board-ready copy of the rubric

**Set:** Show a photo of the front of your house and ask the students, using think-pair-share, how your house is the same as or different from the one they live in. Next, ask what it would be like to live outside all the time with no shelter. (They would not be protected from danger, climate, and pests.)

**Input:** Read one of the books cited in the materials list. Review the type(s) of shelter in the book. Using think-pair-share, ask the students to discuss how these shelters were made and how they protected the people. Write the answers on the chart or board. If the students do not come up with all of them, suggest climate, danger, and pests. Explain the unit, the performance tasks, and the rubric using the board-ready copy.

**Assessment:** Informally observe whether the students are able to understand the concept of shelter.

**Closure:** Using think-pair-share, ask the students from what three things shelters protect us.

## LESSON 2: USING THE DICTIONARY TO UNDERSTAND KEY VOCABULARY OF SHELTERS

**Standards:**

*National Council for the Social Studies Standard III: People, Places, and Environments G:*   Describe how people create places that reflect ideas, personality, culture, and wants and needs as they design homes.
*NCTE #8:*   Students use a variety of technological and information resources to gather and synthesize information and to create and communicate knowledge.
*AASL #2:*   Draw conclusions, make informed decisions, apply knowledge to new situations, and create new knowledge. 2.1, Skills: 2.1.1, Continue an inquiry-based research process by applying critical-thinking skills (analysis, synthesis, evaluation, organization) to information and knowledge in order to construct new understandings, draw conclusions, and create new knowledge; 2.1.4, Use technology and other information tools to analyze and organize information; 2.1.5, Collaborate with others to exchange ideas, develop new understandings, make decisions, and solve problems.

**Objective:**
Students paraphrase the definitions of key vocabulary words.

**Materials:**

* chart with the students' ideas on shelter from the previous lesson
* visual of rain or snow
* 15 elementary dictionaries
* 30 copies of the paper strip from the CD
* board-ready copy of the paper strip on the CD

**Set:** Ask, "What is the weather like today?" Using think-pair-share, ask "How do people where we live protect themselves from weather?"

**Review:** Review the arrangement of the dictionary and the use of guide words.

**Input:** Pair students and give each pair an elementary dictionary. Choose one of the words on the work sheet, "climate," to look up. Model, thinking aloud, how to look up a word in the dictionary (beginning letter, next letter, etc.). With the students, find the word and read the definition aloud. The students put the definition in their own words, with help from you. Write the paraphrased definition in the space on the paper strip. With the students, read the definition chorally.

**Guided practice:** Give each pair of students two paper strips with the same word to look up in the dictionary. After reading the entry, they write their own paraphrased definition on their paper strip. After the research is completed, the pairs split and two groups of 15 students are formed. Each student explains his or her word to the rest of the group.

**Assessment:** Informally observe whether the students are able to find the word in the dictionary, write its definition in their own words, and explain it to others. If a formal assessment is desired, the work sheets can be assessed.

**Closure:** Using think-pair-share, ask the students how they found the word in the dictionary.

## LESSON 3: RESEARCHING A SPECIFIC EARLY AMERICAN SHELTER IN THE ENCYCLOPEDIA

**Standards:**

*National Council for the Social Studies Standard III: People, Places, and Environments G:* Describe how people create places that reflect ideas, personality, culture, and wants and needs as they design homes.
*AASL #2:* Draw conclusions, make informed decisions, apply knowledge to new situations, and create new knowledge. 2.1, Skills: 2.1.1, Continue an inquiry-based research process by applying critical-thinking skills (analysis, synthesis, evaluation, organization) to information and knowledge in order to construct new understandings, draw conclusions, and create new knowledge; 2.1.4, Use technology and other information tools to analyze and organize information; 2.1.5, Collaborate with others to exchange ideas, develop new understandings, make decisions, and solve problems.
*NCTE #8:* Students use a variety of technological and information resources to gather and synthesize information and to create and communicate knowledge.

**Objective:**
Using an encyclopedia, students do research on their assigned early American shelter.

**Materials:**

- chart with the students' ideas on shelters from the previous lesson
- two sets of encyclopedias
- copies of specific pages of the article "Indians, American"
- visual of a chickee, an early Seminole house
- board-ready copy of the work sheet on the CD
- paper strips with the name of the shelter and the encyclopedia entry (may be a specific tribe or under Indian, American)
- 11 folders with the name of the shelter on the cover, a copy of the rubric, and a work sheet for each student in the group
- 11 upper-grade student helpers, parent helpers, or volunteers

**Set:** Using think-pair-share, ask, "If you lived in a place that was marshy and flooded, what kind of special feature would be needed for your shelter?" Give the answer (put it on stilts) if no one guesses it.

**Review:** Review the organization of an encyclopedia and the use of guide words. Also review that encyclopedias have long and short articles and not everything can be looked up by a specific word. It may need to be placed in a topic.

**Input:** Choose "chickees," and tell the class you are going to find information on that shelter. Look in the "Ch" encyclopedia, but it is not there. Ponder aloud under what other subject you could look. Think aloud that the Seminole Indians made chickees; perhaps the information will be in an article about the Native Americans known as the Seminoles. Look under "S" and find the article with the information. Show the pictures and charts, and read the headings and subheadings. Read aloud the pertinent information, paraphrase it, and write it on the work sheet. Also draw a picture of a chickee that matches the one in the encyclopedia. Arrange the students into 11 groups and assign each an early American shelter. Give each group a folder with the name of the shelter on it: adobe pueblo, dugout, wigwam, tipi (tepee), log cabin, sod house, longhouse, hogan, igloo, plank house, and wickiup. The folder should also contain a copy of the rubric, and the work sheets for the encyclopedia. The students write their names and room numbers on the front of the folder and assign themselves numbers 1, 2, and 3, depending on the size of the group.

**Guided practice:** Students work in the groups to complete the encyclopedia research assisted by a helper. Together the group determines the volume of the encyclopedia needed. Student 1 gets the volume, and the group uses the guide words to locate the article. Student 2 shows the pictures and charts, and reads the headings and subheadings. Student helper skims the article to find the information on the correct shelter and reads, in a whisper to the rest of the group, the pertinent information. Student 1 or 3 paraphrases the information, and the other students write it on their work sheets. All students draw a picture of the shelter to match the one in the encyclopedia. Circulate during guided practice to offer assistance as needed. At the end of the guided practice, collect the group folders.

**Assessment:** Informally observe whether the students are able to find the information and write it in their own words. If a formal assessment is desired, the work sheets can be assessed.

**Closure:** Using think-pair-share, ask the students how they located their shelter in the encyclopedia.

## LESSON 4: USING NONFICTION BOOKS TO FIND FURTHER INFORMATION

**Standards:**

*National Council for the Social Studies Standard III: People, Places, and Environments G:*   Describe how people create places that reflect ideas, personality, culture, and wants and needs as they design homes. *AASL #2:*   Draw conclusions, make informed decisions, apply knowledge to new situations, and create new knowledge. 2.1, Skills: 2.1.1, Continue an inquiry-based research process by applying critical-thinking skills (analysis, synthesis, evaluation, organization) to information and knowledge in order to construct new understandings, draw conclusions, and create new knowledge; 2.1.4, Use technology and other information tools to analyze and organize information; 2.1.5, Collaborate with others to exchange ideas, develop new understandings, make decisions, and solve problems. *NCTE #8:*   Students use a variety of technological and information resources to gather and synthesize information and to create and communicate knowledge.

**Objectives:**

1.   Students use nonfiction books to find out more information about their assigned shelter.
2.   Students paraphrase information on their assigned shelter.

**Materials:**

- easy nonfiction books on different shelters and the people who used them
- 11 copies of the work sheet from the CD
- board-ready copy of the work sheet
- 11 shelter group folders
- 11 upper-grade student helpers, parent helpers, or volunteers

**Set:** Using think-pair-share, say, "I used the encyclopedia to look up information about chickees, a shelter that Seminoles used. Now I'm curious about chickees and want to learn more. Where can I look for more information?"

**Review:** Review the meaning of the word "shelter" and what influences what it is and how it is built (climate, building materials, and building methods).

**Input:** Explain that the library has many resources. One of them is nonfiction books. Show the students where the American history and Native American books are on the shelves, in the 970s. Tell the students that you have pulled books for them on the shelters they are studying and that they are going to look for some interesting facts about the shelter and the people who built them. Model this using a primary nonfiction book about the Seminole people. Look at the pictures and read some captions and a few sentences to find some interesting facts about chickees and the Seminoles. Elicit help from the students in reiterating some of the facts. Write these in your own words on the work sheet, modeling at least two sentences. Write the author and title of the book where the information was found.

**Guided practice:** Distribute the group folders and the nonfiction books for each group. The students look at the pictures in the books to preview the information. Student 2 finds the shelter. The helper reads aloud the information about the shelter and the people who built it. All students in the group decide on the interesting facts and paraphrase them. All of the students write the facts on their work sheet. Student 3 finds the author and title of the book where the information was found, and all the students write the information on their work sheet. After the research is done, collect the folders.

**Assessment:** Informally observe whether the students are able to find the information and write it in their own words. If a formal assessment is desired, the work sheets can be collected.

**Closure:** Each group discusses the new facts they found about why and how the shelter was built.

## LESSON 5:  FINDING FURTHER INFORMATION ON THE INTERNET

**Standards:**

*National Council for the Social Studies Standard III: People, Places, and Environments G:*   Describe how people create places that reflect ideas, personality, culture, and wants and needs as they design homes. *AASL #2:*   Draw conclusions, make informed decisions, apply knowledge to new situations, and create new knowledge. 2.1, Skills: 2.1.1, Continue an inquiry-based research process by applying critical-thinking skills (analysis, synthesis, evaluation, organization) to information and knowledge in order to construct new understandings, draw conclusions, and create new knowledge; 2.1.4, Use technology and other information tools to analyze and organize information; 2.1.5, Collaborate with others to exchange ideas, develop new understandings, make decisions, and solve problems.

*NCTE #8:* Students use a variety of technological and information resources (e.g., libraries, databases, computer networks, video) to gather and synthesize information and to create and communicate knowledge.

*NETS Technology #3: Research and Information Fluency:* Students apply digital tools to gather, evaluate, and use information.

**Objective:**

Using the Internet, students assist in reading and gathering interesting facts about their shelters.

**Materials:**

- projection of an Internet computer screen (must have access to computer, Internet, and means of projection)
- personalized start page or bookmarked Internet sites available on the CD
- 30 copies of the Letter to Parents with the Web sites, available on the CD
- visual of a chickee
- 11 shelter group folders
- 11 copies of the work sheet
- board-ready copy of a work sheet

**Set:** Say, "So far we've looked for information in the dictionary, the encyclopedia, and nonfiction books. Where else could we find information about the early American shelters we are researching?"

**Review:** Review that the Internet is a network of interconnected computers around the world and a source of information and images.

**Input:** Explain that the library has many resources. One of them is the Internet. Show the students a Web page for a chickee and the Seminoles: www.aaanativearts.com/article1157.html or http://en.wikipedia. org/wiki/Chickee. Tell the students that you have bookmarked sites for each type of shelter they are researching. Model this by using the Web site to find information about chickees. Look at the pictures and print one. Read captions and a few sentences to find some interesting facts (making sure that the historical location of the shelter has been noted ). Elicit help from the students in reiterating some of the facts. Write these in your own words on the work sheet, modeling two facts. After you have written the facts, put a copy of the work sheet and the picture of the shelter in the appropriate group's folder. Repeat this for each of the 11 shelters.

**Assessment:** Informally assess whether the students can restate the information presented by the Web sites.

**Closure:** Distribute to the students the letter to the parents with the Web sites and encourage the students to visit the sites at home with their parents.

*Note: This lesson may take several sessions to complete.*

# LESSON 6: LOCATING THE BUILDERS OF SHELTERS ON AN OUTLINE MAP

**Standards:**

*National Council for the Social Studies Standard III: People, Places, and Environments G:* Describe how people create places that reflect ideas, personality, culture, and wants and needs as they design homes. . . .
*AASL #2:* Draw conclusions, make informed decisions, apply knowledge to new situations, and create new knowledge. 2.1, Skills: 2.1.1, Continue an inquiry-based research process by applying critical-thinking skills (analysis, synthesis, evaluation, organization) to information and knowledge in order to construct new understandings, draw conclusions, and create new knowledge; 2.1.4, Use technology and other information tools to analyze and organize information; 2.1.5, Collaborate with others to exchange ideas, develop new understandings, make decisions, and solve problems.
*NCTE #8:* Students use a variety of technological and information resources (e.g., libraries, databases, computer networks, video) to gather and synthesize information and to create and communicate knowledge.
*NETS Technology #3: Research and Information Fluency:* Students apply digital tools to gather, evaluate, and use information.

**Objectives:**

1. Students make a map key to show locations of the shelters used in early America.
2. Students locate their assigned shelter on the outline map.

**Materials:**

- 11 outline maps of the United States, with the states shown, available from www.infoplease.com/statemaps.html under U.S. regions, one in each group folder
- board-ready copy of the outline map
- 11 group shelter folders

**Set:** Remind students what a chickee looks like: on stilts, no sides, and a thatched roof. Using think-pair-share, ask, "Why wouldn't this shelter work in a place that snows?"

**Review:** Review how climate influences what types of shelters are built. Also review north, south, east, and west.

**Input:** Project the outline map of the United States. State that the chickees were built by people who lived in the Everglades of southern Florida, where it is marshy, humid, and hot. Ask the students to locate Florida. Ask the students to locate the southern part of Florida. Make up a symbol for the chickee and put it on the map in southern Florida. Also put the symbol in the map key. Distribute the group folders and ask the students to look in their notes and find the location of their shelter and decide on a symbol for their shelter. One group at a time reports to the class the location of their shelter. Student 1 puts the symbol in the correct place on the board-ready outline map and adds that symbol to the map's key. Student 2 does the same on the outline map in the group folder. Students only record their own shelters on the outline map in their folder. Student 3 writes a title for their map, for example: "Historic Sites of the Longhouse of the Iroquois."

**Assessment:** Informally assess whether the students have information on the location, can find it on a map, and understand symbols and map keys.

**Closure:** Using think-pair-share, ask the students to discuss why the housing today looks very much the same across the United States compared to the housing they researched from 200 years ago.

*Note: You will need to read the information about building the model, print out the directions, and collect the materials before the next lesson. The Web sites and resources are available on the CD. The volunteers or student helpers for the next lesson need to be familiarized with the directions and materials. You will need to make a model of a chickee for the following lesson: www.mce.k12tn.net/indians/reports1/seminole.htm#homes.*


## LESSON 7: MAKING MODELS OF THE SHELTERS

**Standards:**

*National Council for the Social Studies Standard III: People, Places, and Environments G:* Describe how people create places that reflect ideas, personality, culture, and wants and needs as they design homes.
*AASL #2:* Draw conclusions, make informed decisions, apply knowledge to new situations, and create new knowledge. 2.1, Skills: 2.1.1, Continue an inquiry-based research process by applying critical-thinking skills (analysis, synthesis, evaluation, organization) to information and knowledge in order to construct new understandings, draw conclusions, and create new knowledge; 2.1.4, Use technology and other information tools to analyze and organize information; 2.1.5, Collaborate with others to exchange ideas, develop new understandings, make decisions, and solve problems.
*NCTE #8:* Students use a variety of technological and information resources (e.g., libraries, databases, computer networks, video) to gather and synthesize information and to create and communicate knowledge.
*NETS Technology #3: Research and Information Fluency:* Students apply digital tools to gather, evaluate, and use information.


**Objectives:**

1. Students follow written directions to make the assigned shelter they have been researching.
2. Students cooperate and share the tasks.


**Materials:**

- printed directions on how to make each model, from Web sites available on the CD
- 11 lids from copy paper boxes
- materials to make each shelter, placed in the carton lids
- 11 shelter group folders
- 11 parents or older students or volunteers who have been oriented on how to make a specific model
- completed model of a chickee

**Set:** State that today each group will make a model of the shelter they have been researching.

**Review:** Review that it is important to read all the directions before beginning, and that each direction needs to be followed exactly.

**Input:** Show the students your completed model of the chickee. Briefly describe how it was made. Distribute the directions for making the model and the materials needed to the correct groups. The helpers read all the directions aloud and then each direction as needed. The students make the model with assistance from their helper. Last, the students design an environment in which to place the shelter according to their research.

**Assessment:** Informally assess whether the students cooperate, are able to follow the directions to make the shelter, and figure out the environment in which to place it.

**Closure:** Each group reviews the steps in making the shelter. Ask the students to explain the process to their families that evening.

*Note: The guided practice of this lesson may take several sessions to complete.*

## LESSON 8: PREPARING THE MUSEUM PRESENTATIONS

**Standards:**

*National Council for the Social Studies Standard III: People, Places, and Environments G:* Describe how people create places that reflect ideas, personality, culture, and wants and needs as they design homes.
*AASL #2:* Draw conclusions, make informed decisions, apply knowledge to new situations, and create new knowledge. 2.1, Skills: 2.1.1, Continue an inquiry-based research process by applying critical-thinking skills (analysis, synthesis, evaluation, organization) to information and knowledge in order to construct new understandings, draw conclusions, and create new knowledge; 2.1.4, Use technology and other information tools to analyze and organize information; 2.1.5, Collaborate with others to exchange ideas, develop new understandings, make decisions, and solve problems.
*NCTE #8:* Students use a variety of technological and information resources (e.g., libraries, databases, computer networks, video) to gather and synthesize information and to create and communicate knowledge.
*NETS Technology #3: Research and Information Fluency:* Students apply digital tools to gather, evaluate, and use information.

**Objectives:**

1. Students plan their presentation by assigning parts and practicing.
2. Students consult the presentation checklist to make sure all the information is covered.

**Materials:**

- 11 shelter group folders
- large 5″ × 7″ lined index cards at each table

- finished model of the shelters
- board-ready copy of the presentation checklist
- 11 copies of the presentation checklist

**Set:** Ask how many students have been to a museum. Say, "We're going to invite your parents and a first-grade class to see your shelters. Since they can't read, how can the first-graders learn about your shelter?"

**Input:** Distribute and explain the checklist for the presentation. Assign students 1, 2, and 3 specific tasks on the checklist and have them put their names next to the topics. In all groups, students must be assigned more than one topic.

**Guided practice:** Each group looks in their folders for the information required on the checklist. The students in each group write index cards for their assigned topic, and then the students practice their presentations. After the practice is finished, the index cards are placed in the folder and the group folders are collected.

**Assessment:** Informally assess whether the students cooperate and are able to follow the directions in order to practice their presentations.

**Closure:** Ask each group to report how the checklist helped to prepare for the presentation.

## LESSON 9: PRESENTING THE MUSEUM OF SHELTERS

**Standards:**

*National Council for the Social Studies Standard III: People, Places, and Environments G:*    Describe how people create places that reflect ideas, personality, culture, and wants and needs as they design homes.
*AASL #3:*    Share knowledge and participate ethically and productively as members of our democratic society. 3.1, Skills: 3.1.1, Conclude an inquiry-based research process by sharing new understandings and reflecting on the learning; 3.1.3, Use writing and speaking skills to communicate new understandings effectively.
*NCTE #8:*    Students use a variety of technological and information resources (e.g., libraries, databases, computer networks, video) to gather and synthesize information and to create and communicate knowledge.
*NETS Technology #3: Research and Information Fluency:*    Students apply digital tools to gather, evaluate, and use information.

**Objective:**
Students present information on the model of their shelter in the form of a museum exhibit.

**Materials:**

- time for the second graders to set up the museum
- 11 shelter group folders with the presentation index cards

- finished model of the shelters
- class of first-graders to be the visitors to the Shelter Museum
- bell or other signal to switch the groups

**Set:** Welcome the visitors to the Shelter Museum. State that students will be making presentations to the visitors based on the research they have done in the library.

**Review:** Review the manners for visitors in a museum.

**Input:** Explain the procedure for viewing the exhibits. The second-graders in each group stand next to their model. The first-graders are broken into 11 groups and placed in front of a model. Each first-grade group spends three minutes in front of each model. When the bell rings the first-graders move to the next model.

**Guided practice:** The second-grade shelter groups stand next to their models. The first-grade students are broken up into 11 groups, and when the bell rings, the museum "round robin" exhibit viewing begins.

**Assessment:** Informally assess whether the second-grade students are able to speak clearly and explain their presentations.

**Closure:** Using think-pair-share, ask both classes why shelters have changed and why these shelters are no longer in general use.

*Note: This presentation could be done several times for different audiences and at night for parents and the community during curriculum nights, literacy fairs, and so on.*

## LESSON 10: RATING THE MODELS AND FINAL DISCUSSION ON SHELTERS

**Standards:**

*AASL #3:* Share knowledge and participate ethically and productively as members of our democratic society. 3.1, Skills: 3.1.1, Conclude an inquiry-based research process by sharing new understandings and reflecting on the learning; 3.1.3, Use writing and speaking skills to communicate new understandings effectively.

**Objectives:**

1. Students rate the model of their shelter based on a rubric.
2. Students participate in a discussion on key and concluding questions about shelters.

**Materials:**

- finished model of the shelters
- board-ready copy of the "model" rubric available on the CD
- 30 copies of the "model" rubric

**Set:** Using think-pair-share, ask, "How can we tell what kind of job we did in making our model of the assigned shelters?"

**Review:** Review the rubric that will be used to assess the model of the shelters.

**Input:** Project the board-ready "model" rubric on the board. Distribute copies to the students and explain it. Place the model of the chickee on a table. Take one category of the rubric and apply it to the model of the chickee, deciding how you performed on that category. Circle the rating number you have decided to give for that category. Explain that the groups are going to use the rubric to assess the model of their assigned shelter.

**Guided practice:** The students are instructed to get into their shelter groups and get their folders. Each group is given a copy of the "model" rubric and students are asked to rate their model according to the rubric. They are to circle the rating in each category of the rubric. After the groups have finished the assessment of their models, they are asked to report their ratings. Then lead the class to make conclusions based on their research. Do this by using think-pair-share and asking key questions and concluding questions.
    Examples of key questions:

- Why do people make shelters?
- What types of shelters did people use in the past?
- What are the factors that determine the types of shelters in the past?

Example of concluding question:

- Today why do most shelters around the world look the same?

**Assessment:** Informally observe whether the students are able to use the rubric to assess their model and whether they were able to participate in the discussion of shelters.

**Closure:** Using think-pair-share, ask the students to identify their favorite part of the unit.

*Note: The Shelter Museum could be displayed in the library for a time or at a school open house.*

# Chapter 11

# Third Grade: Transportation

## PLANNING

### Stage 1: Identify Desired Results

**Established goals:**

*National Council for the Social Studies Content Standard II: Time, Continuity, and Change, B:* Demonstrate an ability to use correctly vocabulary associated with time such as past, present, future, and long ago; read and construct simple timelines; identify examples of change.

*National Council for the Social Studies Content Standard VIII: Science, Technology, and Society, A:* Identify and describe examples in which science and technology have changed the lives of people, such as in transportation.

**Essential questions:**

1. What is transportation and why is it important?
2. How has transportation changed over the last 10,000 years?
3. What are some forms of transportation?

**Understandings:**

1. Students understand how to place an event on a timeline of the history of transportation.
2. Students understand the innovations of transportation and how it has changed life from long ago, the recent past, and to the present.

**What key knowledge and skills will the students acquire?**

1. Students understand the concept of transportation and some of its forms.
2. Students use the dictionary to understand the key vocabulary of transportation.
3. Students understand how to place changes in transportation on a timeline.
4. Students use a dictionary, the Internet, an atlas, nonfiction books, and an encyclopedia to extract pertinent information on an assigned form of transportation.
5. Students teach others about an assigned form of transportation.

## Stage 2: Determine Acceptable Evidence

**Performance tasks:**

- Students make a class dictionary of the vocabulary of transportation.
- Each group creates a timeline for the forms of transportation assigned.
- Using the cooperative learning jigsaw strategy, students teach each other about the timeline events and dates of their assigned form of transportation.
- As a class, the students create a transportation timeline that includes all of the forms of transportation researched.

**Student self-assessment and reflection:**

Summative assessment: Students assess their final product. Students use the following rubric to assess their performance task:

### Transportation Dictionary Rubric

| Category | 4 Great | 3 Very Good | 2 Okay | 1 Needs More Work |
|---|---|---|---|---|
| Is it easy to understand? | Each entry has a clear meaning. | Almost all the entries have clear meanings. | Most entries have clear meanings. | Less than half of the entries have clear meanings. |
| Are the facts correct? | All facts in the dictionary are correct. | Almost all facts in the dictionary are correct. | Most facts in the dictionary are correct. | Less than half of the facts in the dictionary are correct. |
| Does everyone understand the information? | All students in the group can correctly answer questions related to the dictionary. | Almost all of students in the group can correctly answer questions related to the dictionary. | Most students in the group can correctly answer questions related to the dictionary. | Less than half of students in the group can correctly answer questions related to the dictionary. |
| Grammar | There are no mistakes in spelling or the use of uppercase and lowercase letters. | There are no mistakes in spelling or the use of uppercase and lowercase letters after it was checked by an adult. | There are a few mistakes in spelling or the use of uppercase and lowercase letters after it was checked by an adult. | There are quite a few mistakes in spelling or the use of uppercase and lowercase letters after it was checked by an adult. |

## Stage 3: Plan Learning Experiences

- Read a book about transportation, brainstorm the various forms of transportation, and introduce the performance tasks and rubric for the unit.
- Assign seven forms of transportation to the groups: ship, railroad, airplane, rocket, automobile, balloon, and bicycle (instructor researches submarines).
- Students research their form of transportation using an encyclopedia, nonfiction books, an atlas, the Internet, and an almanac.

- Students locate and paraphrase definitions of the vocabulary words from their assigned form of transportation.
- The class makes a dictionary of transportation terms.
- The students teach each other about the form of transportation they researched.
- The students make a timeline for their assigned form of transportation.
- The students complete a class timeline of the assigned forms of transportation.
- Lead a class discussion using key and concluding questions.

## LESSON 1: BRAINSTORMING

**Standards:**

*National Council for the Social Studies Content Standard II:* Demonstrate an ability to use correctly vocabulary associated with time such as past, present, future, and long ago; read and construct simple timelines; identify examples of change.

*National Council for the Social Studies Content Standard VIII: Science, Technology, and Society, A:* Identify and describe examples, such as in transportation, in which science and technology have changed the lives of people.

**Objectives:**

1. Students understand that there are many forms of transportation.
2. Students understand that science and technology have changed transportation and this has changed peoples' lives.
3. Students understand the performance tasks and rubric required for the unit.

**Materials:**

- chart or empty board-ready paper
- visuals of different forms of transportation, including a Conestoga wagon with the livestock pulling it and a moving van
- one of the following books:
    Baines, Francesca. 1994. *Transportation*. New York: Dorling Kindersley. 49 pp.
    Richards, Jon. 2005. *Transportation*. Mankato, MN: Chrysalis Education. 32 pp.
- board-ready copy of the rubric

**Set:** Show the pictures of the Conestoga wagon and the moving van. Ask the students to raise their hands to identify the form of transportation that is used today to move household belongings from one place to another. Using think-pair-share, ask the advantages of using a moving van. Then ask the disadvantages of using the Conestoga wagon.

**Input:** Read one of the books cited in the materials list. Using think-pair-share, ask the students to identify the forms of transportation. Write these on the chart or board. If the students do not come up with all of them, suggest the forms that will be researched: ship, railroad, airplane, rocket, automobile, balloon, and bicycle (you will research submarines). Assist the students in categorizing the forms into land, air, and water. Using the board-ready copies, explain the unit, the performance tasks, and rubric.

**Assessment:** Informally observe whether the students are able to understand the concept of transportation and its many forms.

**Closure:** Using think-pair-share, ask the students to identify the three categories of transportation.

## LESSON 2: USING THE DICTIONARY TO UNDERSTAND KEY VOCABULARY OF TRANSPORTATION

**Standards:**

*National Council for the Social Studies Content Standard II: Time, Continuity, and Change, B:*  Demonstrate an ability to use correctly vocabulary associated with time such as past, present, future, and long ago; read and construct simple timelines; identify examples of change.
*National Council for the Social Studies Content Standard VIII: Science, Technology, and Society, A:*  Identify and describe examples in which science and technology have changed the lives of people such as in transportation.
*AASL #2:*  Draw conclusions, make informed decisions, apply knowledge to new situations, and create new knowledge. 2.1, Skills: 2.1.1, Continue an inquiry-based research process by applying critical-thinking skills (analysis, synthesis, evaluation, organization) to information and knowledge in order to construct new understandings, draw conclusions, and create new knowledge; 2.1.4, Use technology and other information tools to analyze and organize information; 2.1.5, Collaborate with others to exchange ideas, develop new understandings, make decisions, and solve problems.
*NCTE #8:*  Students use a variety of technological and information resources togather and synthesize information and to create and communicate knowledge.

**Objective:**
Using a dictionary, students paraphrase the definitions of key vocabulary for their assigned form of transportation.

**Materials:**

- chart with the students' ideas on transportation from the first lesson
- visual of a nuclear submarine
- 15 elementary dictionaries
- seven paper strips with the vocabulary words for each assigned form of transportation available from the CD
- copies of the work sheets from the CD, enough for each student in the group to have one
- board-ready copy of the input work sheet on the CD
- seven copies of the rubric
- seven folders, each with the name of one form of transportation on the cover: ship, railroad, airplane, rocket, automobile, balloon, and bicycle

**Set:** Show the visual of a submarine and ask whether the students know what and where a periscope is on a submarine.

**Review:** Review the arrangement of the dictionary and the use of guide words.

**Input:** Pair students and give each pair an elementary dictionary. Look up "periscope" in the dictionary. Model, thinking aloud, how to look up a word in the dictionary (beginning letter, next letter, etc.). Locate the word and direct the student to turn to the correct page. Read the definition aloud. The students put the definition in their own words, with help from you. Write the paraphrased definition in the space on the work sheet. With the students, read the definition chorally.

**Guided practice:** Group the students and give each group a form of transportation and two elementary dictionaries. Distribute the group folders, rubric, paper strips, and work sheets. Students put their names on the folders beside the numbers 1, 2, 3, and 4. Students in each group work together to locate and paraphrase the definitions of the words for their assigned form of transportation. After the guided practice is finished, the work sheets are placed in the folder and the folders are collected.

**Assessment:** Informally observe whether the students are able to find the words in the dictionary and write the definitions in their own words. If a formal assessment is desired, the work sheets can be assessed.

**Closure:** Using think-pair-share, ask the students how they found the word in the dictionary.

## LESSON 3: RESEARCHING A SPECIFIC FORM OF TRANSPORTATION IN THE ENCYCLOPEDIA

**Standards:**

*National Council for the Social Studies Content Standard II: Time, Continuity, and Change, B:* Demonstrate an ability to use correctly vocabulary associated with time such as past, present, future, and long ago; read and construct simple timelines; identify examples of change.

*National Council for the Social Studies Content Standard VIII: Science, Technology, and Society, A:* Identify and describe examples, such as in transportation, in which science and technology have changed the lives of people.

*AASL #2:* Draw conclusions, make informed decisions, apply knowledge to new situations, and create new knowledge. 2.1, Skills: 2.1.1, Continue an inquiry-based research process by applying critical-thinking skills (analysis, synthesis, evaluation, organization) to information and knowledge in order to construct new understandings, draw conclusions, and create new knowledge; 2.1.4, Use technology and other information tools to analyze and organize information; 2.1.5, Collaborate with others to exchange ideas, develop new understandings, make decisions, and solve problems.

*NCTE #8:* Students use a variety of technological and information resources to gather and synthesize information and to create and communicate knowledge.

**Objective:**

Using an encyclopedia, students make a timeline identifying five important dates in the history of their assigned form of transportation.

**Materials:**

- two sets of encyclopedias
- the seven transportation group folders from the previous lesson
- seven copies of the timeline work sheet from the CD
- board-ready copy of the work sheet on the CD
- visuals of a historic submarine and a nuclear submarine

**Set:** Show the two visuals and use think-pair-share to ask which picture is from long ago and why.

**Review:** Review the organization of an encyclopedia and the use of guide words. Also review that encyclopedias have long and short articles and not everything can be looked up by a specific word—it may need to be placed in a topic.

**Input:** Look up "submarine" in the encyclopedia. Ponder aloud under what letter it would be found, realize that the "S" is in two volumes, and select the correct one after checking the spine. Look for the subtopic of "history" and look to see whether there is a listing of dates. As there is no chart or list, read aloud the pertinent paragraphs and model how to pick the five most important dates. Fill out the board-ready timeline work sheet, paraphrasing what happened on each important date. Make sure the dates are in correct chronological order as you write them on the timeline work sheet. State that each group will be creating a timeline for its assigned form of transportation. Give each group their folder and timeline work sheet and assign the tasks. Student 1 will identify the volume needed and get it from the shelf. Student 2 will use the guide words to find the article. Student 3 will find the subtopic "history" and look for a list of dates. Student 4 or 1 will read the dates and events. Together, the students will decide on the five most important dates in the history of their assigned form of transportation. Each student will take a turn at writing a date and event on the timeline work sheet.

**Guided practice:** Students work in their groups to complete the encyclopedia research. Circulate during guided practice to offer assistance as needed. At the end of the guided practice, collect the group folders.

**Assessment:** Informally observe whether the students are able to find the information and write it in their own words. If a formal assessment is desired, the work sheets can be assessed.

**Closure:** Using think-pair-share, ask the students how they located their assigned form of transportation in the encyclopedia.

## LESSON 4: USING NONFICTION BOOKS TO FIND INFORMATION

**Standards:**

*National Council for the Social Studies Content Standard II: Time, Continuity, and Change, B:* Demonstrate an ability to use correctly vocabulary associated with time such as past, present, future, and long ago; read and construct simple timelines; identify examples of change.
*National Council for the Social Studies Content Standard VIII: Science, Technology, and Society, A:* Identify and describe examples in which science and technology have changed the lives of people such as in transportation.

*AASL #2:*   Draw conclusions, make informed decisions, apply knowledge to new situations, and create new knowledge. 2.1, Skills: 2.1.1, Continue an inquiry-based research process by applying critical-thinking skills (analysis, synthesis, evaluation, organization) to information and knowledge in order to construct new understandings, draw conclusions, and create new knowledge; 2.1.4, Use technology and other information tools to analyze and organize information; 2.1.5, Collaborate with others to exchange ideas, develop new understandings, make decisions, and solve problems.

*NCTE #8:*   Students use a variety of technological and information resources to gather and synthesize information and to create and communicate knowledge.

**Objective:**
Students use nonfiction books to find information about their assigned form of transportation.

**Materials:**

- kindergarten through third-grade reading level nonfiction books on transportation
- 30 copies of the work sheet available on the CD
- board-ready copy of the work sheet
- the seven transportation group folders from the previous lesson

**Set:** Using think-pair-share, say, "I used the dictionary and the encyclopedia to look up information about submarines. Where else can I look for information?"

**Review:** Review the meaning of "transportation" and the seven forms of transportation assigned.

**Input:** Explain that the library has many resources. One of them is nonfiction books. Show the students where the transportation books are on the shelves, in the 380s and the 629s. Explain that the nonfiction books are arranged by subject using the numbers in the Dewey Decimal System. Tell the students that you have pulled books for them on the forms of transportation they are studying and that they are going to be looking for specific facts. Model this by using a primary nonfiction book about submarines. Refer to the five dates from the encyclopedia research timeline and focus on information about the development of the submarine. Look at the table of contents to see whether "history" is one of the chapters. If not, look in the index. Note the pages cited. Look at those pages, perusing the pictures, reading the captions, and searching for information about the dates you chose. Read aloud information about one of the dates and elicit help from the students in reiterating some of the facts. Write the facts in your own words on the work sheet, modeling at least two sentences. Write the author and title of the book where the information was found.

**Guided practice:** Distribute the group folders, a work sheet for each student, and the nonfiction books for each group. The directions are for each student to take one of the dates and to look in the nonfiction books for information on the topic and to fill out the work sheet. Students may work in pairs, depending on the availability of the nonfiction books for each form of transportation. Circulate to offer assistance as needed.

**Assessment:** Informally observe whether the students are able to find the information and write it in their own words. If a formal assessment is desired, the work sheets can be collected.

**Closure:** Each group discusses the new facts they found about the history of their form of transportation. Collect the group folders.

## LESSON 5: FINDING INFORMATION ON THE INTERNET

**Standards:**

*National Council for the Social Studies Content Standard II: Time, Continuity, and Change, B:* Demonstrate an ability to use correctly vocabulary associated with time such as past, present, future, and long ago; read and construct simple timelines; identify examples of change.

*National Council for the Social Studies Content Standard VIII: Science, Technology, and Society, A:* Identify and describe examples in which science and technology have changed the lives of people such as in transportation.

*AASL #2:* Draw conclusions, make informed decisions, apply knowledge to new situations, and create new knowledge. 2.1, Skills: 2.1.1, Continue an inquiry-based research process by applying critical-thinking skills (analysis, synthesis, evaluation, organization) to information and knowledge in order to construct new understandings, draw conclusions, and create new knowledge; 2.1.4, Use technology and other information tools to analyze and organize information; 2.1.5, Collaborate with others to exchange ideas, develop new understandings, make decisions, and solve problems.

*NCTE #8:* Students use a variety of technological and information resources (e.g., libraries, databases, computer networks, video) to gather and synthesize information and to create and communicate knowledge.

*NETS Technology #3: Research and Information Fluency:* Students apply digital tools to gather, evaluate, and use information.

**Objectives:**

1. Students use the Internet to find at least two new and interesting facts about their assigned form of transportation.
2. Students understand that the Internet provides information and images on many topics.
3. Students understand that Web sites need to be evaluated for reliability.

**Materials:**

- projection of an Internet computer screen (must have access to computer, Internet, and means of projection)
- personalized start page or bookmarked Internet sites available from the CD
- 30 copies of the letter to parents with the Web sites, available on the CD
- the seven transportation group folders from previous lessons
- 30 copies of the work sheet
- board-ready copy of a work sheet
- 10 to 15 computers with Internet access

**Set:** Ask, "So far we've looked for information in the dictionary, the encyclopedia, and nonfiction books. Where else could we find information about transportation?"

**Review:** Review that the Internet is a network of interconnected computers around the world and a source of information and images.

**Input:** Explain that the library has many resources. One important resource is the Internet. Show the students Web sites for submarines: www.submarine-history.com/, http://en.wikipedia.org/wiki/Submarine, and http://inventors.about.com/library/inventors/blsubmarine3.htm.

Use the Web sites to find information about key dates in the history of submarines. Read captions and a few sentences to find some interesting facts. Elicit help from the students in reiterating some of the facts. Write these in your own words on the work sheet, modeling two facts. Write the names of the Web sites on the work sheet. Tell the students that you have bookmarked sites on the personalized start page for each form of transportation they are researching.

**Guided practice:** Pair students and assign each pair a computer. Have them use the personalized start page to find a Web site on their assigned form of transportation. They will look at the pictures and read some of the information. They will find two interesting facts and paraphrase them for the work sheet. They will write the name of the Web site on the work sheet. Circulate among the computers to offer assistance as needed. After all students complete the assignment, have them meet in their groups to discuss the new facts and place their work sheets in the correct folders. At end of the guided practice, collect the group folders.

**Assessment:** Informally assess whether the students can restate the information presented by the Web sites.

**Closure:** Distribute to the students the letter to parents mentioning the Web sites and encourage the students to visit the Web sites at home with their parents.

## LESSON 6: ENTRIES FOR THE TRANSPORTATION DICTIONARY

**Standards:**

*AASL #2:*   Draw conclusions, make informed decisions, apply knowledge to new situations, and create new knowledge. 2.1, Skills: 2.1.1, Continue an inquiry-based research process by applying critical-thinking skills (analysis, synthesis, evaluation, organization) to information and knowledge in order to construct new understandings, draw conclusions, and create new knowledge; 2.1.4, Use technology and other information tools to analyze and organize information; 2.1.5, Collaborate with others to exchange ideas, develop new understandings, make decisions, and solve problems.

*NCTE #8:*   Students use a variety of technological and information resources (e.g., libraries, databases, computer networks, video) to gather and synthesize information and to create and communicate knowledge.

*NETS Technology #3: Research and Information Fluency:*   Students apply digital tools to gather, evaluate, and use information.

**Objective:**
   Using a computer, students type entries of assigned words for the transportation dictionary.

**Materials:**

   • the seven transportation group folders, which include the definitions from the dictionary lesson
   • 10 to 15 computers
   • computer with printer and capability of projecting its screen display

**Set:** State that today each group will make a dictionary of the transportation vocabulary it has been researching.

**Review:** Review that the definitions were located in a previous lesson. Dictionary entries are in alphabetical order. Their entries must have the correct spelling and definition.

**Input:** Project a computer desktop. Click on "start," find Microsoft Word, and open a page. Type at the top of the page, in Arial font size 28, the word "periscope." Then type in the paraphrased definition. Model pulling down under "file" to save the entry onto the desktop. Then model pulling down "file" to print the entry. Explain that the word and definition should only take up about a quarter of the page by showing the students your printed page.

**Guided practice:** The students meet in their groups and the folders are distributed. Student 1 gathers all the definitions and lays them out. Student 2 assigns words to each group member. Pair the students and assign each pair a computer. The students type the entries. Circulate, offering assistance as necessary. Students collect their entries from the printer and place them in their folders. After the assignment is completed, collect the folders and the printed entries.

**Assessment:** Informally assess whether the students are able to follow the directions to make the entries on the computer.

**Closure:** Each group discusses the process of using the computer to make the entries in the dictionary.

*Note: Cut all the printed dictionary entries pages to half a page and put them back in each group's folder.*

## LESSON 7: ILLUSTRATING AND ARRANGING THE CLASS'S TRANSPORTATION DICTIONARY

**Standards:**

*National Council for the Social Studies Content Standard II: Time, Continuity, and Change, B:* Demonstrate an ability to use correctly vocabulary associated with time such as past, present, future, and long ago; read and construct simple timelines; identify examples of change.

*National Council for the Social Studies Content Standard VIII: Science, Technology, and Society, A:* Identify and describe examples in which science and technology have changed the lives of people such as in transportation.

*AASL #2:* Draw conclusions, make informed decisions, apply knowledge to new situations, and create new knowledge. 2.1, Skills: 2.1.1, Continue an inquiry-based research process by applying critical-thinking skills (analysis, synthesis, evaluation, organization) to information and knowledge in order to construct new understandings, draw conclusions, and create new knowledge; 2.1.4, Use technology and other information tools to analyze and organize information; 2.1.5, Collaborate with others to exchange ideas, develop new understandings, make decisions, and solve problems.

*NCTE #8:* Students use a variety of technological and information resources (e.g., libraries, databases, computer networks, video) to gather and synthesize information and to create and communicate knowledge.

*NETS Technology #3: Research and Information Fluency:* Students apply digital tools to gather, evaluate, and use information.

**Objectives:**

1. Students illustrate some of their transportation dictionary definitions.
2. Students arrange the dictionary in alphabetical order.

**Materials:**

- the seven group folders
- pencils and black thin-tip felt pens at each table
- board-ready copy of the paraphrased definition of "periscope" that has been printed from the computer

**Set:** Open a dictionary, show the pages to the students, and comment that all words in the dictionary do not have pictures. Using think-pair-share, ask why some words in the dictionary have a picture and others don't.

**Review:** Review the arrangement of a dictionary.

**Input:** Project the entry for "periscope." Ask whether a picture would greatly increase a reader's understanding of the definition. Model illustrating the word "periscope." The instructions are for the illustrations to be done first in pencil, and then traced over with the thin-tip felt pens.

**Guided practice:** The folders are distributed to the groups. Student 2 lays out all the half-page typed dictionary entries. As Student 3 reads each definition, the group decides whether the word can and should be illustrated. Student 1 collects the definitions that will be illustrated and assigns them to group members. Student 4 is in charge of the definitions that have not been illustrated. After all the assigned definitions have been illustrated, call out each letter of the alphabet. Students give their entry as the letter is called. If more than one entry starts with the same letter, the class decides in what order the entries should be placed.

**Assessment:** Informally assess whether the students cooperated and were able to follow the directions to illustrate and organize the transportation dictionary.

**Closure:** Using think-pair-share, ask whether it was helpful researching the vocabulary before researching the topic.

*Note: Make 30 copies of the transportation dictionary before the next lesson is taught. This is done by pasting two half-page entries onto a full page and copying the pages double sided. Make very sure that the dictionary is in correct alphabetical order before copying.*

## LESSON 8: READING AND RATING THE TRANSPORTATION DICTIONARY

**Standards:**

*AASL #3:* Share knowledge and participate ethically and productively as members of our democratic society. 3.1, Skills: 3.1.1, Conclude an inquiry-based research process by sharing new understandings and reflecting on the learning; 3.1.3, Use writing and speaking skills to communicate new understandings effectively.

**Objectives:**

1.   Students read their dictionary of transportation.
2.   Students rate their dictionary based on a rubric.

**Materials:**

- 30 copies of the transportation dictionary
- board-ready copy of the rubric available from the CD
- 30 copies of the rubric

**Set:** Using think-pair-share, ask, "How can we tell what kind of job we did in making our transportation dictionary?"

**Review:** Review where and how the students looked up the information they put in the transportation dictionary.

**Input:** Distribute the copies of the class's dictionary. Model reading the first definition. Put the rubric for the dictionary on the board, distribute copies to the students, and explain it. Take one category of the rubric and apply it to the dictionary, deciding how they did on that category. Circle the rating. Each group is assigned a category to assess. Several groups will have the same category. The students are instructed to read and rate the dictionaries.

**Guided practice:** Each group member takes a turn in reading the entries in the transportation dictionary. Student 1 reads their assigned category of the rubric and the ratings. Student 2 leads the discussion on which rating applies. Student 3 circles the agreed-upon rating.

**Assessment:** Informally observe whether the students are able to use the rubric to rate the transportation dictionary.

**Closure:** Lead the students through a summary of their evaluation.

## LESSON 9:   CREATING A TIMELINE OF TRANSPORTATION

*Note: Before this lesson, make a small master timeline from the dates in each group's folder to facilitate the calling of the dates. Start with the earliest date.*

**Standards:**

*National Council for the Social Studies Content Standard II: Time, Continuity, and Change, B:*   Demonstrate an ability to use correctly vocabulary associated with time such as past, present, future, and long ago; read and construct simple timelines; identify examples of change.
*National Council for the Social Studies Content Standard VIII: Science, Technology, and Society, A:*   Identify and describe examples in which science and technology have changed the lives of people such as in transportation.

*AASL #3:* Share knowledge and participate ethically and productively as members of our democratic society. 3.1, Skills: 3.1.1, Conclude an inquiry-based research process by sharing new understandings and reflecting on the learning; 3.1.3, Use writing and speaking skills to communicate new understandings effectively.

*NCTE #8:* Students use a variety of technological and information resources (e.g., libraries, databases, computer networks, video) to gather and synthesize information and to create and communicate knowledge.

**Objectives:**

1. Students use the important dates in the history of their assigned form of transportation to create a class timeline of all the forms of transportation.
2. Students read the timeline and understand that the most innovations in transportation were made in the recent past.

**Materials:**

- the seven group folders
- wall-mounted "Transportation Timeline" with dates marked from earliest date to the present
- scissors and glue sticks on each table

**Set:** Using think-pair-share, say, "Each of the groups has five important dates in the history of their form of transportation. How can we compare when the different forms were first used and later improved?"

**Review:** Review that timelines are a visual representation of events in the correct chronological order, and that the students made a transportation timeline during their encyclopedia research.

**Input:** Read your dates from the "submarine" timeline in chronological order. Model cutting the timeline work sheet apart so that each date and event is on a separate strip of paper. Apply glue to the back of the paper strip with the earliest date. Place the paper strip on the appropriate section of the timeline and read out loud the date and event. Then place the rest of the dates on the appropriate sections of the timeline, reading the dates and events as you post them.

**Guided practice:** Distribute the group folders. Student 1 finds the timeline work sheet. Student 2 cuts the work sheet apart. Student 3 assigns a paper strip with a date and event to each group member. After all the timeline work sheets have been separated, use the master timeline to call out the dates beginning with the earliest date. Make sure to assist those groups having both B.C. and A.D. dates. As each student's date is called, the student reads the date and event on his or her paper strip and glues and posts it in the correct place on the timeline. Once the timeline is completed, lead a class discussion on making conclusions about the forms of transportation based on the timeline. Do this by using think-pair-share and asking key questions on each form of transportation before asking concluding questions.

Examples of key questions for each form of transportation:

- How were peoples' lives changed when boats could go across a large body of water?
- How was life changed when boats were powered by engines and didn't have to rely on manpower or wind?

Examples of concluding questions are:

- During what time span did the most innovations happen in transportation?
- How is the world different now that people can travel easily from one part of the world to another?

**Assessment:** Informally observe whether the students are able to create the timeline, answer the key questions, and draw conclusions.

**Closure:** Using think-pair-share, ask, "How did making the timeline help you understand how transportation changed?"

*Note: The timeline could be placed in the classroom or library for further discussion and display.*

# Chapter 12

# Fourth Grade:  Biomes

---

---

## Stage 1: Identify Desired Results

**Established goal:**

*National Science Education Content Standard C: Life Science:* Organisms and Their Environments: An organism's patterns of behavior are related to the nature of that organism's environment including the kinds and numbers of other organisms present, the availability of food and resources, and the physical characteristics of the environment.

**Essential questions:**

1. What is a biome and what are its characteristics?
2. Where are the biomes on the earth?
3. What are humans doing to change or influence the condition and future of the biomes?
4. Which biome do you live in?

**Understandings:**

1. Students identify the characteristics of a biome.
2. Students identify the seven biomes, their characteristics, and where they are located.
3. Students understand that the plants and animals that live in each biome are interdependent.
4. Students understand that plants and animals have adapted to the biome in which they live.
5. Students understand that human activity affects the basic underlying conditions and future of biomes.

**What key knowledge and skills will the students acquire?**

1. Students define the key vocabulary of the unit: biome, taiga, tundra, grassland, deciduous, forest, desert, tropical, rain forest, savannah, climate, adaptation, annual, arid, atmosphere, basin, community, competition, conserve, drought, evergreen, humid, habitat, landforms, organism, perennial, prairie, species, steppe, symbiosis, and vegetation.
2. Students use the encyclopedia, Internet, dictionary, online catalog, and nonfiction books to research: location, climate, dominant plants, common animals, and impact of humans.
3. Using Microsoft Publisher, students create a brochure on their assigned biome.

## Stage 2: Determine Acceptable Evidence

**Performance tasks:**

1.  Students make a brochure describing the characteristics of their assigned biome.
2.  Using the cooperative learning jigsaw strategy each student presents and teaches their biome brochure to a small group.

**Student self-assessment and reflection:**
Summative assessment: Students assess their final product. Students reflect after the assessment and revise information in the brochure. Students use the following rubric to assess their performance task:

## Rubric for Biome Brochure

| Category | 4 Great | 3 Very Good | 2 Okay | 1 Needs More Work |
|---|---|---|---|---|
| Writing: grammar | There are no grammatical mistakes in the brochure. | There are no grammatical mistakes in the brochure after feedback from an adult. | There are one or two grammatical mistakes in the brochure even after feedback from an adult. | There are several grammatical mistakes in the brochure even after feedback from an adult. |
| Content: accuracy | All facts in the brochure are accurate. | 99–90% of the facts in the brochure are accurate. | 89–80% of the facts in the brochure are accurate. | Fewer than 80% of the facts in the brochure are accurate. |
| Attractiveness & organization | The brochure has exceptionally attractive formatting and well-organized information. | The brochure has attractive formatting and well-organized information. | The brochure has well-organized information. | The brochure's formatting and organization of material are confusing to the reader. |
| Sources | Careful and accurate records are kept to document the source of 95–100% of the facts and graphics in the brochure. | Careful and accurate records are kept to document the source of 94–85% of the facts and graphics in the brochure. | Careful and accurate records are kept to document the source of 84–75% of the facts and graphics in the brochure. | Sources are not documented accurately or are not kept on many facts and graphics. |
| Graphics/pictures | Graphics go well with the text and there is a good mix of text and graphics. | Graphics go well with the text, but there are so many that they distract from the text. | Graphics go well with the text, but there are too few and the brochure seems "text-heavy." | Graphics do not go with the accompanying text or appear to be randomly chosen. |
| Knowledge gained | All students in the group can accurately answer all questions related to facts in the brochure and to technical processes used to create the brochure. | All students in the group can accurately answer most questions related to facts in the brochure and to technical processes used to create the brochure. | Most students in the group can accurately answer most questions related to facts in the brochure and to technical processes used to create the brochure. | Several students in the group appear to have little knowledge about the facts or technical processes used in the brochure. |

### Stage 3: Plan Learning Experiences

- Read a book and discuss the characteristics of a biome: location, climate, plants, animals, conditions, and future. Brainstorm identifying the seven biomes and introduce the performance tasks and rubric for the unit.
- Using a dictionary, students research key biome vocabulary words.
- Each group is assigned a biome (tundra, taiga [boreal forest], deciduous temperate forest, grasslands, savanna, desert, and tropical rainforest) to research using the encyclopedia, nonfiction books, and Web sites. Using a Web site, students create a map of the location of their assigned biome.
- Each group makes a brochure about their assigned biome. The brochure must contain information about the location, climate, dominant plants, common animals, conditions, and future of the biome.
- After the first draft, students use the rubric to rate and revise their biome brochure.
- Using the cooperative learning jigsaw strategy, each student presents and teaches his or her group's biome brochure to a small group.
- Lead a class discussion using key and concluding questions.

## LESSON 1: BRAINSTORMING

**Standards:**

*National Science Education Content Standard C: Life Science:* Organisms and Their Environments: An organism's patterns of behavior are related to the nature of that organism's environment including the kinds and numbers of other organisms present, the availability of food and resources, and the physical characteristics of the environment.

**Objectives:**

1. Students identify the characteristics of a biome: location, climate, dominant plants, common animals, conditions, and future.
2. Students understand the performance tasks and rubric required for the unit.

**Materials:**

- chart or empty board-ready paper
- board-ready copy of the biome rubric available from the CD
- one of the following books:
    Burnie, David. 2003. *Scrublands*. Austin, TX: Steck-Vaugh. 64 pp.
    Kalman, Bobbie. 2005. *What Is a Biome?* New York: Crabtree Publishing Company. 32 pp.
    Tocci, Salvatore. 2004. *The Chaparral Life on the Scrubby Coast*. New York: Franklin Watts. 65 pp.
    Warhol, Tom. 2007. *Chaparral and Scrubs*. New York: Marshall Cavendish. 80 pp.
- 30 copies of the biome brochure rubric available from the CD
- visual of tundra

**Set:** Say, "There is a part of the world where it is very cold and dark in the winter, polar bears roam, and the land is flat and frozen. What one word could you use to describe this region of the world?" Give the answer, "tundra," if no one guesses it correctly.

**Input:** Before you read sections of the book, tell the students to notice the following characteristics: location, climate, dominant plants, and common animals. After the reading, use think-pair-share and ask the students to name or describe the biome mentioned in the book. Record their descriptions. Using think-pair-share, ask the students to brainstorm other biomes they know. Record the biomes that match the ones that will be covered in the unit. Add any biomes that are missing. Explain the unit and the performance tasks. Project the board-ready biome brochure rubric. Hand out a copy of the rubric to the students. Go over the categories and the rating system from 4 to 1, making sure that the students understand the rubric. Then arrange the students into seven groups and assign each group a biome: tundra, taiga (boreal forest), deciduous temperate forest, grassland, savanna, desert, and tropical rainforest. Give each group a folder and tell the students to write on the front of the folder their assigned biome, their names, and their room number. Students are then to number themselves from 1 to 4.

**Guided practice:** The students meet with their groups and write their biome and room number on the folder as well as their names next to the numbers 1 through 4. They put copies of the biome brochure rubric in their folder. Collect the group folders.

**Assessment:** Informally observe whether the students can describe the characteristics of biomes and whether they understand the performance tasks and rubric as explained.

**Closure:** Using think-pair-share, ask, "What are some characteristics of biomes?"

## LESSON 2: USING THE DICTIONARY TO UNDERSTAND THE VOCABULARY OF BIOMES

**Standards:**

*National Science Education Content Standard C: Life Science:* Organisms and Their Environments: An organism's patterns of behavior are related to the nature of that organism's environment including the kinds and numbers of other organisms present, the availability of food and resources, and the physical characteristics of the environment.

*AASL #2:* Draw conclusions, make informed decisions, apply knowledge to new situations, and create new knowledge. 2.1, Skills: 2.1.1, Continue an inquiry-based research process by applying critical-thinking skills (analysis, synthesis, evaluation, organization) to information and knowledge in order to construct new understandings, draw conclusions, and create new knowledge; 2.1.4, Use technology and other information tools to analyze and organize information; 2.1.5, Collaborate with others to exchange ideas, develop new understandings, make decisions, and solve problems.

*NCTE #8:* Students use a variety of technological and information resources to gather and synthesize information and to create and communicate knowledge.

**Objective:**
Using a dictionary, students paraphrase the definitions of biome vocabulary words.

**Materials:**

- chart on the characteristics of biomes from the CD
- 15 intermediate dictionaries
- 30 copies of the work sheet from the CD

- copies of paper strips with two vocabulary words from the CD
- board-ready copy of the work sheet
- visual of a desert

**Set:** Using think-pair-share, ask, "There is an area where it only rains about 6 inches a year and the summer is extremely hot and dry. What biome is that?" (Desert.)

**Review:** Review the chart of biomes and their characteristics: location, climate, dominant plants, common animals, conditions, and future. Name the seven biomes. Also review the arrangement of the dictionary and the use of guide words.

**Input:** The students are grouped by tables of four students, and then paired within each group. Each pair is given an intermediate dictionary. Choose "chaparral" to look up. Model, thinking aloud, how to look up a word in the dictionary (beginning letter, next letter, etc.). With the students, find the word. Read the definition aloud, and then put it in your own words. Write the paraphrased definition in the space on the work sheet. With the students, chorally read the definition.

**Guided practice:** Each pair is assigned two words to look up in an intermediate dictionary. The pair is given two work sheets and a paper strip with two words. Student 1 looks up the first word, reads the entry, and paraphrases a definition of the word. Both students write it on their own work sheet. The students switch roles for the second word. The students are put into two large groups, one student from each pair, to explain their words. After the presentations of the vocabulary words, the students are instructed to get back into their biome groups and put the vocabulary work sheets in their folder. Collect the group folders.

**Assessment:** Informally observe whether the students are able to find the word in the dictionary and write it in their own words. If a formal assessment is desired, the work sheets can be assessed.

**Closure:** Using think-pair-share, ask the students how they found the word in the dictionary.

## LESSON 3: RESEARCHING BIOMES USING THE ENCYCLOPEDIA

**Standards:**

*National Science Education Content Standard C: Life Science:*   Organisms and Their Environments: An organism's patterns of behavior are related to the nature of that organism's environment including the kinds and numbers of other organisms present, the availability of food and resources, and the physical characteristics of the environment.
*AASL #2:*   Draw conclusions, make informed decisions, apply knowledge to new situations, and create new knowledge. 2.1, Skills: 2.1.1, Continue an inquiry-based research process by applying critical-thinking skills (analysis, synthesis, evaluation, organization) to information and knowledge in order to construct new understandings, draw conclusions, and create new knowledge; 2.1.4, Use technology and other information tools to analyze and organize information; 2.1.5, Collaborate with others to exchange ideas, develop new understandings, make decisions, and solve problems.
*NCTE #8:*   Students use a variety of technological and information resources to gather and synthesize information and to create and communicate knowledge.

**Objective:**
Using an encyclopedia, students research and record the characteristics of their assigned biome.

**Materials:**

- chart on characteristics of biomes from the CD
- two sets of the latest edition of the *World Book Encyclopedia*
- 30 copies of the work sheet from the CD
- board-ready copy of the work sheet
- board-ready copy of the "Major Land Biomes" from the *World Book Encyclopedia*
- seven copies of the "Major Land Biomes" from the *World Book Encyclopedia*
- seven biome group folders
- visual of a tropical rain forest

**Set:** Using think-pair-share, ask, "There is a region of the world that has very heavy rainfall, a large, canopied, humid forest, and many colorful birds and insects. Which biome is it?" (Tropical rain forest.)

**Review:** Review the characteristics of biomes: location, climate, dominant plants, common animals, conditions, and future. Read the names of the biomes. Review the organization of an encyclopedia and the use of guide words. Remind the students to look at and read the pictures, captions, charts, and graphs in an article before reading the information.

**Input:** Choose the biome "chaparral," which was not assigned to a group to research. Model looking up the word "biome" in the encyclopedia and filling out the board-ready work sheet in your own words. Use information on the board-ready chart "Major Land Biomes." Then model looking at the end of the encyclopedia article on "biome" to discover what related articles the encyclopedia has. Find that the encyclopedia has an article on "chaparral" and turn to that article. Read the article, and in your own words add any information needed to the board-ready work sheet. Then go over the bibliographic entries for the biome and chaparral articles on the work sheet.

**Guided practice:** Students get into their assigned groups. Student 1 is in charge of materials. Student 1 gets the group folder and distributes a copy of the "Major Land Biomes" chart and work sheet to each group member. Student 2 leads the group in reading the chart, in order to locate the information on their assigned biome. Once the information is pinpointed, each student fills out a work sheet. Student 1 then gets the encyclopedia volume, when it is decided by the group which letter is needed. Student 2 uses the guide words to find the article on their assigned biome. Student 2 shows the pictures and charts, and reads the headings and subheadings if any. Student 3 reads aloud, in a whisper to the other members of the group, the information the students deem important in the article. After each student makes suggestions, student 4 helps them paraphrase the information into notes. Students add the information to their work sheets. Student 1 is in charge of helping all members of the group write the bibliographic entry correctly. Circulate during guided practice to offer assistance as needed. At the end of the guided practice, collect the group folders.

**Assessment:** Informally observe whether the students are able to find the information from the encyclopedia and write it in their own words. If a formal assessment is desired, the work sheets can be assessed.

**Closure:** Using think-pair-share, ask the students to give examples of the information they found on their assigned biome in the encyclopedia.

## LESSON 4: USING NONFICTION BOOKS TO RESEARCH BIOMES

**Standards:**

*National Science Education Content Standard C: Life Science:* Organisms and Their Environments: An organism's patterns of behavior are related to the nature of that organism's environment including the kinds and numbers of other organisms present, the availability of food and resources, and the physical characteristics of the environment.

*AASL #2:* Draw conclusions, make informed decisions, apply knowledge to new situations, and create new knowledge. 2.1, Skills: 2.1.1, Continue an inquiry-based research process by applying critical-thinking skills (analysis, synthesis, evaluation, organization) to information and knowledge in order to construct new understandings, draw conclusions, and create new knowledge; 2.1.4, Use technology and other information tools to analyze and organize information; 2.1.5, Collaborate with others to exchange ideas, develop new understandings, make decisions, and solve problems.

*NCTE #8:* Students use a variety of technological and information resources to gather and synthesize information and to create and communicate knowledge.

**Objective:**
Students use nonfiction books to locate information about their assigned biome.

**Materials:**

- nonfiction books on the different biomes in their correct location in the library
- 30 copies of the work sheet available from the CD
- board-ready copy of the work sheet
- computers with online catalog access
- Look for a Book form available from the CD
- seven biome group folders
- chart on the characteristics of biomes from the CD

**Set:** Using think-pair-share, say, "I used the dictionary and encyclopedia to look up information about the characteristics of the chaparral biome. It had some information but certainly not all that I needed in order to make the best brochure I can. Where else could I look for information?"

**Review:** Review the characteristics of biomes: location, climate, dominant plants, common animals, conditions, and future. Also review the procedure for using the online catalog to find books by their subjects.

**Input:** Explain that the library has many resources. One of main resources is nonfiction books. Model going to a computer, accessing the online catalog, typing in "chaparral," "biome," "habitat," and so on to find a book. Use the Look for a Book form to write the call number and title of a nonfiction book. Then find the book on the shelf. Peruse it and read a few facts that apply to the characteristics of the chaparral biome. Model writing the facts on the board-ready work sheet. Make a point of reading the facts, and then only writing down the important words, not complete sentences. Then write the bibliographic information about the book you have used on the board-ready work sheet.

**Guided practice:** Students get into their assigned groups. Student 2 is in charge of materials. She or he gets the folder and hands out the work sheets. Student 3 leads the search on the online catalog for non-fiction books on the assigned biome. He or she writes the call number and titles of books that will be helpful. While the other group members return to their seats, student 2 takes the Look for a Book forms and find the books on the shelf. Student 1 assigns the books to group members in pairs, depending on the number of books found. Each pair looks in the table of contents and the index to pinpoint pages that may be helpful and writes them on the work sheet. The students take turns finding the pages, determining whether the information is useful, and taking notes in the appropriate place on the work sheet. All students write a bibliographic entry for the nonfiction books they used.

**Assessment:** Informally observe whether the students are able to find the information and write it in their own words. If a formal assessment is desired, the work sheets can be collected.

**Closure:** Using think-pair-share, ask, "What additional information did the nonfiction books give you?"

*Note: The guided practice of this lesson can be repeated if the groups don't have enough time to complete their research. The nonfiction books and group folders can also be given to the teacher and the research can continue in the classroom.*

## LESSON 5: INFORMATION AND A BIOME MAP FROM THE INTERNET

**Standards:**

*AASL #2:* Draw conclusions, make informed decisions, apply knowledge to new situations, and create new knowledge. 2.1, Skills: 2.1.1, Continue an inquiry-based research process by applying critical-thinking skills (analysis, synthesis, evaluation, organization) to information and knowledge in order to construct new understandings, draw conclusions, and create new knowledge; 2.1.4, Use technology and other information tools to analyze and organize information; 2.1.5, Collaborate with others to exchange ideas, develop new understandings, make decisions, and solve problems.

*NCTE #8:* Students use a variety of technological and information resources (e.g., libraries, databases, computer networks, video) to gather and synthesize information and to create and communicate knowledge.

*NETS Technology #3: Research and Information Fluency:* Students apply digital tools to gather, evaluate, and use information.

**Objectives:**

1. Using the Internet, students locate information on their biome.
2. Using the Internet, students color a world map of the locations of their assigned biome.
3. Students understand that the Internet provides information and images on many topics.
4. Students understand that Web sites need to be evaluated for their reliability.

**Materials:**

- projection of an Internet computer screen (must have access to computer, Internet, and means of projection)
- personalized start page or bookmarked Internet sites available from the CD
- 10 to 15 computers with Internet access
- board-ready copy of a world map from www.infoplease.com/statemaps.html (under "continents")

- seven copies of world map, one for each group
- seven work sheets available from the CD
- board-ready copy of the work sheet
- the seven biome group folders
- chart on the characteristics of biomes from the CD
- 30 copies of the Letter to Parents with the Web sites, available on the CD

**Set:** Ask, "So far we've looked for information in the dictionary, the encyclopedia, and nonfiction books. Where else could we find information about biomes?"

**Review:** Review the characteristics of biomes: location, climate, dominant plants, common animals, conditions, and future. Read the names of the biomes. Review that the Internet is a network of interconnected computers around the world and a source of information and images. Web sites need to be evaluated for reliability. Also review the rules of using the Internet at school.

**Input:** Explain that the library has many resources. One of them is the Internet. Show the students a Web page on the chaparral biome, www.blueplanetbiomes.org/chaparral.htm. Model reading for information and filling out the work sheet. Then click on www.worldbiomes.com/biomes_map.htm and http://users.rcn.com/jkimball. ma.ultranet/BiologyPages/B/Biomes.html and model coloring a world map with the location of "chaparral." Then model taking the information from the Web site to create a bibliographic entry. Using think-pair-share, ask, "On what basis were the Web sites reliable?"

**Guided practice:** The students are instructed to get into their biome groups. Student 1 gets their folder, a world map, and a work sheet. Pair students and assign computers. One pair is given the task of clicking on a biome map Web site from the personalized start page and using it to color the world map with the locations of their assigned biome. The other pair is instructed to use the personalized start page to find Internet sites on their assigned biome. They are to read for information and fill out the work sheet. The students are also instructed to make a bibliographic entry on the work sheet for every Web site from which they get information. Circulate around the room, offering assistance when necessary. At the end of the guided practice, collect the group folders.

**Assessment:** Informally assess whether the students can restate the information presented by the Web sites.

**Closure:** Distribute to the students the letter to the parents with the Web sites and encourage the students to visit the sites at home with their parents.

## LESSON 6: WRITING A BIOME BROCHURE

**Standards:**

*AASL #2:* Draw conclusions, make informed decisions, apply knowledge to new situations, and create new knowledge. 2.1, Skills: 2.1.1, Continue an inquiry-based research process by applying critical-thinking skills (analysis, synthesis, evaluation, organization) to information and knowledge in order to construct new understandings, draw conclusions, and create new knowledge; 2.1.4, Use technology and other information tools to analyze and organize information; 2.1.5, Collaborate with others to exchange ideas, develop new understandings, make decisions, and solve problems.

*NCTE #8:*    Students use a variety of technological and information resources (e.g., libraries, databases, computer networks, video) to gather and synthesize information and to create and communicate knowledge.
*NETS Technology #3: Research and Information Fluency:*    Students apply digital tools to gather, evaluate, and use information.

**Objective:**
Students use a checklist to write the first draft of a biome brochure from the information on their work sheets.

**Materials:**

- checklist for biome brochure available from the CD
- 30 copies of the draft work sheet
- the seven biome group folders
- board-ready checklist available from the CD
- board-ready "chaparral" research work sheets from previous lessons
- board-ready draft work sheet
- chart on the characteristics of biomes from the CD

**Set:** Using think-pair-share, ask, "How can putting information in a brochure help others understand the characteristics of your assigned biome?" After some class discussion, say, "Today we are going to write the first draft of a biome brochure."

**Review:** Review the characteristics of biomes: location, climate, dominant plants, common animals, conditions, and future. Read the names of the biomes.

**Input:** Project the board-ready checklist for the biome brochure and go over each point. Model comparing your board-ready research work sheets on the "chaparral" biome with the checklist requirements. Model making sure that all the sections on the research work sheets have been filled out with enough information. Model taking the research information on "location" and "climate" and writing those sections in complete sentences with correct grammar, spelling, and punctuation on the board-ready draft work sheet.

**Guided practice:** Instruct students to get into their biome groups. Student 1 gets the group folder, a checklist, and a draft work sheet. Student 2 gets out the research work sheets and uses the checklist to make sure that all the required information is on the work sheets. Student 3 assigns each group member a section of the draft work sheet to write using complete sentences, with correct grammar, spelling, and punctuation. Once each section has been written, student 4 does a final editing. Circulate around the room, offering assistance when necessary. At the end of the guided practice, collect the group folders.

**Assessment:** Informally assess whether the students have completed their checklist and rewritten each section of their biome brochure.

**Closure:** Using think-pair-share, ask, "How did the checklist help in the writing of the draft of the biome brochure?"

*Note: The guided practice of this lesson can be repeated if the groups don't have enough time to finish writing their biome brochures.*

## LESSON 7: DESIGNING A BIOME BROCHURE USING A STORYBOARD

**Standards:**

*AASL #2:* Draw conclusions, make informed decisions, apply knowledge to new situations, and create new knowledge. 2.1, Skills: 2.1.1, Continue an inquiry-based research process by applying critical-thinking skills (analysis, synthesis, evaluation, organization) to information and knowledge in order to construct new understandings, draw conclusions, and create new knowledge; 2.1.4, Use technology and other information tools to analyze and organize information; 2.1.5, Collaborate with others to exchange ideas, develop new understandings, make decisions, and solve problems.
*NCTE #8:* Students use a variety of technological and information resources (e.g., libraries, databases, computer networks, video) to gather and synthesize information and to create and communicate knowledge.
*NETS Technology #1: Creativity and Innovation:* Students demonstrate creative thinking, construct knowledge, and develop innovative products and processes using technology.

**Objective:**
Students use a storyboard to design a biome brochure.

**Materials:**

- 35 storyboards for "page one" and 35 storyboards for "page two" available on the CD
- the seven biome group folders
- two copies each of the board-ready storyboard forms for "page one" and "page two"
- chart on the characteristics of biomes from the CD
- 30 copies of the encyclopedia brochure available on the CD

**Set:** Say, "Today we are going to design a biome brochure using a device called a storyboard."

**Review:** Review the characteristics of biomes: location, climate, dominant plants, common animals, conditions, and future. Read the names of the biomes.

**Input:** Distribute copies of the encyclopedia brochure. Guide the students in discovering the placement of the title, subtitles, information, and graphics in relationship to how the brochure is folded and read. Project "page one" of the board-ready storyboard and discuss ways a title, information, and graphics on "chaparral" could be arranged on the page. Then project "page two" of the board-ready storyboard and discuss the placement of subtitles, information, graphics, and bibliographic entries on the page. Using the two storyboard forms, with the class design "page one" and "page two" of at least two unique biome brochures. Individual facts are not written for the brochure at this time.

**Guided practice:** Instruct students to get into their biome groups. Student 1 gets their folders and storyboards. Student 2 leads the group members in a discussion of where to place the title, information, and graphics on page one and page two of the storyboard. The group works together until a final agreed-upon storyboard for "page one" and "page two" of the brochure is made. Circulate around the room, offering assistance when necessary. At the end of the guided practice, collect the group folders.

**Assessment:** Informally assess whether the students have completed their storyboards.

**Closure:** Using think-pair-share, ask, "How did having the storyboard help you in designing the biome brochure?"

*Note: The guided practice of this lesson can be repeated if the groups don't have enough time to finish designing their biome brochure in the library. The designing of the brochure can also be done in the classroom. The storyboards for the biome brochures must be completed before the next lesson is taught.*

## LESSON 8: MAKING A BIOME BROCHURE USING MICROSOFT PUBLISHER

**Standards:**

*National Science Education Content Standard C: Life Science:* Organisms and Their Environments: An organism's patterns of behavior are related to the nature of that organism's environment including the kinds and numbers of other organisms present, the availability of food and resources, and the physical characteristics of the environment.

*AASL #2:* Draw conclusions, make informed decisions, apply knowledge to new situations, and create new knowledge. 2.1, Skills: 2.1.1, Continue an inquiry-based research process by applying critical-thinking skills (analysis, synthesis, evaluation, organization) to information and knowledge in order to construct new understandings, draw conclusions, and create new knowledge; 2.1.4, Use technology and other information tools to analyze and organize information; 2.1.5, Collaborate with others to exchange ideas, develop new understandings, make decisions, and solve problems.

*NCTE #8:* Students use a variety of technological and information resources to gather and synthesize information and to create and communicate knowledge.

**Objectives:**

1. Students understand the procedure for creating a brochure.
2. Using Microsoft Publisher, students create a brochure on their assigned biome.

**Materials:**

- projection of an Internet computer screen (must have access to computer, Internet, and means of projection)
- 10 to 15 computers with Microsoft Publisher and Internet access if graphics from Web sites are desired
- the seven biome group folders
- chart on the characteristics of biomes from the CD
- seven floppy disks or CDs
- visual of a deciduous temperate rain forest

**Set:** Using think-pair-share, ask, "There is an area where it rains about 80 inches a year, the winters are cold and wet, and bears, deer, and elk roam through an evergreen forest. Which biome is it?" (Deciduous temperate rain forest.)

**Review:** Review the characteristics of biomes: location, climate, dominant plants, common animals, conditions, and future. Read the names of the biomes.

**Input:** Project a computer desktop and under "Start" or "Programs" go to "Microsoft Publisher." Scroll down to "Brochures," click on "Informational," and select a brochure (accessory bar informational brochure) to teach the procedure for creating a brochure. Show the students how to:

- delete a box, picture, or writing if not needed
- add a graphic from Microsoft Clips Online
- add a title using WordArt Gallery
- go from page one to page two
- change the color of the bar decoration
- change style and font

**Guided practice:** Instruct the students to get into their biome groups. Student 1 gets their group folders. Pair students within their group and assign each pair to a computer. One pair works on page one and one pair works on page two. Circulate among the computers, offering assistance when necessary. At the end of the lesson, the groups should print what they have done so far and save their brochure to a disk or CD. At the end of the guided practice, collect the group folders and the disks or CDs.

**Assessment:** Informally assess whether the students are able to use Microsoft Publisher to create a biome brochure.

**Closure:** Using think-pair-share, ask, "How did having the storyboard form and the brochure draft work sheet already done help in the making of the biome brochure on the computer?"

*Note: The guided practice of this lesson can be repeated if the groups don't have enough time to finish making their biome brochures. The making of the brochure can also be done in the classroom or computer lab. The biome brochures must be completed before the next lesson is taught.*

## LESSON 9: READING, RATING, AND CHANGING THE BIOME BROCHURES

**Standards:**

*AASL #3:* Share knowledge and participate ethically and productively as members of our democratic society. 3.1, Skills: 3.1.1, Conclude an inquiry-based research process by sharing new understandings and reflecting on the learning; 3.1.3, Use writing and speaking skills to communicate new understandings effectively.

**Objectives:**

1. Students read their biome brochure.
2. Students rate their biome brochure based on a rubric.
3. Students make any final changes on their biome brochure.

**Materials:**

- two copies of each group's biome brochure
- board-ready copy of the biome brochure rubric
- instructor-made chaparral brochure
- 30 copies of the biome brochure rubric
- seven biome group folders
- 10 to 15 computers with Microsoft Publisher and Internet Access
- seven disks or CDs with each group's biome brochure
- chart on the characteristics of biomes from the CD

**Set:** Using think-pair-share, ask, "How can we tell what kind of job we did in making our biome brochure?"

**Review:** Review that a rubric is a tool to assess a product.

**Input:** Project the biome brochure rubric on the board, distribute copies to the students, and explain it. Take one category of the rubric and apply it to the "chaparral" biome brochure, deciding how you performed on that category. Circle the rating number you have decided to give for that category. Explain that the groups are going to use the rubric to assess their biome brochures and they should make any final changes they need on their biome brochures.

**Guided practice:** The students are instructed to get into their biome groups. Student 1 gets the folder and two copies of the "almost final" biome brochure. Student 2 is the leader of the discussion and makes sure that all group members are able to voice their rating and reasons. Student 3 reads a section of the brochure, and this is followed by a rating session. Student 2 circles the agreed-upon rating. This continues until all sections have been rated. After the group has finished the assessment of their brochure, they are to change anything on the biome brochure that was not given at least a "3." Student 3 assigns any agreed-upon rewriting of the brochure. Circulate around the room, offering assistance when necessary. At the end of the guided practice, the students save their biome brochure. Collect the group folders and the disks or CDs.

**Assessment:** Informally observe whether the students are able to use the rubric to assess and change their biome brochure.

**Closure:** Using think-pair-share, ask, "How did you use the rubric to revise your brochure?"

*Note: The biome brochures must be completed before the teaching of the next lesson.*

## LESSON 10: PRESENTATION OF THE BIOME BROCHURES

**Standards:**

*AASL #3:* Share knowledge and participate ethically and productively as members of our democratic society. 3.1, Skills: 3.1.1, Conclude an inquiry-based research process by sharing new understandings and reflecting on the learning; 3.1.3, Use writing and speaking skills to communicate new understandings effectively.

*NCTE #8:* Students use a variety of technological and information resources (e.g., libraries, databases, computer networks, video) to gather and synthesize information and to create and communicate knowledge.

*NETS Technology #2: Communication and Collaboration:* Students use digital media and environments to communicate and work collaboratively to support individual learning and contribute to the learning of others.

**Objective:**
Each student orally presents and teaches his or her biome brochure to a group.

**Materials:**

- 30 copies of each group's biome brochure
- a bell or timer
- chart on the characteristics of biomes from the CD

**Set:** Say, "Today you are going to teach each other about the seven biomes of the world."

**Review:** Review the cooperative learning jigsaw strategy. Remind students that effective presenters speak loudly and clearly, and the listeners are silent and attentive during the presentations.

**Input:** Students get into their biome groups, and student 3 collects their biome brochures and distributes seven copies to each group member. Let the students know that they will have five minutes to present and teach their biome brochure. Students bring their chairs with them when their student number is called. All student 1s are directed to a one location in the library, all the student 2s to another location, and so on. Once at their assigned locations, instruct the students to form a circle.

**Guided practice:** Decide ahead of time the order of the presentations. Begin by calling out the first biome and then ring a bell after five minutes are up. Make sure the students have finished their presentations and then call out the next biome. Students present their information when their biome is called. They distribute a copy of the brochure to each person in the group just before they present. After all the biomes have been called and all the presentations are complete, the students take their chairs back to the tables and wait for instructions. Using think-pair-share, lead the class to make conclusions based on their research. Do this by leading a discussion and asking key questions before asking the concluding questions.
   Examples of key questions:

- What is a biome and what are its characteristics?
- What are the biomes on the earth?
- What are humans doing to change or influence the condition and future of the biomes?
- What biome do you live in?

Examples of concluding questions:

- What can a person or communities do to ensure that all the biomes on the earth are not damaged by human activity?
- What can governments and nations do to ensure that all the biomes on earth are not damaged by human activity?

**Assessment:** Gather from the answers to the discussion questions whether the students have acquired the desired understandings. Using the biome brochure rubric, you can formally assess each biome brochure for a final grade for each group.

**Closure:** Using think-pair-share, ask the students to identify their favorite part of the unit.

# Chapter 13

# Fifth Grade:  Natural Weather Hazards

## PLANNING

### *Stage 1:  Identify Desired Results*

**Established goals:**

*National Science Education Standards Content Standard F: Natural Weather Hazards:*
- Internal and external processes of the earth system cause natural weather hazards, events that change or destroy human and wildlife habitats, damage property, and harm or kill humans. Natural weather hazards include earthquakes, landslides, wildfires, volcanic eruptions, floods, storms, and even possible impacts of asteroids.
- Natural weather hazards can present personal and societal challenges because misidentifying the change or incorrectly estimating the rate and scale of change may result in either too little attention and significant human costs or too much cost for unneeded preventive measures.

**Essential questions:**

1. How have natural weather hazards affected people, animals, and land?
2. How have people tried to lessen the effects of natural weather hazards?

**Understandings:**

1. What are natural weather hazards?
2. How do natural weather hazards form?
3. Where do natural weather hazards happen around the world?
4. What are the effects of natural weather hazards on people and property?
5. What are the emergency procedures needed before, during, and after a specific natural weather hazard?

**What key knowledge and skills will the students acquire?**

1. Students define natural weather hazards, understand how they are formed and where, and research early warning and measuring systems.

2. Students understand the scope of destruction of a natural weather hazard.
3. Students understand and use the procedure for making an emergency procedure flyer.
4. Students use the dictionary, encyclopedia, Internet, online catalog, nonfiction books, atlas, and almanac to extract information on a natural weather hazard.

## Stage 2: Determine Acceptable Evidence

**Performance task:**
Students create a one-page emergency procedure flyer for the community about a natural weather hazard, including what to do before, during, and after it occurs.

**Student self-assessment and reflection:**
Summative assessment: Students assess their final product. Students reflect after the assessment and revise their flyer. Students use the following rubric to assess their performance task:

### Rubric for Emergency Procedure Flyer

| Category | 4 Great | 3 Very Good | 2 Okay | 1 Needs More Work |
|---|---|---|---|---|
| Research/Statistical Data | Students include 4 or more high-quality examples or pieces of data to support their campaign. | Students include at least 3 high-quality examples or pieces of data to support their campaign. | Students include at least 2 high-quality examples or pieces of data to support their campaign. | Students include fewer than 2 high-quality examples or pieces of data to support their campaign. |
| Campaign/Product | Students create an original, accurate, and interesting product that adequately addresses the issue. | Students create an accurate product that adequately addresses the issue. | Students create an accurate product, but it does not adequately address the issue. | The product is not accurate. |
| Sources: Quality | Students include 4 or more high-quality sources. | Students include 2–3 high-quality sources. | Students include 2–3 sources, but some are of questionable quality. | Students include fewer than 2 sources. |
| Sources: Citation | Information in all source citations is correct and in the format assigned. | Information in all source citations is correct, but there are minor errors in formatting. | Information in almost all source citations is correct *and* there are minor errors in formatting. | The information is often incorrect *or* there are major errors in formatting. |

## Stage 3: Plan Learning Experiences

- The instructor shows short video clips of several natural weather hazards or reads passages from non-fiction books on natural weather hazards. The instructor leads a discussion about natural weather hazards: thunderstorms, hurricanes, tornadoes, blizzards, tsunamis, floods, cyclones, and typhoons (which the instructor uses as a model for the input of many of the lessons). The performance task and rubric for the unit are introduced.
- Each group is assigned a natural weather hazard.

- Students use the dictionary to define key vocabulary.
- Students take notes on information from the encyclopedia.
- Students use the online catalog to find nonfiction books and take notes on their assigned hazard.
- Students use the Internet to find safety information.
- Students use the almanac to find the human cost of natural weather hazards.
- Students use the atlas to locate the places that a specific natural weather hazard occurs.
- Students write a rough draft of their one-page natural weather hazard emergency procedures flyer.
- Students use the rubric to revise their emergency procedures flyer.
- Students use the cooperative learning jigsaw strategy to teach other students about their assigned natural weather hazard.
- Using think-pair-share, the instructor leads a class discussion with key and concluding questions about natural weather hazards.

## LESSON 1: BRAINSTORMING

**Standards:**

*National Science Education Standards Content Standard F: Natural Weather Hazards:*
- Internal and external processes of the earth system cause natural weather hazards, events that change or destroy human and wildlife habitats, damage property, and harm or kill humans. Natural weather hazards include earthquakes, landslides, wildfires, volcanic eruptions, floods, storms, and even possible impacts of asteroids.
- Natural weather hazards can present personal and societal challenges because misidentifying the change or incorrectly estimating the rate and scale of change may result in either too little attention and significant human costs or too much cost for unneeded preventive measures.

**Objectives:**

1. Students understand that there are many types of natural weather hazards.
2. Students understand that natural weather hazards have an effect on people and property.
3. Students understand the performance task and rubric required for the unit.

**Materials:**

- chart or empty board-ready paper
- videos or video clips of natural weather hazards such as tornadoes, tsunamis, or hurricanes, or passages from the following books:
  Challen, Paul. *Hurricane and Typhoon Alert!* New York: Crabtree Publishing Company, 2004.
  Harrison, Carol. *Weather and Climate*. Chicago: Gareth Stevens Publishing, 2004.
  Maisner, Heather. *Amazing Weather*. Grand Rapids, MI: School Specialty, 2007.
- board-ready copy of the rubric

**Set:** Show video clips of natural weather hazards or read some passages from the books in the materials list. Ask the students to identify the natural weather hazards that were in the videos or books.

**Input:** Students use think-pair-share to identify other natural weather hazards. Write all of the hazards. Circle the ones that are weather related (thunderstorms, hurricanes, tornadoes, blizzards, tsunamis, floods, and cyclones) and state that they will be the focus of the research. Explain the unit, the performance task, and the rubric using the board-ready copies.

**Assessment:** Informally observe whether the students are able to understand the concept of natural weather hazards.

**Closure:** Using think-pair-share, ask the students to name some of the natural weather hazards.

## LESSON 2: USING THE DICTIONARY TO UNDERSTAND KEY VOCABULARY OF NATURAL WEATHER HAZARDS

**Standards:**

*National Science Education Standards Content Standard F: Natural Weather Hazards:*
- Internal and external processes of the earth system cause natural weather hazards, events that change or destroy human and wildlife habitats, damage property, and harm or kill humans. Natural weather hazards include earthquakes, landslides, wildfires, volcanic eruptions, floods, storms, and even possible impacts of asteroids.
- Natural weather hazards can present personal and societal challenges because misidentifying the change or incorrectly estimating the rate and scale of change may result in either too little attention and significant human costs or too much cost for unneeded preventive measures.

*AASL #2:* Draw conclusions, make informed decisions, apply knowledge to new situations, and create new knowledge. 2.1, Skills: 2.1.1, Continue an inquiry-based research process by applying critical-thinking skills (analysis, synthesis, evaluation, organization) to information and knowledge in order to construct new understandings, draw conclusions, and create new knowledge; 2.1.4, Use technology and other information tools to analyze and organize information; 2.1.5, Collaborate with others to exchange ideas, develop new understandings, make decisions, and solve problems.

*NCTE #8:* Students use a variety of technological and information resources to gather and synthesize information and to create and communicate knowledge.

**Objectives:**

1. Using a dictionary, students paraphrase the definitions of key vocabulary for the unit.
2. Students teach each other about the words they have researched.

**Materials:**

- chart with the students' ideas on natural weather hazards from the first lesson
- visual of a typhoon
- 30 copies of the work sheet from the CD
- four or five copies of each of seven paper strips with four weather words each, available on the CD
- board-ready copy of the work sheet on the CD

- 30 intermediate dictionaries
- seven group folders with the performance task rubric from the CD

**Set:** Show the visual of a typhoon and ask whether the students know what kind of natural weather hazard it is.

**Review:** Review the arrangement of the dictionary and the use of guide words.

**Input:** Give students an intermediate dictionary. If there aren't enough dictionaries, the students can do this activity in pairs. Look up "typhoon" in the dictionary. Model, thinking aloud, how to look up a word in the dictionary (beginning letter, next letter, using guide words, etc.). Locate the word and read the definition aloud. The students put the definition in their own words, with help. Write the paraphrased definition in the space on the work sheet. With the students, chorally read the definition.

**Guided practice:** Students at each table are given paper strip with the same four words and copies of the work sheets. Each table has different words. The students work together to locate and paraphrase the definitions of the words. They make sure everyone in the group understands all four words. Each student writes the paraphrased definitions on his or her individual work sheet. After the research is completed, the students are numbered, 1 through 4 or 5 at each table. All the 1s are grouped together, all the 2s, and so on. Each student teaches the four words from his or her work sheet, on which he or she is an expert. Then group the students into their natural weather hazard groups. The group folders are distributed with the natural weather hazard indicated on the cover (thunderstorms, hurricanes, tornadoes, blizzards, tsunamis, floods, and cyclones). Students write their names next to the number on the cover, 1 through 4 or 5. Collect the group folders.

**Assessment:** Informally observe whether the students are able to find the words in the dictionary, paraphrase the definitions, and teach the words to the other students. Students are directed to take their dictionary work sheets home and share the definitions with their parents.

**Closure:** Using think-pair-share, ask the students how they found the words in the dictionary.

## LESSON 3: RESEARCHING NATURAL WEATHER HAZARDS IN THE ENCYCLOPEDIA

**Standards:**

*National Science Education Standards Content Standard F: Natural Weather Hazards:*
- Internal and external processes of the earth system cause natural weather hazards, events that change or destroy human and wildlife habitats, damage property, and harm or kill humans. Natural weather hazards include earthquakes, landslides, wildfires, volcanic eruptions, floods, storms, and even possible impacts of asteroids.
- Natural weather hazards can present personal and societal challenges because misidentifying the change or incorrectly estimating the rate and scale of change may result in either too little attention and significant human costs or too much cost for unneeded preventive measures.

*AASL #2:* Draw conclusions, make informed decisions, apply knowledge to new situations, and create new knowledge. 2.1, Skills: 2.1.1, Continue an inquiry-based research process by applying critical-thinking skills (analysis, synthesis, evaluation, organization) to information and knowledge in order to construct new understandings, draw conclusions, and create new knowledge; 2.1.4, Use technology and

other information tools to analyze and organize information; 2.1.5, Collaborate with others to exchange ideas, develop new understandings, make decisions, and solve problems.
*NCTE #8:*    Students use a variety of technological and information resources to gather and synthesize information and to create and communicate knowledge.

**Objective:**
Using an encyclopedia, students record the characteristics, locations, formation, and effects of natural weather hazards.

**Materials:**

* two sets of the *World Book Encyclopedia*
* 30 copies of the work sheet from the CD
* 30 copies of a world map from www.infoplease.com/statemaps.html (under "continents")
* board-ready copy of work sheet
* board-ready outline map of the world
* visual of a typhoon
* seven group folders (from previous lesson)

**Set:** Show the visual of the typhoon and ask, "Where in the world does this type of storm occur?"

**Review:** Review the organization of an encyclopedia and the use of guide words. Remind the students to look at and read the pictures, captions, charts, and graphs in an article before reading the information.

**Input:** Look up "typhoon" in the encyclopedia. Ponder aloud under what letter it would be found, "T." Realize that the second letter is a "y," so the article will be at the very end of the "T" encyclopedia volume. Select the correct one after checking the spine and find the article on "typhoon." Read the work sheet aloud to see what information is required. Read aloud the pertinent information from the encyclopedia and model how to paraphrase the information, writing notes, not complete sentences. Show the students that not all the sections of the work sheet have been filled in because the encyclopedia did not contain all the information required. Put the outline map of the world on the board and model how to use the information in the encyclopedia to locate the areas of the world where typhoons occur. Model writing the bibliographic entry for the article you used.

**Guided practice:** Students get into their assigned groups from the previous lesson. In each group, student 1 is in charge of materials. He or she gets the group's folder, the work sheets, the world map, and the encyclopedia volume, when it is decided by the group which letter is needed. Student 2 uses the guide words to find the article, shows the pictures and charts, and reads the headings and subheadings, if any. Student 3 reads aloud, in a whisper to the rest of this group, the information the students deem important in the article. After each student makes suggestions, student 4 helps the group paraphrase the information and indicates the location of the natural weather hazard on the world map. Students fill out individual work sheets and world map. Student 1 is in charge of helping all members of the group write the bibliographic entry correctly. Circulate during guided practice to offer assistance as needed. At the end of the guided practice, collect the group folders.

**Assessment:** Informally observe whether the students are able to find the information and write it in their own words.

**Closure:** Using think-pair-share, ask the students what problems they experienced while paraphrasing the information.

## LESSON 4: USING NONFICTION BOOKS TO FIND INFORMATION

**Standards:**

*National Science Education Standards Content Standard F: Natural Weather Hazards:*
- Internal and external processes of the earth system cause natural weather hazards, events that change or destroy human and wildlife habitats, damage property, and harm or kill humans. Natural weather hazards include earthquakes, landslides, wildfires, volcanic eruptions, floods, storms, and even possible impacts of asteroids.
- Natural weather hazards can present personal and societal challenges because misidentifying the change or incorrectly estimating the rate and scale of change may result in either too little attention and significant human costs or too much cost for unneeded preventive measures.

*AASL #2:* Draw conclusions, make informed decisions, apply knowledge to new situations, and create new knowledge. 2.1, Skills: 2.1.1, Continue an inquiry-based research process by applying critical-thinking skills (analysis, synthesis, evaluation, organization) to information and knowledge in order to construct new understandings, draw conclusions, and create new knowledge; 2.1.4, Use technology and other information tools to analyze and organize information; 2.1.5, Collaborate with others to exchange ideas, develop new understandings, make decisions, and solve problems.

*NCTE #8:* Students use a variety of technological and information resources to gather and synthesize information and to create and communicate knowledge.

**Objective:**
Students use nonfiction books to find information on their assigned form of natural weather hazard.

**Materials:**

- nonfiction books on the different natural weather hazards in their correct location in the library
- computers with online catalog access
- Look for a Book form from the CD
- seven group folders (from previous lesson)
- 30 copies of the work sheet available from the CD

**Set:** Using think-pair-share, say, "I used the encyclopedia to look up information about the characteristics of the typhoon. It had some information, but certainly not all that I needed in order to make the best emergency procedure flyer I can. Where else could I look for information?"

**Review:** Review the procedure for finding books by subject using the online catalog.

**Input:** Explain that the library has many resources. One of main resources is nonfiction books. Model going to a computer, accessing the online catalog, and typing in "typhoon." Use the Look for a Book form to write the call number and title of a book. Then find the book on the shelf. Project the board-ready work sheet and read it to know what information is required. Peruse the table of contents and the index to find page numbers that are likely to contain the information. Turn to one of the pages noted, read a paragraph aloud, and decide whether the information is on target. If so, paraphrase it and write it on the work sheet. Students chorally read your paraphrased information. After this example, model how to write a bibliographic entry for the book you just used.

**Guided practice:** Students get into their assigned groups from the previous lesson. Student 2 is in charge of materials. He or she gets the folder and hands out the work sheets. Student 3 leads the search on the online catalog for nonfiction books on the assigned natural weather hazard. He or she writes the call number and titles of books that will be helpful. While the other group members return to their seats, student 3 takes the Look for a Book forms and finds the books on the shelf. Student 1 assigns the books to group members in pairs, depending on the number of books found. Each pair looks in the table of contents and the index to pinpoint pages that may be helpful and writes them on the work sheet. The students take turns finding the pages, determining whether the information is useful, and taking notes paraphrasing the information in the appropriate place on the work sheet. All students write a bibliographic entry for the nonfiction books they used.

**Assessment:** Informally observe whether the students are able to find the information and write it in their own words.

**Closure:** Using think-pair-share, ask, "What additional information did the nonfiction books give you?"

*Note: The guided practice of this lesson can be repeated if the groups don't have enough time to complete their research. The nonfiction books and group folders can also be given to the teacher, and the research can continue in the classroom.*

## LESSON 5: FINDING INFORMATION IN THE ALMANAC

**Standards:**

*National Science Education Standards Content Standard F: Natural Weather Hazards:*
- Internal and external processes of the earth system cause natural weather hazards, events that change or destroy human and wildlife habitats, damage property, and harm or kill humans. Natural weather hazards include earthquakes, landslides, wildfires, volcanic eruptions, floods, storms, and even possible impacts of asteroids.
- Natural weather hazards can present personal and societal challenges because misidentifying the change or incorrectly estimating the rate and scale of change may result in either too little attention and significant human costs or too much cost for unneeded preventive measures.

*AASL #2:* Draw conclusions, make informed decisions, apply knowledge to new situations, and create new knowledge. 2.1, Skills: 2.1.1, Continue an inquiry-based research process by applying critical-thinking skills (analysis, synthesis, evaluation, organization) to information and knowledge in order to construct new understandings, draw conclusions, and create new knowledge; 2.1.4, Use technology and other information tools to analyze and organize information; 2.1.5, Collaborate with others to exchange ideas, develop new understandings, make decisions, and solve problems.

*NCTE #8:* Students use a variety of technological and information resources (e.g., libraries, databases, computer networks, video) to gather and synthesize information and to create and communicate knowledge.

**Objectives:**

1. Students use the almanac to find information about when and where specific natural weather hazards have occurred.
2. Students record the information, including loss of life, on a work sheet.

**Materials:**

- 30 copies of the work sheet available on the CD
- board-ready copy of a work sheet
- seven group folders
- 15 copies of the most recent edition of *The World Almanac and Book of Facts*

**Set:** Ask, "So far we've looked for information in the dictionary, the encyclopedia, and nonfiction books. Where can we find information about recent and historical occurrences of natural weather hazards and the statistics on the loss of human life?"

**Review:** Review that the almanac is a current book of facts and statistics. It is necessary to use the index, which is in alphabetical order, to find specific information.

**Input:** Explain that the library has many resources. One of these is the almanac. Distribute the almanacs and the work sheets to each pair of students. Read the work sheet to understand what information is required. Note that the thunderstorm group has a separate work sheet and questions. Model using the index to look up "typhoon," writing down the pages cited. Turn to the first page and skim it. Decide that this will not give you the required information. Turn to the second series of pages cited, and find the heading "Some Notable Hurricanes, Typhoons, Blizzards, Other Storms." Point out the abbreviations for the different storms and the setup of the chart. Model how to transfer the required information on the earliest, most recent, and most deadly occurrence of the weather disaster. Note that sometimes the most deadly disaster will be the earliest or most recent, and students should repeat the information in the space on the work sheet. Model writing the bibliographic entry for *The World Almanac and Book of Facts*.

**Guided practice:** Students get into their groups, and student 3 gets the group folder. Students work in pairs to find the required information and write the bibliographic entry.

**Assessment:** Informally assess whether the students use the index, find the correct information, record it, and write the bibliographic entry.

**Closure:** Direct student 4 of each group to report to the whole class the deadliest incident of their assigned natural weather hazard. Collect the group folders.

## LESSON 6: FINDING INFORMATION ON THE INTERNET

**Standards:**

*National Science Education Standards Content Standard F: Natural Weather Hazards:*
- Internal and external processes of the earth system cause natural weather hazards, events that change or destroy human and wildlife habitats, damage property, and harm or kill humans. Natural weather hazards include earthquakes, landslides, wildfires, volcanic eruptions, floods, storms, and even possible impacts of asteroids.
- Natural weather hazards can present personal and societal challenges because misidentifying the change or incorrectly estimating the rate and scale of change may result in either too little attention and significant human costs or too much cost for unneeded preventive measures.

*AASL #2:* Draw conclusions, make informed decisions, apply knowledge to new situations, and create new knowledge. 2.1, Skills: 2.1.1, Continue an inquiry-based research process by applying critical-thinking skills (analysis, synthesis, evaluation, organization) to information and knowledge in order to construct new understandings, draw conclusions, and create new knowledge; 2.1.4, Use technology and other information tools to analyze and organize information; 2.1.5, Collaborate with others to exchange ideas, develop new understandings, make decisions, and solve problems.

*NCTE #8:* Students use a variety of technological and information resources (e.g., libraries, databases, computer networks, video) to gather and synthesize information and to create and communicate knowledge.

*NETS Technology #3: Research and Information Fluency:* Students apply digital tools to gather, evaluate, and use information.

**Objectives:**

1. Students use Web sites to find information about emergency safety procedures before, during, and after an occurrence of their assigned natural weather hazard.
2. Students understand that the Internet provides information and images on many topics.
3. Students understand that Web sites need to be evaluated for their reliability.

**Materials:**

- projection of an Internet computer screen (must have access to computer, Internet, and means of projection)
- personalized start page or bookmarked Internet sites, available on the CD
- 30 copies of the "Letter to Parents" with the Web sites, available on the CD
- seven group folders from the previous lessons
- 30 copies of the work sheet, available on the CD
- board-ready copy of a work sheet
- 10 to 15 computers with Internet access

**Set:** Ask, "So far we've looked for information in the dictionary, the encyclopedia, nonfiction books, and an almanac. Where else could we find current information about emergency procedures before, during, and after an occurrence of a natural weather hazard?"

**Review:** Review that the Internet is a network of interconnected computers around the world and a source of information and images. Web sites need to be evaluated for reliability. Also review the rules on using the Internet at school.

**Input:** Explain that the library has many resources. One of them is the Internet. Show the students some Web sites: one showing how typhoons are formed, http://news.bbc.co.uk/2/hi/science/nature/4183344.stm; one giving information on emergency procedures for hurricanes (which is what typhoons are called in the Western Hemisphere), www.fema.gov/kids/protect.htm; and the Red Cross, which has a great deal of information for their emergency procedure flyers, www.redcross.org/services/disaster/0,1082,0_501_,00.html. Model searching the Web sites to find information about emergency procedures before, during, and after a hurricane (typhoon). Read the information and paraphrase it. Project the board-ready copy of the work sheet and fill in the required information for one of the procedures. Write the name of the Web site as well as the URL on the work sheet. Discuss why the Web sites you used are considered very reliable (U.S. government, BBC, and Red Cross). Tell the students that you have bookmarked sites on the personalized start page for each natural weather hazard they are researching.

**Guided practice:** Students are paired within their groups (from previous lessons), and each pair is assigned a computer. They use the personalized start page to find Web sites on their assigned natural weather hazard. They look at the Web sites, decide on the pertinent material, and read it. They paraphrase the information and record it on the work sheet. They write the names of the Web sites and the URLs on the work sheet. Circulate among the computers, offering assistance as needed. After all students complete the assignment, they meet in their groups to discuss the new information and place their work sheets in their folders. Collect the group folders.

**Assessment:** Informally assess whether the students can restate the information presented by the Web sites and have written the title and the URL for each Web site.

**Closure:** Distribute to the students the letter to the parents with the Web sites and encourage the students to visit the sites at home with their parents.

## LESSON 7: WRITING THE ROUGH DRAFT OF THE EMERGENCY PROCEDURE FLYER

**Standards:**

*National Science Education Standards Content Standard F: Natural Weather Hazards:*
- Internal and external processes of the earth system cause natural weather hazards, events that change or destroy human and wildlife habitats, damage property, and harm or kill humans. Natural weather hazards include earthquakes, landslides, wildfires, volcanic eruptions, floods, storms, and even possible impacts of asteroids.
- Natural weather hazards can present personal and societal challenges because misidentifying the change or incorrectly estimating the rate and scale of change may result in either too little attention and significant human costs or too much cost for unneeded preventive measures.

*AASL #2:* Draw conclusions, make informed decisions, apply knowledge to new situations, and create new knowledge. 2.1, Skills: 2.1.1, Continue an inquiry-based research process by applying critical-thinking skills (analysis, synthesis, evaluation, organization) to information and knowledge in order to construct new understandings, draw conclusions, and create new knowledge; 2.1.4, Use technology and other information tools to analyze and organize information; 2.1.5, Collaborate with others to exchange ideas, develop new understandings, make decisions, and solve problems.

*NCTE #8:* Students use a variety of technological and information resources (e.g., libraries, databases, computer networks, video) to gather and synthesize information and to create and communicate knowledge.

*NETS Technology #3: Research and Information Fluency:* Students apply digital tools to gather, evaluate, and use information.

**Objectives:**

1. Students use a template to write the rough draft of the emergency procedures flyer for their assigned natural weather hazard.

2.    Students use their research work sheets and bibliographic entries as the information for the emergency procedure flyer.

**Materials:**

- seven group folders from the previous lessons
- 30 copies of the template from the CD
- board-ready copy of the template

**Set:** Using think-pair-share, ask, "Today we're going to write an emergency procedures flyer for the natural weather hazards we have been researching. Why would this flyer be useful for the school and community?"

**Review:** Say, "The purpose of a rough draft is to get the required information in your own words and in complete sentences. The editing will come later, so don't worry about misspellings and punctuation."

**Input:** Lay out the work sheets on typhoons that you have completed. Look at the template to see what information is needed. First, make up a title that will create interest for the reader. A suggestion is "Terrible Typhoons: Emergency Procedures." Model where to find the information for each section of the template. Model the writing of one or two sections.

**Guided practice:** Students get into their assigned groups from previous lessons while student 3 gets the folder and a copy of the template for each group member. First, the group decides on a snappy title. Student 1 assigns each group member a section of the template. Students work individually to write that section using the research work sheets in the folder. Circulate among the tables, offering assistance as needed.

**Assessment:** Informally assess whether the students can use the information to write their sections of the flyer.

**Closure:** Students read their section of the template to the other group members. Collect the group folders.

*Note: The students may need more than one session in the library or classroom to complete the guided practice of this lesson. The first draft of the emergency procedure flyer must be completed before the teaching of the next lesson.*

## LESSON 8:  READING AND RATING THE DRAFT OF THE EMERGENCY PROCEDURE FLYER

**Standards:**

*AASL #3:*    Share knowledge and participate ethically and productively as members of our democratic society. 3.1, Skills: 3.1.1, Conclude an inquiry-based research process by sharing new understandings and reflecting on the learning; 3.1.3, Use writing and speaking skills to communicate new understandings effectively.

**Objectives:**

1.    Students read the draft of their emergency procedure flyer.
2.    Students rate their emergency procedure flyer based on the rubric.

3.    Student make revisions based on their assessment and create a final copy of their emergency procedure flyer.

**Materials:**

- the seven group folders from previous lessons
- board-ready copy of the rubric, available on the CD
- 30 copies of the rubric
- board-ready copy of the instructor's template on typhoons, with two sections written
- 30 copies of the template already in the group folders

**Set:** Using think-pair-share, ask, "How can we tell what kind of a job we have done so far in making our emergency procedure flyers?"

**Review:** Review that a rubric is a tool to assess a product.

**Input:** Read one section of your board-ready flyer. Put the rubric for the project on the board, distribute copies to the students, and review it. Take one category of the rubric and apply it to your emergency procedure typhoon flyer, deciding how you did on that category. Circle the rating.

**Guided practice:** The group folders are distributed. Student 2 in each group is the leader of the discussion and makes sure that all group members are able to voice their rating and reasons. Student 1 reads a section of the flyer. This is followed by a rating session. Student 2 circles the rating and takes suggestions for revisions. This continues until all sections have been rated and suggestions for revision given. Student 3 assigns the rewriting of the sections. Each member of the group rewrites a section of the template to include the revisions. The final drafts are written on new copies of the templates and cut and pasted onto one page.

**Assessment:** Informally observe whether the students are able to use the rubric to rate the product and make revision suggestions.

**Closure:** The group members read the revised sections, in the order of the template, to each other.

*Note: The guided practice of this lesson may need more than one session to be accomplished. Using computers, the students need to type the one-page emergency procedure flyers and add any graphics before the next lesson.*

## LESSON 9:  PRESENTATION OF THE EMERGENCY PROCEDURES FLYERS

**Standards:**

*National Science Education Standards Content Standard F: Natural Weather Hazards:*
- Internal and external processes of the earth system cause natural weather hazards, events that change or destroy human and wildlife habitats, damage property, and harm or kill humans. Natural weather hazards include earthquakes, landslides, wildfires, volcanic eruptions, floods, storms, and even possible impacts of asteroids.

- Natural weather hazards can present personal and societal challenges because misidentifying the change or incorrectly estimating the rate and scale of change may result in either too little attention and significant human costs or too much cost for unneeded preventive measures.

*AASL #3:*    Share knowledge and participate ethically and productively as members of our democratic society. 3.1, Skills: 3.1.1, Conclude an inquiry-based research process by sharing new understandings and reflecting on the learning; 3.1.3, Use writing and speaking skills to communicate new understandings effectively.

*NCTE #8:*    Students use a variety of technological and information resources to gather and synthesize information and to create and communicate knowledge.

**Objective:**

Using the cooperative learning jigsaw strategy, students teach others about their assigned natural weather hazard using the emergency procedures flyer each group has produced.

**Materials:**

- copies of the emergency procedures flyers, 30 per hazard
- bell or timer

**Set:** Say, "It's time to share our performance task and new knowledge so that everyone in the class will know about each of the natural weather hazards we've researched.

**Review:** Review the cooperative learning jigsaw strategy. Remind students that effective presenters speak loudly and clearly, and that listeners are silent and attentive during the presentations.

**Input:** Students get into their natural weather hazard groups, and student 4 in each group collects emergency procedure flyers and distributes seven copies to each group member. Let the students know that they will have five minutes to present and teach their emergency procedure flyer. Students bring their chairs with them when their student number is called. Student 1s are directed to one location in the library, student 2s to another location, and so on. Once at their assigned locations, the students are instructed to form a circle.

**Guided practice:** Decide ahead of time the order of the presentations. Begin by calling out the first hazard and then ring a bell after five minutes are up. Make sure the students have finished their presentations and then call out the next hazard. Students present their information when their hazard is called. They distribute a copy of the emergency procedure flyer to each person in the group just before they present. After all the natural weather hazards have been called and all the presentations are complete, the students take their chairs back to the tables and wait for instructions. Using think-pair-share, lead the class to making conclusions based on their research. Ask key questions before asking concluding questions.

Examples of key questions:

- Which natural weather disaster is the most deadly?
- In what order would you put the destructiveness of the natural weather hazards and why?
- What natural weather hazards do we experience in our town, city, and state?
- How are our local and state governments prepared to deal with a natural weather hazard?

Examples of concluding questions:

- How have natural disasters affected people, animals, and land?
- How have people tried to lessen the effects of natural disasters?

**Assessment:** Informally observe whether the students are able to communicate the information effectively and teach it to the other students. Gather from the answers to the discussion questions whether the students have acquired the desired understandings. If a formal assessment is desired, use the rubric to assign a grade to each emergency procedure flyer.

**Closure:** Using think-pair-share, ask the students what was their favorite part of the unit.

*Note: A copy of the flyers could be presented to interested organizations in the community.*

# Chapter 14

# Sixth Grade: War

---

**PLANNING**

---

*Stage 1: Identify Desired Results*

**Established goals:**

*National Council for the Social Studies Standard IX: Global Connections:*
- b. Analyze examples of conflict, cooperation, and interdependence among groups, societies, and nations.
- e. Describe and explain the relationships and tensions between national sovereignty and global interests, in such matters as territory, natural resources, trade, use of technology, and welfare of people.

**Essential questions:**

1. Are there any common causes of the wars in which the United States has participated?
2. Did the wars accomplish the reasons given by the governments?
3. How does the reality of war affect the soldiers who are fighting?

**Understandings:**

1. Students identify the causes and effects of a nation going to war.
2. Students compare and contrast wars in which the United States participated and conclude if there are similar reasons for the wars.

**What key knowledge and skills will the students acquire?**

1. Students define the key vocabulary of an assigned war.
2. Students use the encyclopedia, dictionary, atlas, almanac, Internet, and online catalog and non-fiction books to extract pertinent information about the causes, outcomes, casualties, length, protests against, and human side of the assigned wars: Revolutionary War in America, Mexican War, Civil War, World War I, World War II, Korean War, Vietnam War, and Persian Gulf War.
3. Students use PowerPoint technology to create a presentation based on their research.
4. Students make a chart comparing and contrasting the wars researched.

## *Stage 2: Determine Acceptable Evidence*

**Performance tasks:**

1. Students create and present a PowerPoint presentation for the war assigned encompassing the causes, effects, outcomes, length, protests, and human toll.
2. Students complete a chart about the war they researched.
3. The class completes a comparative chart of the wars researched.

**Student self-assessment and reflection:**

Summative assessment: Students assess their final product. Students use the following rubrics to assess their performance task:

### Rubric for War Unit PowerPoint

| Category | 4 Great | 3 Very Good | 2 Okay | 1 Needs More Work |
|---|---|---|---|---|
| Background | Background does not detract from text or other graphics. Choice of background is consistent from card to card and is appropriate for the topic. | Background does not detract from text or other graphics. Choice of background is consistent from card to card. | Background does not detract from text or other graphics. | Background makes it difficult to see text or competes with other graphics on the page. |
| Use of Graphics | All graphics are attractive (size and colors) and support the theme/content of the presentation. | A few graphics are not attractive, but all support the theme/content of the presentation. | All graphics are attractive, but a few do not seem to support the theme/content of the presentation. | Several graphics are unattractive and detract from the content of the presentation. |
| Text: Font Choice and Formatting | Font formats (e.g., color, bold, italic) have been carefully planned to enhance readability and content. | Font formats have been carefully planned to enhance readability. | Font formatting has been carefully planned to complement the content. It may be a little hard to read. | Font formatting makes it very difficult to read the material. |
| Content: Accuracy | All content throughout the presentation is accurate. There are no factual errors. | Most of the content is accurate but there is one piece of information that might be inaccurate. | The content is generally accurate, but one piece of information is clearly flawed or inaccurate. | Content is typically confusing or contains more than one factual error. |
| Spelling and Grammar | Presentation has no misspellings or grammatical errors. | Presentation has 1–2 misspellings, but no grammatical errors. | Presentation has 1–2 grammatical errors but no misspellings. | Presentation has more than 2 grammatical and/or spelling errors. |
| Sequencing of Information | Information is organized in a clear, logical way. It is easy to anticipate the type of material that might be on the next card. | Most information is organized in a clear, logical way. One card or item of information seems out of place. | Some information is logically sequenced. An occasional card or item of information seems out of place. | There is no clear plan for the organization of information. |

**Rubric for War Comparison Chart**

| Category | 4 Great | 3 Very Good | 2 Okay | 1 Needs More Work |
|---|---|---|---|---|
| Labels | All items of importance on the poster are clearly labeled with labels that can be read from at least 3 feet away. | Almost all items of importance on the poster are clearly labeled with labels that can be read from at least 3 feet away. | Several items of importance on the poster are clearly labeled with labels that can be read from at least 3 feet away. | Labels are too small to view or no important items were labeled. |
| Required Elements | The poster includes all required elements as well as additional information. | All required elements are included on the poster. | All but 1 of the required elements is included on the poster. | Several required elements were missing. |
| Knowledge Gained | Student can accurately answer all questions related to facts in the poster and processes used to create the poster. | Student can accurately answer most questions related to facts in the poster and processes used to create the poster. | Student can accurately answer about 75% of questions related to facts in the poster and processes used to create the poster. | Student appears to have insufficient knowledge about the facts or processes used in the poster. |
| Content: Accuracy | At least 7 accurate facts are displayed on the poster. | 5–6 accurate facts are displayed on the poster. | 3-4 accurate facts are displayed on the poster. | Less than 3 accurate facts are displayed on the poster. |
| Attractiveness | The poster is exceptionally attractive in terms of design, layout, and neatness. | The poster is attractive in terms of design, layout, and neatness. | The poster is acceptably attractive though it may be a bit messy. | The poster is distractingly messy or very poorly designed. It is not attractive. |
| Mechanics | Capitalization and punctuation are correct throughout the poster. | There is 1 error in capitalization or punctuation. | There are 2 errors in capitalization or punctuation. | There are more than 2 errors in capitalization or punctuation. |

## Stage 3: Plan Learning Experiences

- Read a book and brainstorm why governments go to war. Introduce the performance task and rubrics of the unit.
- Each group is assigned a war and uses the dictionary to become familiar with key vocabulary for that war.
- Students research their assigned war using the encyclopedia, the online catalog and nonfiction books, the almanac, and the Internet.
- Students complete a chart on their assigned war.
- Students learn how to make a PowerPoint presentation.
- Students make a PowerPoint presentation, deciding on what information and graphics are needed.
- Students present their PowerPoint and charts to the class.
- Students assess their PowerPoint and charts according to the rubrics.
- The class makes a comparative chart of the wars researched.
- Lead a discussion on the comparative aspects of the wars.

## LESSON 1: BRAINSTORMING

**Standards:**

*National Council for the Social Studies Standard IX: Global Connections:*
- b. Analyze examples of conflict, cooperation, and interdependence among groups, societies, and nations.
- e. Describe and explain the relationships and tensions between national sovereignty and global interests, in such matters as territory, natural resources, trade, use of technology, and welfare of people.

**Objectives:**

1. Students understand that there are many causes of war.
2. Students brainstorm the names of the wars in which the United States participated.
3. Students understand the performance task and rubrics required for the unit.

**Materials:**

- chart or empty board-ready paper
- one of the following books:
    Conway, John Richard. 2006. *Primary Source Accounts of the Korean War.* Berkeley Heights, NJ: MyReportLinks.com Books.
    Santella, Andrew. *The Korean War.* 2007. Minneapolis, MN: Compass Point Books.
    Stein, Conrad. 2002. *Korean War Veterans Memorial.* New York: Children's Press.
- board-ready copy of the rubrics

**Set:** Ask whether the United States is presently at war. If so, where is it being fought? Use think-pair-share to ask how the war is affecting each student.

**Input:** Read passages from one or more of the books in the materials list. Students use think-pair-share to discuss why the Korean War was fought. Ask the students to name the wars in which the United States participated, writing them on a chart or board as they are named and adding those the students do not name. Circle the wars that will be researched (Revolutionary War in America, Mexican War, Civil War, World War I, World War II, Vietnam War, and Persian Gulf War). Explain the unit, the performance task, and the rubrics using the board-ready copies.

**Assessment:** Informally observe whether the students are able to understand the concept of war.

**Closure:** Using think-pair-share, ask the students why nations go to war. Write these on the board.

## LESSON 2: USING THE DICTIONARY TO UNDERSTAND KEY VOCABULARY OF WAR

**Standards:**

*National Council for the Social Studies Standard IX: Global Connections:*
- b. Analyze examples of conflict, cooperation, and interdependence among groups, societies, and nations.

- e. Describe and explain the relationships and tensions between national sovereignty and global interests, in such matters as territory, natural resources, trade, use of technology, and welfare of people.

*AASL #2:*  Draw conclusions, make informed decisions, apply knowledge to new situations, and create new knowledge. 2.1, Skills: 2.1.1, Continue an inquiry-based research process by applying critical-thinking skills (analysis, synthesis, evaluation, organization) to information and knowledge in order to construct new understandings, draw conclusions, and create new knowledge; 2.1.4, Use technology and other information tools to analyze and organize information; 2.1.5, Collaborate with others to exchange ideas, develop new understandings, make decisions, and solve problems.

*NCTE #8:*  Students use a variety of technological and information resources to gather and synthesize information and to create and communicate knowledge.

**Objective:**

Using a dictionary, students paraphrase the definitions of key vocabulary for the war they are researching.

**Materials:**

- war chart with the students' ideas on causes of war
- 30 intermediate dictionaries
- 30 copies of the work sheet from the CD
- board-ready copy of the work sheet from the CD
- seven group folders, with the name of a war written on the cover of each: Revolutionary War in America, Mexican War, Civil War, World War I, World War II, Vietnam War, and Persian Gulf War. Inside are the performance task rubrics and an outline map of the world or the United States available at www.infoplease.com/statemaps.html (under "U.S. regions") or www.infoplease.com/statemaps.html (under "continents").
- visual of the Korean War
- paper strips of vocabulary for each war available in the CD

**Set:** Show a visual of the Korean War and ask whether anyone knows why the Korean War was fought.

**Review:** Review the arrangement of the dictionary and the use of guide words.

**Input:** Distribute the intermediate dictionaries. Tell the students you are going to look up the meaning of the word "communism." Model, thinking aloud, how to look up a word in the dictionary (beginning letter, next letter, using guide words, etc.). Locate the word and read the definition aloud. Note that this word was modeled in order to understand one of the causes of the Korean War. The students put the definition in their own words, with help from you. Write the paraphrased definition in the space on the work sheet. With the students, read the definition chorally. The students are grouped and given the folders, which have already been labeled with a war. The students write their names next to the numbers 1 through 4 or 5.

**Guided practice:** Each group is given a paper strip with vocabulary words of their assigned war and a work sheet. The students work together to locate and paraphrase the definitions of the words and write them on their individual work sheets. They make sure everyone in the group understands all the words. Students place their work sheets in the group folder. Collect the folders.

**Assessment:** Informally observe whether the students are able to find the words in the dictionary and write the definition in their own words, and make sure all group members understand the definitions of the words.

**Closure:** Using think-pair-share, ask the students what clues the definitions of the words gave them about the war they were assigned.

## LESSON 3: RESEARCHING WAR IN THE ENCYCLOPEDIA

**Standards:**

*National Council for the Social Studies Standard IX: Global Connections:*
- b. Analyze examples of conflict, cooperation, and interdependence among groups, societies, and nations.
- e. Describe and explain the relationships and tensions between national sovereignty and global interests, in such matters as territory, natural resources, trade, use of technology, and welfare of people.

*AASL #2:* Draw conclusions, make informed decisions, apply knowledge to new situations, and create new knowledge. 2.1, Skills: 2.1.1, Continue an inquiry-based research process by applying critical-thinking skills (analysis, synthesis, evaluation, organization) to information and knowledge in order to construct new understandings, draw conclusions, and create new knowledge; 2.1.4, Use technology and other information tools to analyze and organize information; 2.1.5, Collaborate with others to exchange ideas, develop new understandings, make decisions, and solve problems.

*NCTE #8:* Students use a variety of technological and information resources to gather and synthesize information and to create and communicate knowledge.

**Objective:**
Using an encyclopedia, students research who, where, when, why, and outcome of their assigned war.

**Materials:**

- two sets of encyclopedias
- group folders from the previous lesson
- 30 copies of the work sheet
- board-ready copy of work sheet
- board-ready copy of the world or U.S. map already in the group folders
- visual of a map showing North and South Korea

**Set:** Show the visual and ask what groups fought the Korean War.

**Review:** Review the organization of an encyclopedia and the use of guide words. Remind the students to look at and read the pictures, captions, charts, and graphs in an article before reading the information.

**Input:** Look up "Korean War" in the encyclopedia. Ponder aloud under what letter it would be found and "realize" that the second letter is an "o" so the article will be in the middle of the "K's" in the "J–K" encyclopedia volume. Select the correct one after checking the spine and find the article on "Korean War," remembering to use the guide words. Show the pictures and charts, and read the headings and subheadings. Read the work sheet aloud to see what information is required. Find the subtopic and read aloud the pertinent information from the encyclopedia. Model how to paraphrase the information, writing notes, not complete sentences. Put the outline map of the world on the board and model how to use the words in the encyclopedia to locate the area of the world in which the war occurred. Model the bibliographic entry for the article used.

**Guided practice:** Students get into their assigned group. Student 1 in each group is in charge of materials. She or he will get the group folder, work sheets, and the encyclopedia volume when it is decided what volume is needed. Student 2 uses the guide words to find the article. Student 2 shows the pictures and charts and reads the headings and subheadings if any. Student 3 reads aloud, in a whisper to the rest of the group, the information the students deem important in the article. After each student makes suggestions, Student 4 helps the students paraphrase the information into notes. Students fill out individual work sheets and the world or U.S map. Student 1 is in charge of helping all members of the group write the bibliographic entry correctly. Circulate during guided practice to offer assistance as needed. At the end of the guided practice, collect the group folders.

**Assessment:** Informally observe if the students are able to find the information and write it in their own words.

**Closure:** Using think-pair-share, ask the students how they found required information.

## LESSON 4: USING NONFICTION BOOKS TO FIND INFORMATION

**Standards:**

*National Council for the Social Studies Standard IX: Global Connections:*
- b. Analyze examples of conflict, cooperation, and interdependence among groups, societies, and nations.
- e. Describe and explain the relationships and tensions between national sovereignty and global interests, in such matters as territory, natural resources, trade, use of technology, and welfare of people.

*AASL #2:* Draw conclusions, make informed decisions, apply knowledge to new situations, and create new knowledge. 2.1, Skills: 2.1.1, Continue an inquiry-based research process by applying critical-thinking skills (analysis, synthesis, evaluation, organization) to information and knowledge in order to construct new understandings, draw conclusions, and create new knowledge; 2.1.4, Use technology and other information tools to analyze and organize information; 2.1.5, Collaborate with others to exchange ideas, develop new understandings, make decisions, and solve problems.

*NCTE #8:* Students use a variety of technological and information resources to gather and synthesize information and to create and communicate knowledge.

**Objective:**
Students use nonfiction books to find out information about their assigned war, the number of casualties, the effects on the civilian population, the outcomes, and the protests against it.

**Materials:**

- nonfiction books on the different wars in their correct location in the library
- computers with online catalog access
- Look for a Book form from the CD
- seven group folders from previous lessons
- 30 copies of the work sheet available from the CD
- board-ready copy of the work sheet
- visual of the symbols of communism and capitalism (the New York City skyline can be used as a symbol for capitalism)

**Set:** Show the visuals and say "These are visuals of communism and capitalism. They represent one of the causes of the Korean War. The communists in the northern part of Korea wanted to control all of the territory of Korea. The economic system in the southern part of Korea was capitalism. Capitalism allows private property and private ownerships of goods, companies, and services. The South Koreans asked the United Nations for assistance so they could avoid being controlled by the communists."

**Review:** Review the procedure for finding books by subject using the online catalog.

**Input:** Explain that the library has many resources. One of main resources is nonfiction books. Model going to a computer, accessing the online catalog, and typing in "Korean War." Use the "Look for a Book" form to write the call number and title of a book. Find the book on the shelf. Project the board-ready work sheet and read it to know what information is required. Peruse the table of contents and the index to find page numbers that are likely to have the information. Turn to one of the pages you've noted and read the facts that apply to the causes of the Korean War. Read a paragraph aloud and decide whether the information is on target. If so, paraphrase it and write notes on the work sheet under the space for "causes." Students chorally read your notes. After this example, model how to write a bibliographic entry for the book you just used.

**Guided practice:** Students get into their assigned groups. Student 2 is in charge of materials, gets the group folder, and hands out the work sheets. Student 3 leads the search on the online catalog for nonfiction books on the assigned war. She or he writes the call numbers and titles of books that will be helpful. While the other group members return to their seats, Student 3 takes the filled-out Look for a Book forms and finds the books on the shelf, not more than six at a time. Student 1 assigns the books to group members in pairs, depending on the number of books found. Each pair looks in the table of contents and the index to pinpoint pages that may be helpful and writes them on the work sheet. The students take turns finding the page, determining whether the information is useful, and taking notes in the appropriate place on the work sheets. All students write bibliographic entries for the nonfiction books they use.

**Assessment:** Informally observe whether the students are able to find the information and write it in their own words.

**Closure:** Using think-pair-share, the students share whether they found additional or conflicting reasons for the war from the nonfiction books as compared to the encyclopedia.

*Note: The guided practice of this lesson can be repeated if the groups don't have enough time to complete their research. The nonfiction books can also be checked out to the teacher and the research can continue in the classroom.*

## LESSON 5: FINDING PERTINENT INFORMATION IN THE ALMANAC

**Standards:**

*National Council for the Social Studies Standard IX: Global Connections:*
- b. Analyze examples of conflict, cooperation, and interdependence among groups, societies, and nations.
- e. Describe and explain the relationships and tensions between national sovereignty and global interests, in such matters as territory, natural resources, trade, use of technology, and welfare of people.

*AASL #2:* Draw conclusions, make informed decisions, apply knowledge to new situations, and create new knowledge. 2.1, Skills: 2.1.1, Continue an inquiry-based research process by applying critical-thinking skills (analysis, synthesis, evaluation, organization) to information and knowledge in order to construct new understandings, draw conclusions, and create new knowledge; 2.1.4, Use technology and other information tools to analyze and organize information; 2.1.5, Collaborate with others to exchange ideas, develop new understandings, make decisions, and solve problems.

*NCTE #8:* Students use a variety of technological and information resources (e.g., libraries, databases, computer networks, video) to gather and synthesize information and to create and communicate knowledge.

**Objectives:**

1. Students use an almanac to find information about the casualties of the U.S. forces for their assigned war.
2. Students record the information on a work sheet.

**Materials:**

- 30 copies of the work sheet available in the CD
- board-ready copy of the work sheet
- seven group folders from previous lessons
- 15 copies of the most recent edition of *The World Almanac and Book of Facts*
- visual of a flag-draped casket

**Set:** Show the visual and ask, "So far we've looked for information in the dictionary, the encyclopedia, and nonfiction books. Where can we find statistics about the casualties of the U.S. forces for each war?"

**Review:** Review that the almanac is a current book of facts and statistics. It is necessary to use the index, which is in alphabetical order, to find specific information.

**Input:** Explain that the library has many resources. One of them is the almanac. Distribute the almanacs and the work sheets to pairs of students in each group. Project and read the board-ready work sheet to understand what information is required. Model using the index to look up "Korean War," writing down the pages cited. Turn to the first page and skim it. Decide whether this will give the required information. Turn to the second series of pages cited, and find the heading "Casualties, U.S. Forces." Model how to transfer the required information onto the work sheet. Model writing the bibliographic entry for *The World Almanac and Book of Facts*.

**Guided practice:** Students get into their groups, and Student 3 gets the group folder. Students work together as a group or in pairs to find the required information and write the bibliographic entry. You should assist the Civil War group to fill out their work sheet, because they have to record information for both the North and the South.

**Assessment:** Informally assess whether the students use the index, find the correct information, record it, and write the bibliographic entry correctly.

**Closure:** Ask Student 4 of each group to report to the whole class the number of American soldiers killed in the war they researched. Students compare the loss of life and decide which was the deadliest war for Americans. Collect the group folders.

## LESSON 6: FINDING INFORMATION ON THE INTERNET

**Standards:**

*National Council for the Social Studies Standard IX: Global Connections:*
- b. Analyze examples of conflict, cooperation, and interdependence among groups, societies, and nations.
- e. Describe and explain the relationships and tensions between national sovereignty and global interests, in such matters as territory, natural resources, trade, use of technology, and welfare of people.

*AASL #2:* Draw conclusions, make informed decisions, apply knowledge to new situations, and create new knowledge. 2.1, Skills: 2.1.1, Continue an inquiry-based research process by applying critical-thinking skills (analysis, synthesis, evaluation, organization) to information and knowledge in order to construct new understandings, draw conclusions, and create new knowledge; 2.1.4, Use technology and other information tools to analyze and organize information; 2.1.5, Collaborate with others to exchange ideas, develop new understandings, make decisions, and solve problems.

*NCTE #8:* Students use a variety of technological and information resources (e.g., libraries, databases, computer networks, video) to gather and synthesize information and to create and communicate knowledge.

*NETS Technology #3: Research and Information Fluency:* Students apply digital tools to gather, evaluate, and use information.

**Objectives:**

1. Students use Web sites to find and print the text of a letter from an American soldier for the war assigned.
2. Students search for more information on who, what, where, when, and why the war was fought.
3. Students note the Web sites that contain graphics they may want to use in their PowerPoint presentation.
4. Students understand that the Internet provides information and images on many topics.
5. Students understand that Web sites need to be evaluated for reliability.

**Materials:**

- projection of an Internet computer screen (must have access to computer, Internet, and means of projection)
- personalized start page or bookmarked Internet sites, available on the CD
- 30 copies of the Letter to Parents with the Web sites, available on the CD
- seven group folders from the previous lessons
- 30 copies of the work sheet
- board-ready copy of the work sheet
- 10 to 15 computers with Internet access
- "Letter to home" from an American soldier who fought in the Korean War

**Set:** Read the most interesting parts of a letter from an American soldier during the Korean War from www.koreanwar-educator.org/topics/letters_warzone/p_index.htm.

**Review:** Review that the Internet is a network of interconnected computers around the world and a source of information and images. Web sites need to be evaluated for reliability. Also review the rules of using the Internet at school.

**Input:** Explain that the library has many resources. One of these is the Internet. Navigate to the Web site on war letters from www.koreanwar-educator.org/topics/letters_warzone/p_index.htm. Model how to find a letter from the Korean War. Navigate to a Web site for the Korean War, http://korea50.army.mil. Project the board-ready copy of the work sheet and model how to find the required information and record it. State that the two sites are reliable because of the sponsors. Write the name of the Web site as well as the URL on the work sheet. Tell the students that you have bookmarked sites on the personalized start page for each war they are researching.

**Guided practice:** Students are paired within their group and assigned a computer. They use the personalized start page to find a Web site on war letters. They look at the Web site, decide on the best example, and print it. They then find Web sites from the personalized start page for their assigned war. They paraphrase the information found on the Web sites and record it as notes on the work sheet. They write the name of the Web sites and the URL on the work sheet. You should circulate among the computers, offering assistance as needed. After all students complete the assignment, they meet in their groups to discuss the new information. Collect the group folders.

**Assessment:** Informally assess whether the students can restate the information presented by the Web sites and have the title and the URL for the Web site.

**Closure:** Ask student 2 from each group to read a few sentences from their letter from a soldier. Using think-pair-share, the students discuss the similarities and differences among the letters. Distribute to the students the letter to the parents with the Web sites and encourage the students to visit the sites at home with their parents.

## LESSON 7: CREATING A CHART FROM INFORMATION ALREADY GATHERED

**Standards:**

*National Council for the Social Studies Standard IX: Global Connections:*
- b. Analyze examples of conflict, cooperation, and interdependence among groups, societies, and nations.

- e. Describe and explain the relationships and tensions between national sovereignty and global interests, in such matters as territory, natural resources, trade, use of technology, and welfare of people.

*AASL #2:*    Draw conclusions, make informed decisions, apply knowledge to new situations, and create new knowledge. 2.1, Skills: 2.1.1, Continue an inquiry-based research process by applying critical-thinking skills (analysis, synthesis, evaluation, organization) to information and knowledge in order to construct new understandings, draw conclusions, and create new knowledge; 2.1.4, Use technology and other information tools to analyze and organize information; 2.1.5, Collaborate with others to exchange ideas, develop new understandings, make decisions, and solve problems.

*NCTE #8:*    Students use a variety of technological and information resources (e.g., libraries, databases, computer networks, video) to gather and synthesize information and to create and communicate knowledge.

**Objective:**
Students use information already gathered to make a chart organizing the information.

**Materials:**

- seven group folders from previous lessons
- 30 copies of the template for the chart
- board-ready copy of the template for the chart

**Set:** Ask, "Today each group is going to create a chart on the war they're researching. Why would this be useful before making the PowerPoint?"

**Review:** Charts are graphic organizers and do not need complete sentences, just ideas and facts.

**Input:** Project the template of the chart. Look at the template to see what information is needed. First, make a title that will create interest in the reader. A suggestion is "The Korean War: Communism versus Capitalism." Model where to find the information for each section of the template. Model the writing of one or two sections.

**Guided practice:** Students get into their assigned groups while Student 3 gets the folder and a copy of the template for each group member. First, the group decides on a snappy title. Student 1 assigns each group member several sections of the chart. Students work individually to write their sections using the work sheets in the folder.

**Assessment:** Informally assess whether the students can use the information to write their sections of the chart.

**Closure:** Students read their section of the chart to the other group members.

*Note: The students may need more than one session to complete the guided practice of this lesson. All sections of the chart must be completed before the teaching of the next lesson.*

---

## LESSON 8:  DESIGNING A POWERPOINT PRESENTATION

*Note: If students are experienced in making PowerPoint presentations, skip the tutorial Web site on making PowerPoint presentations.*

**Standards:**

*NETS Technology #1: Creativity and Innovation:* Students demonstrate creative thinking, construct knowledge, and develop innovative products and processes using technology.

**Objectives:**

1.  Students understand how to use PowerPoint software.
2.  Students write the cards for the PowerPoint presentation.

**Materials:**

*   projection of an Internet computer screen (must have access to computer, Internet, and means of projection)
*   Web site for a tutorial on making a PowerPoint presentation, www.actden.com/pp/
*   instructor-made PowerPoint presentation of the Korean War
*   seven copies of the card list for the PowerPoint presentation
*   board-ready copy of the card list for the PowerPoint presentation
*   lined paper to write the cards
*   seven group folders

**Set:** Show part of a PowerPoint presentation on the Korean War that includes at least one graphic.

**Review:** If the students already have experience in creating a PowerPoint, review the steps with them.

**Input:** If the students do not have experience in creating a PowerPoint presentation, click on www.actden.com/pp/ and lead them through the PowerPoint tutorial. Project the board-ready of the Power-Point card list. Write the card on "where and when the war was fought." Model writing a paragraph or two to present the information. Explain the information required on the other cards.

**Guided practice:** The group folders are distributed. Student 2 in each group assigns each group member several cards. Using the previous lesson's work sheets, students work individually to write the cards, seeking the advice of other group members as needed. You should circulate, assisting students in writing the cards.

**Assessment:** Informally observe whether the students are able to use the research to write the cards.

**Closure:** The group members read the cards they've created to each other.

*Note: The guided practice continues for as many sessions as necessary, either in the library or the classroom, until the all the cards are written and edited.*

## LESSON 9: MAKING A POWERPOINT PRESENTATION

**Standards:**

*NETS Technology #2: Communication and Collaboration:* Students use digital media and environments to communicate and work collaboratively to support individual learning and contribute to the learning of others.

**Objective:**
Students create a PowerPoint presentation about their assigned war.

**Materials:**

- projection of an Internet computer screen (must have access to computer, Internet, and means of projection)
- 10 to 15 computers with Internet access if graphics from Web sites are desired
- instructor-made PowerPoint presentation of the Korean War
- seven group folders with completed cards for the PowerPoint presentation
- seven floppy disks or CDs to save each group's PowerPoint presentation

**Set:** Show part of a PowerPoint presentation on the Korean War that includes at least one graphic.

**Review:** Review the procedures for making a PowerPoint presentation.

**Input:** Open the PowerPoint on the Korean War to create card number 3 about who fought in the war, including all the countries involved. Type one or two paragraphs you have previously written about who fought in the war and the countries involved. Search for a graphic to place on the card. You can either use Microsoft clips online, search on Google images, or copy and paste a picture from a Web site.

**Guided practice:** Students get into their groups and collect the cards they wrote for the PowerPoint. They are assigned computers and take turns making the cards and finding and inserting the graphics. After each session, each group needs to save their work on either a diskette or a CD.

**Assessment:** Informally observe whether the students are able to type the information and find the graphics in a time-effective manner.

**Closure:** Students in each group decide who is going to read each card of the presentation and which student will run the slide show for the presentation to the class.

*Note: It may take several sessions of the guided practice for each group to complete their PowerPoint presentations. If the school has a computer lab, the lessons on the PowerPoint can be taught there. All the PowerPoints must be completed before the next lesson.*

## LESSON 10: PRESENTING THE POWERPOINT

**Standards:**

*National Council for the Social Studies Standard IX: Global Connections:*
- b. Analyze examples of conflict, cooperation, and interdependence among groups, societies, and nations.
- e. Describe and explain the relationships and tensions between national sovereignty and global interests, in such matters as territory, natural resources, trade, use of technology, and welfare of people.

*AASL #3:* Share knowledge and participate ethically and productively as members of our democratic society. 3.1, Skills: 3.1.1, Conclude an inquiry-based research process by sharing new understandings and reflecting on the learning; 3.1.3, Use writing and speaking skills to communicate new understandings effectively.

*NCTE #8:* Students use a variety of technological and information resources to gather and synthesize information and to create and communicate knowledge.

**Objectives:**

1. Each group presents its PowerPoint presentation to the class.
2. Using the performance task PowerPoint rubric, each group assesses its presentation.

**Materials:**

- projection of a computer screen
- group PowerPoint presentations already loaded into a folder on the computer, in chronological order of the assigned wars
- board-ready copy of the rubric
- 30 copies of the rubric
- one hardcopy of each PowerPoint presentation

**Set:** Say, "It's time to share our performance task and new knowledge so everyone in the class will know about all of the wars we've researched. We're going to start with the war that happened first and proceed in order."

**Review:** Review that effective presenters speak loudly and clearly, and the listeners are silent and attentive during the presentations.

**Input:** Students get into their research groups. Call the group on the Revolutionary War in America to come to the computer and do their presentation. Each group is called in order. After the presentations, show the board-ready rubric and distribute copies to the students. Distribute the hard copies of the PowerPoint presentations to each group. Review the categories. Students are instructed to circle their agreed-upon rating in each category for their PowerPoint presentation.

**Guided practice:** Student 3 is the leader of the discussion in each group and makes sure that all group members are able to voice their ratings and reasons. This is followed by a rating session. Student 2 circles the rating. This continues until all sections have been rated.

**Assessment:** Informally observe whether the students are able to present their PowerPoint effectively and rate it using the rubric. You may choose to rate each PowerPoint for a letter grade.

**Closure:** Using think-pair-share, ask the students to compare writing a research report and making a PowerPoint.

*Note: The presentations could be done for other classes, parents, and the community.*

## LESSON 11: MAKING A CLASS CHART TO COMPARE THE WARS

**Standards:**

*National Council for the Social Studies Standard IX: Global Connections:*
- b. Analyze examples of conflict, cooperation, and interdependence among groups, societies, and nations.

- e. Describe and explain the relationships and tensions between national sovereignty and global interests, in such matters as territory, natural resources, trade, use of technology, and welfare of people.

*AASL #2:*   Draw conclusions, make informed decisions, apply knowledge to new situations, and create new knowledge. 2.1, Skills: 2.1.1, Continue an inquiry-based research process by applying critical-thinking skills (analysis, synthesis, evaluation, organization) to information and knowledge in order to construct new understandings, draw conclusions, and create new knowledge; 2.1.4, Use technology and other information tools to analyze and organize information; 2.1.5, Collaborate with others to exchange ideas, develop new understandings, make decisions, and solve problems.

*NCTE #8:*   Students use a variety of technological and information resources to gather and synthesize information and to create and communicate knowledge.

**Objective:**

Students will create a class chart to compare the wars researched.

**Materials**

- the seven group folders
- wall chart, large enough to accommodate sections of the students' charts, with the categories and wars filled in (template available on the CD)
- glue sticks
- scissors on each table

**Set:** Say, "Each group has researched their assigned war and presented the information. Today we are going to make a classroom chart."

**Review:** Remind the students that they have made charts with the categories of who, when, and where, participants, causes, casualties, effects on civilians, and outcomes.

**Input:** Students get into their research groups. Student 4 in each group gets the group folder and hands out the charts they made previously. Student 1 checks that every category of the chart has been filled out. Student 3 hands out the scissors. All members of the group cut the sections from the charts so that they can be affixed to the classroom chart. Direct each group in affixing the sections by category. The students read the section to the class before they are affixed to the chart.

**Assessment:** Informally observe whether the students are able to communicate the information on the chart effectively.

**Closure:** Using think-pair-share, ask, "What kind of questions about war does the information on the chart bring up?" Write down the questions for discussion in the next lesson.

*Note: Make an 8½" × 11" master of the War Comparison Chart, because it will be needed in the next lesson.*

## LESSON 12:  RATING THE WAR COMPARISON CHART

**Standards:**

*AASL #3:*   Share knowledge and participate ethically and productively as members of our democratic society. 3.1, Skills: 3.1.1, Conclude an inquiry-based research process by sharing new understandings and reflecting on the learning; 3.1.3, Use writing and speaking skills to communicate new understandings effectively.

**Objectives:**

1. Students read the War Comparison Chart.
2. Students rate the chart using a rubric.
3. Using the War Comparison Chart, students answer key and concluding questions.

**Materials:**

- seven copies of the War Comparison Chart rubric
- board-ready copy of the War Comparison Chart rubric
- 30 copies of the War Comparison Chart

**Set:** Say, "We have created a War Comparison Chart and now we are going to use a rubric to assess the chart. Then we will draw conclusions about war in general."

**Review:** Review that a rubric is a tool to assess a product.

**Input:** Show the board-ready rubric and distribute copies to the students. Distribute copies of the War Comparison Chart to each student. Review the categories. Students are instructed to circle their agreed-upon rating in each category.

**Guided practice:** Direct the students to get into their research groups. Student 3 is the leader of the discussion in each group and makes sure that all group members are able to voice their rating and reasons. This is followed by a rating session. Student 2 circles the rating. This continues until all categories have been rated. Using think-pair-share, lead the class in a discussion of the War Comparison Chart.

Examples of key questions:

- Which was the most deadly war?
- What did the winning side gain in each war?
- What was the effect for the side that lost the war?
- Which war lasted the longest?
- Which war was the most costly?
- Which wars were fought in the United States?

Examples of concluding questions:

- Were there common causes of wars that the United States fought?
- Did the wars accomplish the reasons given by governments?
- How did the reality of war seem to people not directly involved?

Also ask the questions that were generated in the preceding lesson.

**Assessment:** Informally observe whether the students are able to use the rubric to rate the chart. Gather from the answers to the discussion questions whether the students have acquired the desired understandings.

**Closure:** Using think-pair-share, ask the students what was their favorite part of the unit.

# PART III

## GAMES AND CONTESTS

# Chapter 15

# Games to Practice Reference Skills

The four reference games and the estimation contest were designed to enable students to practice their reference information skills. Using an encyclopedia, almanac, atlas, the Internet, and an online catalog to answer questions in order to win prizes gives students an opportunity to practice their information skills for an educational and fun purpose.

The games have been developed over many years and have been used successfully with every type of school population. The students usually do the games before school or during their lunch recess. However, if students have time after checking out their books, a librarian could allow students to look for an author using the online catalog for the "Between the Pages" game, fill in an estimation guess for the "Counting Corner" contest, or perform other game tasks.

There are three monthly games and two weekly games to place throughout the library. The games require some poster making, some library shelves, counter space, and the purchase of a commercially produced ten-questions game. The plastic sign holders, pencil holders, brochure holders, and two ballot boxes are available from any office supply store. The answer forms should be arranged to fit as many on a sheet as possible when printing out. The prizes require a ready supply of pencils and bookmarks and some type of food treat or other special prize for the winning students.

Three years of the matching and ten-questions reference games are provided, so that they can be used in the library in a three-year cycle. Different sizes of jars or containers should be used for the estimation contest so that estimating skills can be developed using a variety of containers.

The "Between the Pages" six weekly winners should be announced every Monday, and the "Counting Corner" ten winners should be announced at the end of the month. It is suggested that the winners collect their prizes before school and during their lunch recess. Prizes for the reference, matching, and "Use Your Brain" games should be given when a correct answer form is presented to the librarian.

The signs and questions and answers for each game can be found on the CD-ROM.

## MONTHLY 10 QUESTIONS REFERENCE GAMES

**Materials:**

- one plastic $8^{1}/_{2}'' \times 11''$ sign holder for game instructions
- one pencil holder with four pencils
- one brochure holder with 20 answer sheets
- ten $24'' \times 31''$ Reference Game posters from a poster-making machine or made by hand, in color if possible, one for each month with that month's game title, an appropriate graphic, and the 10 questions

- pencils and bookmarks for all students who turn in correct answer sheets
- prizes for the first eight correct answer sheets, either toys or novelties or food treats such as packaged crackers or cookies

**Setup:** Place the $8\frac{1}{2}'' \times 11''$ sign from the CD in a holder, along with a pencil holder and a brochure holder with the answer forms in front of the month's Reference Game poster in the library.

## MONTHLY MATCHING GAME

**Materials:**

- one plastic $8\frac{1}{2}'' \times 11''$ sign holder for game instructions
- one pencil holder with four pencils
- one brochure holder with 20 answer sheets
- ten $24'' \times 31''$ posters from a poster-making machine or made by hand, in color if possible, one for each month with that month's game title, an appropriate graphic, and the 12 items and the 12 matching answers
- pencils and bookmarks for all students who turn in correct answer sheets
- prizes for the first eight correct answer sheets, either toys or novelties or a food treat such as packaged crackers or cookies
- computers with the suggested Internet sites bookmarked

**Setup:** Place the $8\frac{1}{2}'' \times 11''$ sign from the CD in a sign holder in front of the month's Matching Game poster, along with a pencil holder and brochure holder for the answer sheets.

## "BETWEEN THE PAGES" WEEKLY GAME

**Materials:**

- one plastic $8\frac{1}{2}'' \times 11''$ sign holder for game instructions
- one plastic $8\frac{1}{2}'' \times 11''$ sign holder for the five clues
- one pencil holder with four pencils
- one brochure holder with 20 answer sheets
- one piece of construction paper per week to uncover one clue per day. The students would be able to get the right title usually on the fourth or fifth day.
- one plastic clear ballot box, $6'' \times 4''$, with a sign holder showing a graphic of Sherlock Holmes and the words: Between the Pages Answer Box
- pencils and bookmarks for all students who turn in correct answer sheets
- prize for six winners to be drawn from all correct answer sheets, either a toy or novelty or a food treat such as packaged crackers or cookies

**Setup:** Place the $8\frac{1}{2}'' \times 11''$ sign from the CD in a sign holder next to a pencil holder, brochure holder, and answer box for the "Between the Pages" weekly game somewhere in the library.

## "USE YOUR BRAIN" WEEKLY GAME

**Materials:**

- one plastic $8^{1}/_{2}'' \times 11''$ sign holder for game instructions
- one plastic $8^{1}/_{2}'' \times 11''$ sign holder with a white sheet with "Use Your Brain" at the top next to a graphic of a student thinking, a brain, or similar image to express the concept. Every week, tape ten questions from a commercially produced 10-questions game for children (can usually be found at chain book stores) in the middle of the page. The suggested grade levels to buy are third, fourth, or fifth according to the ability of the population of the school.
- one pencil holder with four pencils
- one brochure holder with 20 answer sheets
- pencils and bookmarks for all students who turn in correct answer sheets
- prizes for the first eight correct answer sheets, either a toy or novelty or a food treat such as packaged crackers or cookies

**Setup:** Place the $8^{1}/_{2}'' \times 11''$ sign from the CD in a sign holder with a pencil holder, brochure holder with 20 answer sheets, and $8^{1}/_{2}'' \times 11''$ sign holder with the ten questions somewhere in the library.

## THE "COUNTING CORNER" ESTIMATION JAR MONTHLY GAME

**Materials:**

- one plastic $8^{1}/_{2}'' \times 11''$ sign holder for game instructions
- one pencil holder with four pencils
- one brochure holder with 20 "Counting Corner" answer forms
- different-sized glass or plastic containers
- one plastic clear ballot box, $6'' \times 4''$, with a sign holder showing a math or counting graphic and the words: Counting Corner Answer Box
- prizes for the 10 closest estimates, either a toy or novelty or a food treat such as packaged crackers or cookies

**Suggested months and items for the estimation jar:**

| | |
|---|---|
| August: sea shells | January: buttons |
| September: pine cones | February: Valentine candy |
| October: candy corn | March: M&Ms |
| November: blue corn kernels | April: jelly beans |
| December: red and green pasta trees | May: marbles |

**Setup:** Place the $8^{1}/_{2}'' \times 11''$ sign from the CD in a sign holder next to a pencil holder, brochure holder, and answer box for the "Counting Corner" somewhere in the library.

# Index

**V**

verbs
    second-grade lessons, 36–37
    sixth-grade lessons, 43–44
    thesaurus lessons, 36–37, 43–44
*Visual Dictionary of Baseball, A* (Buckley), 12
visual learners, 4
visual library catalogs, 115–117
visuals as teaching assist, 4
volunteers, classroom, 146

**W**

war (lesson plans), 227–243
    almanacs, 235–236
    brainstorming, 230
    chart making, 237–238, 241–242
    dictionaries, 230–232
    encyclopedias, 232–233
    Internet sources, 236–237
    library use, 233–234
    PowerPoint, 238–241
    presentation skills, 239–241
weather
    almanacs, 105–106, 218–219
    brainstorming, 213–214
    creating flyers, 221–222
    dictionaries, 214–215
    encyclopedias, 215–216
    fourth-grade lessons, 105–106
    integrated lesson plans, 211–225
    Internet sources, 219–221
    library use, 217–218
    presentation skills, 223–225
    third-grade lessons, 20–21
    vocabulary, 20–21
*Weather and Climate* (Harrison), 213
Web site evaluation, 132–133, 136–137, 140–141
Web sites
    animals, 124–125, 128–129, 160
    atlases, 92–93
    biographical, 139–140
    biomes, 202–203
    country information, 92–93, 137–139
    dictionaries, 21–22, 24–25
    dinosaurs, 129
    disasters, 127–128
    diversity, 135–136
    earthquakes, 127–128
    encyclopedias, 61–62, 65–67
    folktales, 126

    geography, 90, 92–93
    government, 92–93, 127–128, 135–136, 138
    history, 88, 135–136
    maps, 82, 86, 90, 92–93
    snowflakes, 123–124
    wolves, 125
    writing bibliographic entries, 133–136, 202–203
Web sites in instruction, 21–22
*Webster's Intermediate Dictionary*, 42
*What Is a Biome?* (Kalman), 197
*Where Do I Live?* (Chesanow), 73
*Where in the World Is Henry?* (Balian), 73
white boards, 3
*Why Do Tigers Have Stripes?* (Dell), 155
Wiggins, Grant, 145–146
Wikipedia, 4, 134
wolves
    first-grade lessons, 124–125
    Internet, 124–125
    Web sites, 125
women
    encyclopedias, 59–60
    fourth-grade lessons, 59–60
WordCentral.com, 21–22
word maps, 41–42
word origins, 27–28
Warhol, Tom, 197
working in pairs, 6
    fifth-grade, 41–42
    first-grade, 13–14
    second-grade, 170–171
    third-grade, 21–22
working in pairs, by source
    almanacs, 101–102, 105–106
    atlases, 77–78, 79–81
    dictionaries, 13–14, 21–22, 22–23, 24–25, 26–27
    encyclopedias, 68–69
    Internet, 128–131, 137–139
    online catalogs, 116–122
    thesaurus lessons, 34–35, 37–41
work sheets, 4
*World Almanac and Book of Facts 2006, The*, 5
    lessons using, 104–114, 218–219, 235–236
*World Almanac for Kids 2007*, 5
    lessons using, 95–103
*World Book Encyclopedia*, 4, 5, 150–151
    lessons using, 47–51, 54–57, 60–70, 199–200, 215–216
World Book Online, 61–62, 65–67
World Factbook Web site, 92–93, 138
writing summaries, 58–59, 67–71

# About the Authors

Susan Garvin has been involved in libraries and education for over 30 years. She earned her bachelor's degree from Northern Arizona University and her master's degree in education with a focus on library science from Arizona State University. She also earned an academic certificate in storytelling from South Mountain Community College. All of her school library experience has been in the metro Phoenix, Arizona, area. Susan spent 25 years as a librarian in the Roosevelt School District and her last two years in Kyrene School District. She also served for three years as a collaborative peer teacher in math, science, and technology. Susan won the Arizona Progressive Library Media Award in 1994. She has taught storytelling for Mesa Community College.

Currently, Susan chairs the Intermediate committee of the Grand Canyon Readers' Award, substitutes, volunteers mentoring new school librarians, tells stories professionally, and will weed anyone's collection for fun. She has served as president of the School Library Media Division of the Arizona Library Association, served on the American Association of School Librarians (AASL) Affiliate Assembly, and presented numerous sessions at state and national conferences.

Annie Weissman has been involved in libraries and education for over 35 years. She earned her bachelor's degree from the University of Rochester and her master's degree from Case Western Reserve's School of Library Science. She taught in a high school for dropouts before working as a children's librarian at Phoenix Public Library. All of her school library experience has been in Phoenix, Arizona. Annie spent many years as a librarian in the Roosevelt School District, concurrently teaching gifted reading. She was an assistant principal in the Madison School District and a principal and librarian in Alhambra School District.

Annie won the Arizona Progressive Library Media Award in 1998. She has taught library science and folklore classes for Arizona State University, and storytelling and children's literature for Paradise Valley Community College. She currently substitutes, supervises student teachers for Arizona State University, writes books, and travels. Annie has served as president of the School Library Media Division of the Arizona Library Association; served on the AASL Affiliate Assembly, as well as on several committees for the Grand Canyon Readers' Award; and presented numerous sessions at state and national conferences.

She is the author of *Transforming Story Times into Reading and Writing Lessons* (Linworth, 2001), *Do Tell! Storytelling for You and Your Students* (Linworth, 2002), and the memoir *As One Door Closes* (Xlibris, 2002).

Susan Garvin and Annie Weissman have collaborated with each other for over 30 years, dreaming up projects, puppet shows, workshops, and programs for Arizona's students and teachers.